ST. PAUL
AMONG THE PHILOSOPHERS

Indiana Series in the Philosophy of Religion

Merold Westphal, editor

St. Paul among the Philosophers

∾

EDITED BY

John D. Caputo & Linda Martín Alcoff

Indiana University Press

Bloomington & Indianapolis

This book is a publication of

Indiana University Press
601 North Morton Street
Bloomington, IN 47404-3797 USA

http://iupress.indiana.edu

Telephone orders   800-842-6796
Fax orders   812-855-7931
Orders by e-mail   iuporder@indiana.edu

Manufactured in the United States of
America

**Library of Congress Cataloging-in-
Publication Data**

St. Paul among the philosophers / edited
by John D. Caputo and Linda Martín
Alcoff.
    p. cm. — (Indiana series in the phi-
losophy of religion)
    Proceedings of a conference held Apr.
14–16, 2005 at Syracuse University.
    Includes bibliographical references and
index.
    ISBN 978-0-253-35317-7 (cloth : alk.
paper) — ISBN 978-0-253-22083-7
(pbk. : alk. paper) 1. Bible. N.T. Epistles
of Paul—Criticism, interpretation, etc.—
Congresses. 2. Paul, the Apostle, Saint—
Congresses. 3. Truth—Congresses. 4.
Universalism—Congresses. I. Caputo,
John D. II. Alcoff, Linda. III. Title: Saint
Paul among the philosophers.
    BS2650.52.S7 2009
    227'.06—dc22
                                    2008048653

1 2 3 4 5 14 13 12 11 10 09

To Cathryn R. Newton,
Dean of the College of Arts and Sciences, Syracuse University

For her leadership and support

CONTENTS

ACKNOWLEDGMENTS

The editors wish to acknowledge the support of Cathryn R. Newton, Dean of the College of Arts and Sciences, Syracuse University (2000–2008), for her generous support and leadership in making possible a series of conferences entitled Postmodernism, Culture and Religion, the first of which, St. Paul Among the Philosophers, was held at Syracuse University on April 14–16, 2005, on which this volume is based.

We are very grateful for the grant we received from the Ray Smith Symposium of Syracuse University, which was a major contribution to the financial support of the conference.

We thank in particular Sherry Hayes and Deborah Pratt, on the staff of the Religion Department at Syracuse University, for their indefatigable energy, unflagging good spirits, and astonishing mastery of the details of running a conference, which made everything easy for us.

ST. PAUL
AMONG THE PHILOSOPHERS

Postcards from Paul:
Subtraction versus Grafting

JOHN D. CAPUTO

"There is no longer Jew or Greek, there is no longer slave or free, there is no longer male or female" (Gal 3:28). As Paula Fredriksen says in the roundtable included in this volume, that is a great sound bite. That is exactly what we want St. Paul to say, we being contemporary democratic, fair-minded pluralists. Viewed more closely, however, Fredriksen adds, Paul was nothing of the sort. He did not affirm the alterity and diversity of Mediterranean culture. He took it for a culture of idol worshipers who, as Fredriksen puts it, "were going to fry." That particularly colorful excerpt from the conversation that took place at Syracuse University in April 2005 is a good example of the sort of problem posed by the contemporary interest shown by secular philosophers in St. Paul. It points out the difficulties encountered in the exchange between the systematizers (philosophers but also the theologians) who want to put Paul to a contemporary purpose and the historians who are interested in reconstituting the original context of Paul's work. They are brought together in the present volume.

Is the proper work of reading to reconstitute what the original author said to the original audience? Or it is to retrieve something implied, implicit, a tendency that is possible, repressed, but astir in the text and thus gives the text a history, a future? The name of a thinker—here "Paul"—is the name of a matter to be thought (*eine Sache des Denkens*), as Heidegger famously said. Or is it better to concede that reading is one thing and thinking another? If, as one is likely to say when faced with such a choice, we want to engage in a bit of both, how then is the one related to the other? What limits does the actual context put on our right to say that Paul says this or that? In *The Postcard* Derrida defended the structural possibility of lost mail. By this he meant not only that a letter can be lost or damaged in the mail, which has certainly been the fate with most of Paul's letters, but that even if it is sent and received it may always be misunderstood, which has also happened to Paul, and beyond that even if it is sent, received, and interpreted in terms of its original context, to the extent that is possible, it is always structurally possible to understand it differently, to recontextualize it. But is there no limit to this? Can any constraints be set in advance to understanding differently?

In this volume we focus on the work of Alain Badiou and Slavoj Žižek, who (along with Georgio Agamben) are at the center of the current retrieval of Paul. These are secular philosophers who pointedly do not share Paul's core belief in the resurrection of Christ but regard his project as centrally important for contemporary political life and reflection. The Pauline project, as they see it, is the universality of truth, the conviction (*pistis*) that what is true is true for everyone and that the proper role of the subject is to make that truth known, to fight the good fight on behalf of the truth, to all the ends of the earth (*apostolos*). They have in mind the dramatic conversion of Paul—the event!—and Paul's subsequent dispute with the leaders of the early Jewish Christian community in Jerusalem that Christ belongs to all, that in Christ there is neither Jew nor Greek, male nor female, master nor slave, and the militant vigor with which Paul promulgated that belief across Asia Minor. In Paul's view, one does not need to be a Jew or first become one in order to receive the word of the gospel. The historians in this volume agree that while this is true enough, what Paul had in mind was that the gentiles would finally be "grafted" onto "the tree of Israel," that Christ is the fulfillment of a specifically Jewish promise, not a Greek one. "Remember that it is not you [the gentiles] that support the root [Israel] but the root that supports you" (Rom 11:18). What Paul is saying is analogous to saying that Buddhism belongs to all, that in the Buddha there is neither Greek nor Jew, that we are all to be grafted onto the Bodhi tree.

Thus we may take the Pauline project in two different directions. On the one hand, there is Badiou's more formalizing method of "subtraction," that the power of truth is to subtract itself from or annul local differences or identities in order to announce and then implement a true universal where there is neither Greek nor Jew. On the other hand, there is the more historically situated model of grafting, where the gentiles would be grafted onto the one true tree of Israel. One universal tree of truth—or one true tree? One truth without identity or one true identity? Actually, it is Žižek himself who puts this point well:

> Saint Paul conceives of the Christian community as the new incarnation of
> the chosen people: it is Christians who are the true "children of Abraham."

> What was, in its first incarnation, a distinct ethnic group is now a commu-
> nity of free believers that suspends all ethnic divisions. . . . Thus we have a
> kind of *"transubstantiation" of the chosen people:* God kept his promise of
> redemption to the Jewish people, but, in the process itself, he changed the
> identity of the chosen people. . . . [Paul's] universe is no longer that of the
> multitude of groups that want to "find their voice," and assert their particu-
> lar identity, their "way of life," but that of a fighting collective grounded in
> the reference to an unconditional universalism.[1]

But this very point, for Žižek, is to be interpreted as a method of subtraction
—a universal subtracting itself from ethnic particularity—rather than as
grafting of all the nations onto the historically identifiable tree of Israel.
Down each road lies an ominous specter. Down the one, the *extra ecclesiam
nullus salus est*, the work of a militant missionary who wants to convert
everyone to the religion of Israel, now fulfilled in Christ, which requires a
work of global missionary conversion, of world Christianization. Down the
other, the specter of the militant revolutionary ready to spill blood on behalf
of his view of what the universal is. Still, is the fear of these specters a fear
of truth, as Badiou and Žižek claim? Is such fear the product of what they
consider a timid postmodern pluralism, in which nothing is really true since
no truth claim really has a universal traction, for which there is a whole for-
est of trees, the tree of Israel, the Bodhi tree, and trees still to be discovered?
Is it the best we can do to accommodate as many different takes on what is
true as possible?

While they are not unsympathetic with the philosophers, the historians gathered in this volume are interested in adding back what Badiou has
subtracted. For Badiou, the Christ-event has abolished Greek and Jew; it has
removed or annulled the defining characteristics of each one, and produced
an absolute and true universal. But such a universal for the historians would
be a gray-on-gray neutral, a neutered and ahistorical structure in which the
historical Paul himself would have no interest. For the historians, the un-
qualified universality of the cross, of the gospel that Paul announces, lies in
the universal extension of the Jew to include everyone, to all the "peoples"
(gentile or pagans), which for Paul includes the Jews who have rejected Jesus,
like branches broken from the olive tree of Israel. Pauline universality is
the universality of the inclusion of the Greek in the Jew, and this—here was
Paul's revolutionary gesture—without having to pass through the narrow
gate of the Jew, of circumcision or the law. God's promise to the Jews was
fulfilled in Christ, a Jew, whom Paul announces is available to all, Greek or
Jew, so that in the end we will all be Jews, spiritually, Jews not according to

the flesh but according to the spirit, having all come to acknowledge and to be acknowledged by the God of Israel. Everyone would be brought under the wing of the One God of Israel. Paul's universalism is the universalism of a monotheist who calls on all people to acknowledge the One God and who claims that the One God makes all people one. This is the universalism of conversion to something quite concrete (grafting), not the formalism of a philosophical universal (subtraction), like the principle of causality, or a mathematical universal, like the Pythagorean theorem. This universal is in fact a paradox, quite like Kierkegaard's paradox. In just the way that Kierkegaard said our eternal happiness is based on a particular point in history, Paul is saying that the well-being of all humanity is based on the events surrounding the death and resurrection of a Galilean Jew named Jesus, at the sound of whose name every knee should bend in heaven and on earth.

So it is not that all differences or distinctions are abolished, but that one difference or distinction in particular, the Jewish difference, is transformed and in being transformed proves to be transcendent, or better self-transcendent, in Christ Jesus, in whom it is able to break out of the particularity of the first form it took in the law and to trump and assimilate other differences, both its own early Jewish form and the Greek difference. Christ fulfills a Jewish promise, not a Greek one; he effects the fulfillment of the law and the prophets, not of Plato and Aristotle. The Christ-event is an event only in the context of the Jewish promise, and he is foretold—at least in the retrospective Christian (or strong) reading—by Jewish prophets and not by Greek wisdom. The crucifixion and resurrection of Christ is not an event for the Greeks; it makes no sense to them. Events require prior context or else they misfire or fail to register. Events must be inserted and exerted within an existing frame which they subvert, pervert, twist, or reinvent in a way that can catch on and cause things to reconfigure. The Copernican theory was an event in the sixteenth century; the same theory could be found in earlier premodern contexts where it was not an event; it simply made no sense. Events cannot simply happen out of the blue, ahistorically, and the subject of the event, however much fidelity he or she displays toward the event, cannot make it happen, cannot make it a success if the context is wrong. Events are like metaphors; they have to differ *from* the existing discourse while having enough purchase *in* the existing discourse to be recognized as a metaphor. They must have enough of an anchor in the existing usage for their novelty to be felt or for them to have any bite; otherwise, they are just gibberish.

Badiou and Žižek: St. Paul among the Philosophers

One way to see the significance that Paul holds for Badiou and Žižek is to go back to the debate about the economy of desire and recall that there are at least two alternatives to locating the origin of desire in a simple need or lack. One is René Girard's notion that desire is mimetic, that we desire the desire of the other, we desire what others desire; what constitutes the object of desire is our desire to have what others have. But we also desire to have what we are forbidden to have, which is no less constitutive of what we desire; we desire to have what we may not have. That story is as old as the second creation myth—where Yahweh precisely constitutes the tree of life as an object of desire by forbidding it—and that is the one that Paul makes famous in his critique of the law. The law chains us to an object precisely by forbidding it, and then, when we transgress the law, we are driven by guilt to reinforce the law, which sends us through the cycle one more time. When we live under the rule of the law, we are under the dark power of sin, where sin is not an individual deed but a domain or kingdom that holds us in its grip. We are dead under the law, slaves to sin and guilt, robots or automatons endlessly reenacting the pattern of prohibition and transgression. Paul does not want to say that the law *is* sin (although at times he seems to suggest it), but that the law is trapped in this unfortunate cycle of transgression. What the law wants, what it enjoins and prohibits, is good and holy and from God, but the system or schema to which law belongs is imperfect, for it has the effect of entrenching us more deeply in sin, like a driver spinning his wheels in a snowbank. The law is implicated in the system of death, trapped within the rule of "flesh" (desire). What is needed is a whole new order, one that is liberated from the economy of desire as a whole and breaks the entire circuit or cycle of transgression and prohibition, thereby introducing a new domain of life in which the rule of flesh is replaced with that of spirit. That is effected by the Christ-event, the pure grace and gratuitousness of the death and resurrection of Christ, which has purchased our freedom from the law and made us free, now children of God and no longer slaves of sin. Thus in place of a law that prohibits murder, there is the reign (or kingdom) of God, of the love of neighbor and even of one's enemies, in which what was negatively prohibited by the law is superseded by affirmation, by love of the other. At that point, the economy of the desire to have—to have what I lack, to have what the other has, or to have what I cannot have—is suspended in favor of something purely an-economic, which is not a desire to have at all. We reach a point that is either not well described as desire or is a desire that has become pure love and pure affirmation beyond having. Following an analysis first made by Lacan, this Pauline point has drawn the interest of both Badiou and Žižek.

In "St. Paul, Founder of the Universal Subject," Badiou condenses the general outlines of his approach to St. Paul.[2] He is a case in point for Badiou, an illustration and a confirmation of a theory that had been in place long before he turned to Paul. But Paul proves to be such a perfect example that it is as if Badiou could have just started there. In order to see what purpose Paul serves for Badiou, it is helpful to see Paul as the apostle of new life, of life victorious over death. For Paul, we were dead under the law and now are born again in Christ. For Badiou, what Paul calls death and life are allegories of our contemporary condition.

To see how Paul is our contemporary according to Badiou, we need to see the sense in which we too are dead and in need of a new life. This "death" Badiou locates in the deadly cycle of homogeny (sameness) and identitarianism (difference). On the one hand, there is the rule of "abstract homogenization," by which Badiou means "capital," the reign or rule of the world market, which can turn anything into a commodity, which can make money off anything. The market counts—it is interested in anything that can be added up and for which a profit margin can be calculated, without regard to content—anything from organic peppers to prostitution to pictures of the pope. It can turn a profit on Christianity or baseball, on religious paraphernalia no less than on adult bookstores. The dollars earned from one can easily be spent on the other; the market is a system of general equivalence. On the other hand, there is the proliferation of identity politics, of women's rights, gay rights, the rights of the disabled, of anti-Jewish or anti-Hispanic or anti-Italian defamation organizations, and so on, which both Badiou and Žižek treat with great cynicism. Žižek recently quipped that he wanted to start up a necrophiliac rights group. Each segment of identity politics creates a new market of specialty magazines, books, bars, websites, DVDs, radio stations, a lecture circuit for its most marketable propagandizers, and so on. By creating an endless series of proliferating differences, of new specialty markets, cultural identity fits hand in glove with the ever-proliferating system of global capital. According to Badiou, each side maintains and makes use of the other—and what the two sides have more deeply in common is that nobody on either side holds anything to be deeply true. An investment capitalist is as happy to make a buck on an automobile that pollutes the environment as on one that conserves fuel, and will shift from one to the other as the market demands. Identity rights advocates, in the view struck by Badiou and Žižek, are happy to have as many closed cultural identities as desired, however mutually contradictory they may be, so long as everyone is able to rent their own space. Nothing anywhere has any starch or pulp. The whole process, on both sides, Badiou maintains, is "without truth." The market has no interest in the truth value of what it sells, and those who practice identity politics are simply defending their own will to power, their own right to be different, not that anything they claim is true. But—and this is central to Badiou—what is "true" must be true for all, no matter who you are or whether it will turn a profit.

It is in the sense that the process is without truth that on Badiou's view we are "dead," that we are "under the law," caught up in the rule or kingdom of death, and that we need a new St. Paul, a Pauline fix. On the one hand, we need someone to hold and say something that is not just one more market-able idea, something that is withdrawn or subtracted from the market's ability to count and that is not counting on having a local appeal. The market is driven the way the Hegelian system is driven, which feeds on the principle of opposition; if you oppose it, that drives the dialectic, which is spurred on by an opposing principle. If you oppose the system of capital, write a good book on it, and get on the lecture circuit, you may have a best-seller on your hands. So Badiou thinks we need something *different* (a singularity) subtracted or excepted from the rule of homogeneity; we need a "truth procedure" that in-terrupts the rule of the received knowledge that everywhere prevails. Truths erupt as a singularity. On the other hand, we need a difference that is not just one more plea for the right to be different, one more identity, which Badiou regards as a political dead end. The singularity from which truth erupts must be genuinely universalizable: "Universalizable singularity necessarily breaks with identitarian singularity."[3]

When one attempts to universalize identitarian singularity—like "white" or "German" or "Christian"—the result is a catastrophe. We need a singularity, an innovation, a breakthrough, the grace of an event, from which all such differences have been subtracted. But when the rule of the market remains unbroken, the result is no less destructive. Then the truth of the work of art is displaced by cultural artifacts, products of the culture of the group, whose axiom is that you have to belong to the group to under-stand the culture. Then the truth of science is replaced by the technically useful or even the culturally popular—herbal teas have the same worth as antibiotics. Then the truth of politics is replaced by managers who negoti-ate among identitarian differences. Then the truth of genuine human love is replaced by the politics of sexuality, like the war between advocates of classical conjugal fidelity and homosexual rights. For Badiou, the system of abstract homogeneity and identity formation is a function of the interplay of the symbolic and the imaginary, while the singularity of the event has to do with the real, with the truth, which is why we get simulacra (culture/technique/management/sexuality) instead of the real thing (art/science/politics/love) and hence are incapable of genuinely disturbing the rule of capital. The result is a generalized culture war—between family values and feminists, scientists and creationists, all of whom belong to the same system that lacks a universalizable singularity.

Badiou calls on the Pauline paradigm to proclaim an event that trumps identitarian differences. For Paul, this meant proposing an alternative to the Greek discourse on wisdom, whose figure is the philosopher, on the one hand, and to the Jewish discourse on law, whose figure is the prophet, on the other hand. In so doing Paul announced something new that is true for all, something that was previously left out of the count, which interrupts the prevailing paradigms and in so doing introduces the new figure of the apostle who proclaims a new and universal order. This eventuates in a new configuration in which there is neither Jew nor Greek, slave nor free man, male nor female, where nationality, class status, and gender are annulled as differences that no longer count. Paul thus supplies a paradigm of a truth procedure. First, the truth erupts as a singular event that interrupts the existing order—for Paul, Christ crucified and raised again, which is foolishness to the Greeks and a stumbling block to the Jews, something that did not count in either discourse (see 1 Cor 1). Next, this event, which completely transforms Paul's life, is taken to constitute the subject. The subject is the one who is galvanized by the event. The event constitutes those who have accepted the event in their heart and proclaimed it on their lips as subjects. The event, in turn, must be named and offered to everyone without regard to the contingent conditions of their existence. The naming of the event is part of the event, and if the event is not successfully named, it does not happen (*arrive*). In point of fact, Badiou says that Paul himself names the event in a way that is completely fictional—the Pauline content of the event, the resurrection of the dead, is a fable, he says. But given his own theory, that could not be entirely true; otherwise the Pauline event would have misfired or fallen flat. In practice, Badiou actually keeps less of a distance from Paul than he is letting on; his actual treatment of the resurrection is less to dismiss it as a pure fable than to interpret it as a figure to which he attaches great allegorical importance. By adapting Paul's figure of a passage from death to a new life, the figure of rebirth and a certain resurrection, Badiou is signing on to part of the content of the Pauline event. But Badiou seeks to interpret this figure allegorically, to find the contemporary equivalent of this figure, the sense in which we today are dead (his critique of capitalism is that it is draining the life out of our world) and need a new life, need to be reborn, which is to adopt a view that is not far removed from radical theology or death of God theology, a point to which we will return below. Finally, this proclamation requires fidelity, a Pauline willingness to be shipwrecked, jailed, snakebitten, persecuted, and run out of town, a militant belief in something from which neither powers nor dominations can separate us, a militancy full of conviction (faith), indefatigability (love), and assurance (hope). Paul fought the good fight and stuck to his guns unto death, visiting and sending letters to a small band of brothers and sisters, at a great personal peril, and eventually effected a revolution under which we today still live.

For Žižek, the problem is also (and even more so than for Badiou) to escape the deadly cycle of law and transgression, and like Badiou he turns to Paul for help in finding a way out, a way that is singularly one of life. Like Badiou, Žižek expends considerable rhetoric criticizing the ethics of the other in liberalism and postmodernism, but one might well wonder, when their views are scrutinized, whether their criticism is directed at the principle itself or against the tepid, lukewarm, and compromised way in which they think it is honored in postmodernism. In *The Fragile Absolute* (2000) Žižek treats the Christian command of neighbor love, "the elementary Christian gesture—best designated by Pauline *agape*,"[4] as a more radical affirmation of the other than can be accounted for by the Lacanian triad of the imaginary, the symbolic, and the real:

> This injunction prohibits nothing; rather, it calls for an activity *beyond* the confines of the Law, enjoining us always to do more and more, to "love" our neighbor—not merely in his imaginary dimension (as our *semblant*, mirror image), on behalf of the notion of Good that we impose on him, so that even when we act and help him "for his own Good," it is *our* notion of what is good for him that we follow.[5]

As the famous case of the veil in France reveals, "our post-political liberal-permissive society"[6] honors the other only when the other is also a tolerant liberal just like ourselves; we honor the other only when the other is the same (narcissism; the imaginary), "a narcissistic (mis)recognition of my mirror-image."[7] The same text continues:

> [enjoining us to "love" our neighbor . . .] not merely in his symbolic dimension (the abstract symbolic subject of Rights).[8]

We ought to be accountable to individuals in the concreteness of their existence, not as instances or pure rational being in general (Kant), or as cases covered by the Decalogue, which belong to the sphere of the symbolic, where the cycle of law and transgression identified by Paul makes its nest.

> . . . but as the Other in the very abyss of its Real, the Other as properly *inhuman* partner, "irrational," radically evil, capricious, revolting, disgusting . . . in short, beyond the Good. This enemy-Other should not be punished (as the Decalogue demands), but accepted as a neighbor.[9]

As a case in point, Žižek mentions Sister Helen Prejean, whose stand against capital punishment is memorably portrayed in *Dead Man Walking* (1995), in which she advocates the cause of a homicidal rapist, Matthew Poncelet. The other person here is not idealized, not excused, but accepted with all his or her faults and flaws, accepted even as the "enemy" as such—like the Roman soldiers who crucified Christ and were forgiven by him—accepted qua thing (*Ding*), qua impossible, unknowable Real. This is a Lacanian rendering of the great paradox of the Sermon on the Mount, whose message has been compromised by any individual, institution, or state calling itself Christian. From a theological point of view, Žižek's account at this point is not immune from supersessionism; he treats this as a case of "going beyond the Decalogue" and gives no consideration to the argument that this established saying of Jesus is not offered by the Galilean rabbi Jesus in opposition to the Torah but as interpretation of it. Furthermore, Žižek curiously associates himself here with a radical pacificist strain in Christianity of the sort found in John Howard Yoder, with which he otherwise would have little patience. Žižek, who is an admirer of Lenin and on occasion even Stalin, thinks that changing the conditions of an unjust world requires something more than pacifism and nonviolence; the idea of nonviolent change by way of democratic elections is the ultimate illusion of democracy.[10]

Žižek compares Pauline *agape* to a shift in Lacan from an earlier masculine logic, in which the point of psychoanalysis is to reconcile the subject with the Big Other and eliminate the symptom, to a "feminine" logic in Seminar 20, in which the law itself is counted as one more symptom or "sinthome." This is more like "Christian charity, much closer to the dimension of the Other (subject) *qua* real . . . Christian charity is rare and fragile, something to be fought for and regained again and again."[11] Love is the "fragile absolute" which puts individuals directly in touch with the truly universal, with the Holy Spirit, and requires us to "'unplug' from the organic community into which we were born," from Jew and Greek, male and female, master and slave, to withdraw from the pagan One-All. The message of Jesus is directed to "those who belong to the very bottom of the social hierarchy," to those who are unplugged from social systems of power, and requires us to love each one qua Real, as a "unique person."[12] For example, "a new understanding of the father emerges, the moment the son, in effect, gets rid of the shadow of paternal authority . . . [and] the son perceives his father no longer as the embodiment of socio-symbolic function, but as a vulnerable subject 'unplugged' from it."[13] The process by which the subject dies to the law, one's social substance, and is reborn, begins afresh, is called the new creation. The fragile absolute is another dimension that breaks through to us in fleeting and fragile moments, like the love that can be detected in the smile or gesture of someone who has otherwise seemed to us cold and rude. That is sublimation, not idealization, because it has no illusions about the other's weakness, which is why Kierkegaard was right to say that love is a *work* of love and that while love believes all, love is not deceived.[14] For Žižek, unplugging does not mean to drop out of the social order but to invent an alternative one. With respect to the law, Christianity moves us beyond "masculine sexuation," which is to transgress the law and in so doing to reinforce it, to "feminine sexuation," which is an act of freedom and autonomy that abstains from it, suspends it, and refuses to be a part of it. That puts a new Žižekian spin on the crucifixion: God the Father, like Medea and like Sethe in Toni Morrison's *Beloved,* sacrifices his own Son rather than be a part of the blood sacrifice system of the law, and he does this precisely to open up a new order of freedom and grace beyond the law.

Three years later, in *The Puppet and the Dwarf,* Žižek returns to Paul by way of the very question Badiou first raised in 2002 as a way of casting his reading of Paul: who is really alive today?[15] Those in the West who aim low and focus on sustaining and enjoying the easy drift of the good life, where everything is safe but tedious, where nothing happens—no event—which is what Badiou calls happiness (Freud's pleasure principle)? Or those who aim high, beyond life, who put life on the line, those for whom something is really happening—an event—just because there is something more important than mere life, some excess of life (something, like freedom or dignity, say) for the sake of which it is worth putting life itself at risk (Freud's death drive)?[16] For example (citing G. K. Chesterton, along with Paul the other theological hero of this book), a soldier surrounded by enemies on all sides has a chance to escape only if he shows a courageous indifference to his own life, while a coward timidly trying to protect his life is done for. (Jesus on the other hand proposed a third alternative: putting down your sword and turning the other cheek!) Žižek then goes on to denounce opponents of the death penalty as defenders of the tepid, painless anemic life, Sister Helen Prejean to the contrary notwithstanding! The icon of this tepid life, he quips, is decaffeinated coffee or alcohol-free beer—deprived of the Real!—and its goal is a long, pleasurable life protected from every risk and every real pleasure.

We today, Žižek says, are like those "anemic Greek philosophers" who laughed at Paul's doctrine of the resurrection.[17] We lack the living power to affirm something dangerous and have only the half-dead negative power to whine about suffering; the only absolute today being absolute evil, like the Holocaust. We are ghosts, the living dead, the undead, not living spirits.[18] Paul is not saying to suspend the law so as to embrace wanton transgression, but (in effect) to obey the laws as if you are not obeying them, to suspend the law, the rule or reign of prohibition that provokes transgression and draws us down its dark corridors (its "obscene underside"), just in order to put on the new being.[19] The law (the symbolic order) is not jettisoned, but we strike up a new relationship to what the law commands. To turn Kant against himself, we do things that are comfortable to duty, this time not out of pure duty, *pace* Kant, but out of love. The "time of the event," the shock of the Real, and of subsequent fidelity to the event, spells the difference between life and death.[20] Žižek focuses on Pauline love as what he calls a "fighting universal," a *work* of love, that wrestles with the Other in all its unpleasantness or even repulsion, which must succeed in concretizing or carrying out the event in day-to day-existence (which Paul would have called filling up what is missing in the body of Christ). The event means "it is consummated," something happened—and now the real work of implementation begins. In Christianity, as opposed to the Jewish messianisms, the Messiah has already come and died and done his work, which leaves us not with the luxury of coasting on or living off this event but with the burden of carrying out the messianic event, making it live. As Deleuze would have said, we must make ourselves worthy of this event. Žižek's interpretation of Christianity here is reminiscent of Bonhoeffer's—God expects us to assume responsibility for the direction of our lives and not wait for him to show up in the nick of time to bail us out. God is the one who took the risk here: "by dying on the cross, He made a risky gesture with no guaranteed final outcome . . . the divine act stands, rather, for the openness of a New Beginning, and it is up to humanity to live up to it, to decide its meaning." God steps into his own creation, "exposing himself to the utter contingency of existence." We live "in the aftermath of the Event, of drawing out the consequences—of what? Precisely of the new space opened up by the Event."[21]

But beyond Bonhoeffer, Žižek also reminds us of various traditions of radical theology that go back to Hegel, like death of God theology, in which the death of the Christ is the beginning of the kingdom of God on earth, which we are responsible to realize. The view Žižek strikes at this point comes close to Vattimo's recent work on Christianity, which is importantly influenced by the theory of the three ages in Joachim of Fiore, the age of the Father (the Old Testament), the age of the Son (the New Testament), and finally the age of the Spirit, of the kingdom of God on earth, where we are no longer servants but friends, when we must complete and carry out what the Son initiated.[22] The death of Christ represents the commencement of the age of the Spirit for Žižek, for whom "'Holy Spirit' designates a new collective."[23] "The Perverse Core of Christianity," the subtitle of *The Puppet and the Dwarf*, turns out to be a play on words. It means that the orthodox view—God has died for our sins in the economy of salvation—is perverse because it reinscribes us in the economy of debt and payment. But the core of Christianity is exactly the opposite ("an-economic"), introducing "another dimension," a "religion of atheism," which perverts that perversion—for an event perverts an already perverted or subversive system—which recognizes that there is no such economy. The true core of Christianity is the perversion of a perversion, the death of death. What better summary of contemporary death of God theology than the following text from Žižek, in which, comparing his position to Lacanian psychoanalysis, Žižek brings his book to the following conclusion:

> The treatment is over when the patient accepts the non-existence of the big Other . . . the patient accepts the absence of such a guarantee. . . . The point of this book is that, at the very core of Christianity, there is another dimension. When Christ dies, what dies with him is the secret hope discernible in "Father, why hast thou forsaken me?": the hope that there is a father who has abandoned me. The "Holy Spirit" is the community deprived of its support in the big Other.[24]

But this critique of religion is not to be confused with a modernist critique of the big Other, which just reinstates the big Other by another name:

> . . . rather it attacks the religious hard core that survives even in humanism, even up to Stalinism, with its belief in History as the "big Other" that decides on the "objective meaning" of our deeds. . . . it is possible to redeem this core of Christianity only in the gesture of abandoning the shell of its institutional organization. . . . That is the ultimate heroic gesture that awaits Christianity: in order to save its treasure, it has to sacrifice itself—like Christ, who had to die so that Christianity could emerge.[25]

At this point Žižek effectively (if unwittingly) rehearses the argument of Mark C. Taylor in *Erring* on behalf of a "postmodern a/theology," beyond a modernist atheism.[26] The age of the spirit is not to be a "vulgar humanist" (modernist) death of God, which puts Man (Feuerbach) or History (Marxism) in the place of God, but a posthumanist one—what virtually anyone working in the field would call a "postmodern" theology, a term regularly denounced by Žižek.

What do Badiou and Žižek desire? What do they want? Cast in its most positive terms, what is finally at stake for Žižek, as for Badiou, is what Paul calls "life," that is, the new order, the new space opened up by the event, the freedom and ambience of grace, beyond the law, where we find such fragile treasure as life has to offer in the midst of life's risky and contingent course. With the event comes the ethics of the event, the responsibility to make ourselves worthy of the event (Deleuze)—to produce something new, something genuinely *alive,* which will break the rule of death, of the not-quite dead. In the superficial quasi-life of consumption and "happiness," all real risk has been removed and replaced with virtual risk—like watching TV thrillers broadcast in surround sound and high definition in a safe and privileged cultural-political site sitting atop a mountain of global injustice. The genuinely vital life, on the other hand, would be marked by the eruptive event of justice, of a genuinely political act, and the turmoil of its aftermath.

In his contribution to the present volume Žižek comes back to the theme of Christian atheism laid out in *The Puppet and the Dwarf.* Here Žižek returns to Paul not exactly as Badiou's apostolic militant, nor as a proto-Lacanian who leads us out of the circle of transgression, but as the first death of God theologian. By focusing our attention on the death and resurrection of Jesus, Paul deserves credit both for inventing Christianity and for seeing Christianity through to its end in the "death of God," whose meaning Žižek has more and more been attempting to plumb. The present essay might be seen to have three stages: (1) an interpretation of the radical atheism with which his favorite Christian theologian, G. K. Chesterton, wrestles; (2) the ethical implications of this atheism, which can be seen in the book of Job; (3) finally, a radicalized—as opposed to the garden variety—Hegel, in whom the Pauline death of God is laid out in the most decisive manner possible.

The point of departure is a reading of G. K. Chesterton's novel *The Man Who Was Thursday,* which is an allegory of the two-sidedness of God who from one side (the back) looks like evil itself and from another (the front) like the good and beautiful. Taken together with Chesterton's *Orthodoxy,* this novel reveals what Žižek regards as Chesterton's "darkest moment," that God is the site of the highest contradiction, the identity of opposites, which shows up in the last words on the Cross where God (in Jesus) laments that he too is forsaken by God, which means that God too is for an instant an atheist, that God doubts, that God rebels against himself. (The political equivalent of this unity of opposites today, Žižek points out, is the masquerade under which the anarchy of lawlessness—capitalist greed, the war in Iraq—mask themselves as law and order, God and nation, a point made in Shelley's "The Mask of Anarchy.")

This metaphysical atheology has enormous consequence for ethics, which means for Žižek that this figure of Jesus on the cross must be linked with the figure of Job before God, who laments the inscrutable way in which God has abandoned him (Job) to the worst. For Žižek the insight with which Chesterton is grappling can be adequately articulated only by a radicalized Hegel. To begin with, God is not the reconciling unity of opposites, but the site of strife and endless antagonism. God falls into his own creation and is torn asunder by it in a battle of good and evil. But as long as one remains in the raw antagonism of God's two sides—good and evil, peace and rage—the framework remains pagan. The specifically Christian element enters only with the notion of a suffering God, which Chesterton explains in his book on Job. Žižek, who both shares and savors Chesterton's taste for paradox, underlines Chesterton's claims that order is the greatest miracle, law the greatest anarchy, orthodoxy the greatest rebellion—and the authoritarianism of the Church is the greatest way to protect reason, for if faith in the authority of God and his Church fails, nothing will be left standing, including reason itself. That is how to understand the long discourse God delivers to Job on the wonders of the natural world he has made. For God himself is surprised by the world's marvels and by the fact that each and every thing, however commonplace it may seem, is exceptional, a mystery and a miracle all its own, a belief that today motivates not religion but the natural sciences. On Žižek's telling, the masculine logic of God the creator who has reasons Job's reason cannot understand gives way to a feminine logic of God embodied in the natural sciences which is truly open to the unforeseeable surprises that nature holds, as the paradoxes of relativity theory and quantum physics confirm. The book of Job ends with the dismissal of the ontotheologians, of the theological rationalizers of the problem of evil, and with Job's acceptance that there is no rationale for his suffering, no deeper meaning. God is not the one who knows the meaning of what seems to us like meaningless suffering, nor is there anything God can do about it except to look on sympathetically and suffer along with Job (us).

Enter (Žižek's) Hegel—and a certain (atheistic) Christianity. For Žižek, the received wisdom about Paul as the inventor of Christianity is actually right—Paul made the messenger into the message—and for him the Pauline trail is the one picked up in Protestantism (whereas Greek Orthodoxy is Johannine and Catholicism is Petrine). Paul focused exclusively on the death and resurrection of Jesus, and the interpretation of that death is still being worked out today. If we do not want to reduce it to sacrifice, which is a pagan-mythic schema, or to a payment for sin, which is an economic schema, then what are we to think is happening in this death on the cross? What dies—in Job's and then again in Jesus' lamentations—is the big story that suffering is a short-term pain for a long-term gain and the God who guarantees a happy outcome. What dies along with it is the hand-in-glove unity of the natural world God made with the God who made it, which one sees in Thomas Aquinas. This death and dying shows up in Protestantism, where a war breaks out between a godless universe which is the object of Enlightenment reason, on the one hand, and trusting in a transcendent God with a faith that is pure feeling, devoid of cognitive status, the result of which is to debase both reason and faith. This predicament, Žižek thinks, can be seen in Kant, where Newtonian knowledge, up against an unknowable in-itself, has to content itself with appearance and make room for Protestant faith that cannot understand what it believes. These are opposing forces with which Hegel tried to come to grips in "Faith and Knowledge."

The theoretical center of Žižek's unique Paulinianism lies in what he has recently been calling the parallax, the identity lying behind a double alienation (or *kenosis*). Žižek means that just as modern humanity is alienated from God so God in turn is alienated from himself in Christ. How are we to deal with double alienation? Not by going back to Thomas Aquinas's medievalism but by seeing that just as human beings are called on to rise above their animality and become truly human, so God must descend into his world and assume our miserable status. The abject status of Christ is described in *The Parallax View,* in connection with a provocative reading of Kierkegaard, as the "comedy of Incarnation."[27] These are not two different things, but a parallax, two different ways at looking at the same thing. "The distance of man from God is thus the distance of God from Himself," he writes in the present essay. Or, as Catherine Malabou puts it, "the suffering of God and the suffering of human subjectivity deprived of God must be analysed as the recto and verso of the same event." Our own sense of distance from God is the other side of God's distance from himself. That is what the Marxist critique of religion misses—it is the one ghost too many of religion that Marx dismisses, as Derrida might have put it.

There is thus another Hegel afoot here, for the standard Hegel is complicit with the old God who now has died, with the Absolute Spirit as the immanent Absolute which sees to it that God writes straight with crooked lines. That, Žižek says in the present essay, is a cliché about Hegel that he wants to upend. As the transcendent Father dies in the Son (Incarnation), so the death of the Son on the cross is also the death not only of the Son (crucifixion) but also of the Immanent Spirit ("my God, why have you abandoned me?") if the Spirit is misconstrued as the cunning of the Absolute Spirit, who steers all things wisely and well to their end. What dies is God himself under any Trinitarian description you choose:

> The point this [traditional] reading [of Hegel] misses is the ultimate lesson to be learned from the divine Incarnation: the finite existence of mortal humans is the only site of the Spirit, the site where Spirit achieves its actuality.... Spirit is a *virtual* entity in the sense that its status is that of a subjective presupposition: it exists only insofar as subjects *act as if it exists*. Its status is similar to that of an ideological cause like Communism or Nation: it is the substance of the individuals who recognize themselves in it, the ground of their entire existence, the point of reference which provides the ultimate horizon of meaning to their lives, something for which these individuals are ready to give their lives, yet the only thing that really exists are these individuals and their activity, so this substance is actual only insofar as individuals believe in it and act accordingly. The crucial mistake to be avoided is therefore to grasp the Hegelian Spirit as a kind of meta-Subject, a Mind, much larger than an individual human mind, aware of itself: once we do this, Hegel has to appear as a ridiculous spiritualist obscurantist, claiming that there is a kind of mega-Spirit controlling our history.... This holds especially for the Holy Spirit: our awareness, the (self)consciousness of finite humans, is its only actual site ... although God is the substance of our (human) entire being, he is impotent without us, he acts only in and through us, he is posited through our activity as its presupposition.[28]

The *Aufhebung*, then, is not of finite individuals into the Absolute Spirit, but the exact Žižekian opposite: the Absolute itself into finite individuals. Now if we venture to characterize an *Aufhebung* as a demythologization, we may say that just as the transcendent God is demythologized by Hegel, so Hegel as the philosopher of Absolute Spirit is demythologized by Žižek.

And so is Paul, to return to the point.

Paul between the Jews and Christians

Whether Paul would have recognized himself in any of this is not a concern for Žižek. Historians, on the other hand, especially historians who have been lured and cajoled into the same room with philosophers and theologians, are always worried about anachronism, about shedding too quickly the baggage of historical context in order to soar more freely in the air of speculation. That is a concern of the historians who contribute to this volume, but it is not unmixed with a certain admiration for the case Badiou and Žižek have made, at least on the point of Paul as the founder of universalism (the question of the "death of God" did not come up). If we may be allowed to borrow a venerable distinction from theology, we might say that there are historians who are just and historians who are merciful. In that case, Paula Fredriksen is more just in her approach to the philosophers while Dale Martin, E. P. Sanders, and Daniel Boyarin are more merciful.

Fredriksen, who is concerned with doing strict historical justice to Paul, draws a rigorous epistemological divide between what Paul, a mid-first-century Jewish visionary, thought, and what was made of him in the subsequent history of Western philosophy and theology. While Fredriksen is rigorous in policing this distinction, she is not about to actually call the police on the philosophers or theologians or, in the case of Žižek and Badiou, the atheologians. What the later tradition makes of foundationalist texts is both necessary and necessarily anachronistic—it departs from the original text and context. That is to say, later generations are nourished by the foundational texts in ways that meet the needs of their times and reflect their own standpoints as much as, and perhaps more than, the foundational texts themselves. That is as it should be. The tradition is marked by geniuses who give strong misreadings of foundational texts which shape their own times and that of subsequent generations. Instead of making themselves contemporaries with Paul, they make Paul "Our Contemporary" (the title of Badiou's first chapter), that is, their own contemporary. Fredriksen is not going to fall on her sword over this, but she would feel better about it if the latter-day philosophers and theologians would at least come clean on this point and admit that such is indeed what is going on.

To illustrate her point, Fredriksen compares Origen's Paul, Augustine's Paul, and Badiou's Paul. Origen's Paul is a universalist—the author of a theory of universal salvation. God is good, everything God made is good, which means that everything will return to God—eventually. It's just that some things will return more quickly, depending on how far out on the rim of the material universe their souls have landed. But God does not throw anyone away. Augustine's Paul is also a universalist—but the author of a theory of universal condemnation. Everything is steeped in original sin and deserves eternal condemnation; still God, in his mercy, chooses to intervene here and there and snap a soul or two from the jaws of hell. Why are some chosen and others not? That is beyond Augustine, beyond Augustine's Paul, beyond comprehension. It belongs to the unfathomable mystery of God. So don't ask. Both authors clinch their argument by citing exactly the same texts (Rom 9). Badiou's Paul is also a universalist—the author of a post-Marxist theory of universal equality. But what is missing from all three Pauls is the apocalyptic in-breaking God, the imminent arrival of God in time to bring about the kingdom. Thus philosophers and theologians use their considerable powers to "produce a more consistent apostle" by leaving out—by subtracting what does not fit and using what they can. That is tolerable, for Fredriksen, if only they would confess that it is they who speak, not the apostle.

This discussion of the historical and theological context of Paul's universalism is continued by New Testament historians E. P. Sanders and Dale Martin. They do not deny that there is a universalism in Paul, but they think it has a different meaning than the strictly philosophical sense it takes on in Badiou. For Sanders, the question of universalism in Paul's thought does not turn on a philosophical concept of universality but on the theological motif of God's plan for universal salvation. Sanders begins with the question of Paul's context "between Judaism and Hellenism," which has produced much debate. Paul was at home in the Greco-Roman world and the world of Jewish scripture and interpretation. But which is the more important context for understanding his view of universal salvation, which he held concurrently with the view that some, not all, would be saved? Sanders bases his assessment of Paul's educational background on the quotations made by Paul. In the ancient world, children learned by memorizing, and the quotations used by adults reflected what they had memorized as children. In Paul's surviving letters, one quotation is from a gentile source, but there are dozens from the Greek translation of Jewish scripture. From this Sanders infers that he was most familiar with the Hebrew Bible in Greek translation. Jewish and Greco-Roman conceptions of time and history were quite distinct. The Greeks thought of history as cyclical. The Jewish view was that history runs in a straight line, from creation to a conclusion determined by God. A study of the resurrection in Paul's letters shows that here too his thought was basically determined by Jewish categories, despite Greek touches at various points. Paul's statements of universal salvation appear in the context of the grand climax of history. Paul could have learned the theory of universal truth and universal equality from Greek or Latin philosophers, and they may have contributed to his universalism. In his letters, however, he connects the hope of universal salvation to the coming of Christ and the conclusion of human history: it is a Jewish-Christian theological concept. The reader of Paul does not know how to reconcile his exclusivism (only those in Christ will be saved) with his universalism (God will manage to redeem the entire creation). This is a question for Christian theology that cannot be solved simply by quoting Paul.

The contribution by historian Dale Martin is a pivotal one in the present collection. For Martin, the readings of Paul proposed by Alain Badiou and Slavoj Žižek seem remarkably on target, even when judged from the point of view of current professional historical criticism. Badiou's notion of "event" does sound like Paul's ways of speaking about the Christ-event. But Badiou and Žižek do not provide us with much content, certainly not systematic theological or philosophical *propositions,* for the *meaning* of the event. Paul's emphasis on his universal mission does spring, as Badiou and Žižek maintain, from Paul's monotheism. Badiou is right to see grace as central for Paul, and to note Paul's relative lack of interest in distributive justice or, in mythological terms, hell. In these and many other ways, Badiou and Žižek propose a Paul that can be affirmed also by contemporary Pauline scholars. But the one aspect of the interpretation proposed by Badiou and Žižek that is both central to their appropriations of Paul and rejected by many current scholars of Paul, at least in the past twenty years or so, is the insistence, similar to nineteenth-century interpreters, that Paul's main mission was to found a new and universal nation, a new ethnicity, or, even more mistakenly, a new religion. Recent biblical scholars have increasingly argued that Paul saw his own mission as one of grafting gentiles into the already existing ethnos (nation, people) of Israel. He was not suppressing the variety of ethnicities but grafting them all onto the one true ethnos—the olive tree of Israel. Paul's own universalism (there is a *certain* universalism in him, but the question is how to get a fix on it) is affected by his apocalypticism, which constrained his epistemology and provided him with a teleology much different from that of ancient or modern universalist philosophers. When pressed by Sanders in the roundtable that followed Martin's presentation about the extent of the metaphor of the tree, about whether Paul's final vision of the salvation of all humankind did not push beyond the figure of the tree of Israel, Martin thought that there is simply an ambiguity about this point in Paul. As Sanders remarks, it is not clear that Paul himself knew exactly what he thought about that.

Boyarin's argument follows closely along the lines of Martin and Sanders, both of whom link Paul with his Jewish and even apocalyptic roots, but differs on just this point from Badiou's approach. For Boyarin, Paul is a radical Jew and Boyarin undertakes to abstract (subtract) him from his Christianity. For Badiou, Paul is a radical militant, a pure subject, and

Badiou attempts to abstract (subtract) him from his Christianity and his Jewishness. Apart from Badiou's practice of an extreme abstraction (subtraction), which thinks there is nothing to the material particularities of Paul's life, Boyarin agrees that Badiou does get the idea of a world-transforming and life-transforming event in Paul right. Badiou takes Galatians 3 as subtracting community identities from truth. Truth transcends history and community. But for Boyarin, Paul is not trying to establish universality. Greek (or pagan) and Jew are religious identities for Paul, to which faith in Christ is being contrasted. The law was our baby-sitter until we matured into faith. On Boyarin's interpretation, Paul is warning the Galatians away from slipping back into the Torah, whose observance of days (Sabbath) and annual events determined by the place of the heavenly bodies is like pagan worship of heavenly bodies. We were once slaves to all these things, but not anymore.

Finally, Richard Kearney changes the subject somewhat and draws in the voice of Agamben by exploring the Pauline distinction between two radically different notions of *dunamis*—as power and as possibility. Following Kierkegaard's and Heidegger's disclosure of a post-metaphysical understanding of the possible, Kearney's own work turns on a distinction between a metaphysical conception of potentiality (*dunamis*), the classic expositions of which are found in Aristotle and Thomas Aquinas, in which potentiality is subordinated to and ultimately annulled by actualization, and what he calls the eschatological conception of power as possibility, as possibilizing, as the endlessly spiraling dynamic of a being toward the future. This conception is not ontological but phenomenological, not metaphysical but mystical, religious, and poetic. It is found in a long line of thinkers stretching from Paul's own idea of the power of God through Angelus Silesius and Nicholas of Cusa and the poet Gerard Manley Hopkins. After setting forth this distinction in the first half of this chapter, Kearney offers a critical review of some of the recent readings of Paul by Agamben, Badiou, and Žižek in the second part. Kearney concludes his analysis with an outline of a postmodern hermeneutics of the possible, reflecting the controversial theological turn in continental philosophy, and his own notion of a microeschatology of the least among us, rooted in Paul's affirmation of the "nothings and nobodies of the world" (1 Cor 1:28). Kearney's microeschatology is focused precisely on the point of what Žižek and Badiou call singularity, that is, on the one not counted in the prevailing system of counting, for which we are the most accountable of all, which thereby represents the universalizable singularity par excellence.

Notes

1. Slavoj Žižek, *The Puppet and the Dwarf: The Perverse Core of Christianity* (Cambridge, Mass.: MIT Press, 2003), 130.

2. The book at the heart of the current debate is Alain Badiou, *Saint Paul: The Foundation of Universalism,* trans. Ray Brassier (Stanford, Calif.: Stanford University Press, 2003). Badiou's magnum opus is *Being and Event,* trans. Oliver Feltham (London: Continuum, 2005). The most readable presentation of his thought is *Ethics: An Essay on the Understanding of Evil,* trans. Peter Hallward (London: Verso, 2002). Peter Hallward has also written the most comprehensive guide to his work: *Badiou: A Subject to Truth,* with a foreword by Slavoj Žižek (Minneapolis: University of Minnesota Press, 2003).

For more on Paul among the philosophers in the literature, see Daniel M. Bell Jr., "The Politics of Fear and the Gospel of Life," *Journal of Cultural and Religious Theory* 8, no. 2 (Spring 2007): 55–80; Ward Blanton, "Apocalyptic Materiality: Return(s) of Early Christian Motifs in Slavoj Zizek's depiction of the Materialist Subject," *Journal of Cultural and Religion Theory* 6, no. 1 (December 2004): 10–27; Ward Blanton, "Disturbing Politics: Neo-Paulinism and the Scrambling of Religious and Secular Identities," *Dialog* 46, no. 1 (Spring 2007); 3–13; Roland Boer, *Criticism of Heaven: On Marxism and Theology* (Leiden: Brill, 2007), chap. 7; Alain Gignac, "Taubes, Badiou, Agamben: Reception of Paul by Non-Christian Philosophers of Today," *Society of Biblical Literature Seminar Paper* 41 (2002): 74–110; Adam Kotsko, "Politics and Perversion: Situating Zizek's Paul," *Journal of Cultural and Religious Theory* 9, no. 2 (Summer 2008): 43–52; P. Travis Kroeker, "Whither Messianic Ethics? Paul as Political Theorist," *Journal of the Society of Christian Ethics* 25, no. 2 (Fall-Winter 2005): 37–58; Denis Müller, "Le Christ, relève de la Loi (Romans 10,4): La possibilité d'une éthique messianique à la suite de Giorgio Agamben," *Studies in Religion/Sciences religieuses* 30, no. 1 (2001): 51–63; Gerrit Neven, "Doing Theology without God? About the Reality of Faith in the 21st Century," *Journal of Cultural and Religious Theory* 6, no. 3 (Fall 2005): 30–42.

3. Whatever differences there are between them, Jacques Derrida and Gilles Deleuze, Slavoj Žižek and Alain Badiou all agree on one central point: there is an essential correlation between singularity and universality. Each thing is singularly itself, each and everything. Each and everything, universally, is itself in virtue of its singular structure. That is why the forgotten transcendental in the medieval theory of transcendentals is not the beautiful, as theologian Hans Urs von Balthasar claims, but the *aliquid:* every being, insofar as it is a being, is a "something," something singular, a *hoc aliquid,* as Duns Scotus says. What everything has in common is its unique difference.

4. Slavoj Žižek, *The Fragile Absolute—or Why the Christian Legacy Is Worth Fighting For* (London: Verso, 2000), 113.

5. Žižek, *Fragile Absolute,* 111–12.

6. Žižek, *Fragile Absolute,* 110.

7. Žižek, *Fragile Absolute,* 112.

8. Žižek, *Fragile Absolute,* 112.

9. Žižek, *Fragile Absolute,* 112.

10. Slavoj Žižek, "From Purification to Subtraction: Badiou and the Real," in

Think Again: Alain Badiou and the Future of Philosophy, ed. Peter Hallward (London: Continuum, 2004), 180.

11. Žižek, *Fragile Absolute,* 118.

12. Žižek, *Fragile Absolute,* 123.

13. Žižek, *Fragile Absolute,* 126.

14. Žižek, *Fragile Absolute,* 128.

15. Žižek, *The Puppet and the Dwarf,* 94–96.

16. Žižek, *The Puppet and the Dwarf,* 95.

17. Žižek, *The Puppet and the Dwarf,* 99.

18. Žižek, *The Puppet and the Dwarf,* 100.

19. Fortunately, Žižek says that this is how the law actually works in Judaism (*The Puppet and the Dwarf,* 113), for the Jewish law is not *Sittlichkeit,* not a set of laws regulating social exchange, but a divine justice that separates the Jew from the existing social order, so that the Jews are "unplugged" from the social substance around them (*The Puppet and the Dwarf,* 119).

20. Žižek, *The Puppet and the Dwarf,* 134–36.

21. Žižek, *The Puppet and the Dwarf,* 136–37.

22. Gianni Vattimo, *After Christianity,* trans. Luca D'Isanto (New York: Columbia University Press, 2002), 30–32.

23. Žižek, *The Puppet and the Dwarf,* 130.

24. Žižek, *The Puppet and the Dwarf,* 169–70.

25. Žižek, *The Puppet and the Dwarf,* 171.

26. Mark C. Taylor, in *Erring: A Postmodern A/theology* (Chicago: University of Chicago Press, 1984), 6: deconstruction is the hermeneutic of the death of God.

27. Slavoj Žižek, *The Parallax View* (Cambridge, Mass.: MIT Press, 2006), 103–11. This section of *The Parallax View,* along with pages 179–87, made up the text that Žižek read at the Syracuse conference in April 2005 under the title "St. Paul with Kierkegaard, or, the Comedy of Christianity." Žižek contributes a new piece of writing to this volume.

28. Žižek, "From Job to Christ," chapter 2 in this volume.

PART ONE

Paul among the Philosophers

ONE

St. Paul, Founder of the Universal Subject

ALAIN BADIOU

The Figure of Our World

What is the figure of our world?

- On the one hand, we have the constant extension of the automatisms of capital, which fulfills Marx's brilliant prediction: the configuration of the world as a global market. This is a figure of abstract homogenization, that is, a generalization of the count unit. In short, it is a singularity that allows for no singularity. All this is nothing else but a singularity of the homogeny that is situated by the paradigm of the general equivalent.
- On the other hand, we have a process of fragmentation into closed identities. These identities are drawn from two sources: (1) the insignificance of reality—identity comes to signify insignificance; and (2) the over-significance of mythic imaginary, for example, racial identity, which is the absolute insignificance of the corporal trait, or else the mythic over-significance of religion or origins.

But each identification, whether a creation or a contrived fabrication of identity, creates a figure which becomes the material for its being invested by homogenization. The semblant of a non-equivalence is necessary for equivalence to be itself a process of identity. This leads us to a major correlation: any construction of identity is destructive. Capital needs destruction, and even massive destruction, to redevelop. A correlation exists between the process of homogeny and the process of identity: that of the destructive submission of identity to homogeny.

The set articulated here is organically without truth. In effect, any process of truth is at variance with the figure of the same. It interrupts the repetition and cannot then be sustained by homogeny. No truth can be sustained by the expansion of homogeny, but neither can it be by the construction of identities, for singularity is universalizable. But universalizable singularity is necessarily at variance both with the singularity constructed from identity and with homogeny. The world is the arena for the play of both axiomatic homogeny (market, capital) and mythological identity. We might say that the world is, in part, an interplay of the symbolic and the imaginary in response to the collapse of the real. And this eliminates the event, and so fidelity to the event, which is the subjective essence of the truth. The world is then hostile to the process of truth insofar as it resists the universal of identity through homogeny or the adhesion to constructed identities. The symptom of this hostility is an effect of the overlapping of names: where the name of a truth procedure would have its place, another name appears which expels it in the direction of homogeny. The name "culture" thus obliterates the name of "art," for the cultural can be inscribed within the market. The name "technique" obliterates the name "science," as Heidegger said. The word "management" obliterates the word "politics." The word "sexuality" obliterates "love." This system of culture, technique, management, sexuality is the superposition of the registers of homogeny.

Take the problem from the point of view of identity. In the case of art, we have a superposition of culture, but since the culture of the group is self-destined, it is un-universalizable. In the case of science, we have a superposition of the technical; in the case of the political, a superposition of religious determination as "fundamentalism"; in the case of love, the superposition of marriage, of the conjugal. The two systems mirror each other; each is legitimated by the discredit of the other. In fact, there is no superiority of the cultivated, the competent, the managerial, the sexually liberated, over the fanatic believer, submitted to a hypocritical morality.

Paul and the Topic of the Discourses

Our question is then, Where and how can we hold forth that universal singularities exist? With respect to this we must call on St. Paul, because his question was not different from ours (which explains his conflicts concerning Jewish identity, including that of Christ). For him, if an event has taken place, and if the truth consists in declaring it (and subsequently being faithful to it), it must be held that the truth is evental when it occurs and that it is singular (neither structural, nor axiomatic, nor legal).[1] It must also be held that, for the same reason, this truth cannot be reserved only to some, but that it is offered to all, universal, destined to each and every one with no identitary definition.[2] It favors no origin. The singularity of the event thus breaks the law, for every truth is illegal, that is to say, incommensurable with the law.

In the 50s of the Christian era, Paul instituted universal singularity and the subject that is its support. In the epistle to the Galatians, he writes, "Christ redeemed us from the curse of the law" (Gal 3:13). Christ, then, is the name of an event, and in fidelity to this Christ-event identities are dissolved: "There is no longer Jew or Greek, there is no longer slave or free, there is no longer male and female" (Gal 3:28).

At the moment St. Paul is speaking, three major circumstances are in place:

- The known world is unified within a powerful political structure, the Roman Empire. In other words, the world is situated under the sign of the One.
- There are two dominant discourses; one is Jewish, the other Greek.
- For one very small group, an event has taken place whose meaning is obscure.

When Paul speaks here of the Greek or the Jew and then of the *ethnoi*, we must understand that the referents of these words are different types of discourses. It is not for him a question of a historical or objective location, but of two subjective figures to which he opposes a third discourse, his own, the Christian discourse. We need to apprehend this delimitation.

A discourse is Jewish if it is founded on the requisition of a sign, if it calls for the sign, if it authorizes the spoken word inasmuch as it constitutes a sign. The subjective figure attached to it is the prophet. Ultimately this figure is a sign of transcendence. A discourse is Greek if it is a discourse of wisdom, that is to say, of the appropriation of the order of the world, and if it thus depends on the pairing of the logos with Being. It is any cosmic discourse in the etymological sense. It is the philosophic discourse, the discourse that loves wisdom. The discourse of totality, by which the subject asserts his place within the totality, is Greek; it is the discourse of the *physis*, of inclusion within totality as natural harmony. The discourse of the exception is Jewish. The sign, the miracle, election indicate transcendence beyond natural totality. The Jewish people itself is exceptional in this sense. The discourse that disposes the order of the world in order to adjust to it is Greek. The discourse that argues from the exception to the order of the world as a sign of transcendence is Jewish. The Christians oscillated between these two discourses, Judeo-Christian or Pagano-Christian.

But Paul's fundamental inspiration is neither Judeo-Christian nor Greco-Christian. This is why it makes no difference to him whether he addresses the

Jews or the Greeks (the Greek discourse). What is important is to be done with the articulation of the two. Paul's endeavor is to effectuate not a synthesis but a diagonal of the two discourses. His aim is to trace a third figure of discourse.

This attempt can only be accomplished if there is a collapse of the figure of the master. For Paul, in effect, there are two possible figures of the master.

- the master who is authorized by the totality: a master of wisdom, the Greek master, who determines what constitutes a rightful inclusion within the totality.
- the master who is authorized by the power of the exception, by the sign as such: the Jewish master, who prophesies.

The figure Paul attempts to construct includes the collapse of mastery. Paul is thus neither a prophet nor a philosopher, but he occupies a third posture. The triangulation proposed is: prophet—philosopher—apostle.

The Evental Declaration

What does the word "apostle" name? For Paul, this name has no empirical or historical signification. It is not, for example, a synonym for "companion of Christ." It is a discursive and subjective figure: the apostle is the one who declares the Christ-event. The gospel is news that is strictly evental. It is neither a matter of producing signs nor of proposing wisdom, but of declaring an event. The authorization for this declaration has no anecdotal basis. There was no witness to what was declared. There was only a pure calling to be the one who would make the declaration: "Paul, called to be the apostle of Jesus Christ." This calling is supernumerary; it is pure grace. It is co-included in the event itself. The event being what must be declared, the subjective figure of the apostle is authorized by what he declares, and so strictly by himself. Paul reminds us often of this. We obtain then the two following theses starting from the beginning of the first epistle to the Corinthians.

First thesis: The announcement of the gospel is made without the wisdom of language (*ouk en sophia logou*), "so that the cross of Christ might not be emptied of its power" (1 Cor 1:17). If we were within this order of wisdom, the Christ-event would be vain, for the nature of the event is such that the wisdom of the logos is unable to declare it. Whatever it can declare is inappropriate to the cross. The underlying thesis is that, if there is an event, it must always be manifested by a point of impasse affecting the language. "Event" means that the established

figures of discourse are powerless to declare it. In the framework of
established discourses, there is no naming process available for an
event. For anyone who is installed in the wisdom of language, the
event is as if it had not taken place; it is vain. We must then begin
with an "evental naming." Paul thus declares that Christ has risen
and that this constitutes the "having-taken-place." The event has
taken place and we are no longer co-present to it in the sense of being
witnesses. It must then be received into the language, and that alone
will constitute a subject. Neither of the two discourses available, that
of the philosopher or that of the prophet, can declare the event.

Second thesis: The declaration is, as such, sheer folly, a nonsensical
discourse. It is devoid of reason and so we have the "folly of the
predication" against the logos. If there is an event, its declaration
appears as madness, that is to say, none of the figures of discourse
has the capacity to assume it. The death of Christ is appropriate
neither to the totality nor to the manifest power of the register
of the exception. Someone's being crucified does not constitute a
sign for any transcendence whatsoever. The ignominious death
of the slave does not in itself constitute the sign of any power.

From these theses, Paul elaborates a series of oppositions: foolish things opposed to wise things, folly opposed to wisdom; weakness and insignificance
opposed to strength and over-significance; for the declaration of the event
supposes weakness and folly. So in the declaration, we find neither the God of
wisdom nor the God of power. He is not even the God of Being, for God chose
what is not over what is. He intermingled the two. It is a matter of declaring
in the Christ-event the non-being, folly, weakness. Paul puts forth a third
discursive figure. To the wisdom of Greek discourse, he opposes the folly of
the cross, and thus the event, establishing the anti-philosophic characteristic
of the Christian discourse as he understands it. Paul is hostile to any reconciliation of Christian discourse with philosophy. To the signs of power and
election, he opposes the scandal of weakness and the ignominy of the death
of Christ (*asthêneia/ischus*).

It can all be recapitulated in what Paul names the choice of non-being
(*ta mê onta*) over those things which are. In his eyes, the Christian discourse
is in an absolutely new relationship to its object. It is effectively a question
of another figure of the real. This figure will be deployed by the revelation
that there are two subjective figures and not one, and so a cleavage of the
subject: the opposition between the way of the flesh and the way of the spirit,

which is not related to the substantial division body/soul but to a subjective division.

In Greek discourse, the object is cosmic totality as appropriated by thought. As a consequence, the real causes desire to take its place in cosmic totality such as it is appropriated by thought; the real is identified with a place one must find one's way to: wisdom. For Paul, on the contrary, the Christ-event indicates precisely the vanity of places, that is to say, that the real appears at the point of the ruin of any place and cannot correspond to a desire to find a place within a totality homogeneous to thought. Thus in 1 Corinthians 4:13: "we have become like the rubbish of the world, the dregs of all things, to this very day." We must then assume the subjectivity appropriate to rejects and that is what Christian discourse assimilates its object to.

In Jewish discourse, the object is to belong to the chosen, the exceptional alliance of God and his people, the seal of the alliance, assented to and manifested in observance of the law. The real can only be attained under the law. But the Christ-event is heterogeneous to the law; it is pure excess with respect to the law. The real cannot be what always finds its place as in Greek discourse; nor can it be that part of an exception that is registered under the immemorial character of the law.

The "folly of predication" will exempt us from Greek wisdom by the disqualification of the regime of places and totality, and free us from the law. The real for Paul is pure event and nothing else. What exists is the Subject who declares this real. For anyone who considers that the real is pure event, the Greek and Jewish discourses remain marked by a difference. This is the incentive for Paul's universalistic conviction. The difference ceases to be significant and operative. The two discourses are no longer distinguished by a real; the distinction is purely rhetorical. In Romans 10:12, Paul points this out: "For there is no distinction between Jew and Greek." More generally, from the moment that the real is identified as an event, the differences between discourses are abolished because the form of the real they propose is exposed as an illusion. The pronunciation of this non-difference establishes precisely the potential universality of Christianity. The Paulinian wager is that a discourse can exist which configures the real as pure event and which, from that point on, addresses everyone without exception. Is it possible? In any case, Paul tries to pursue this path.

What then is the *event* for Paul? It certainly is not the biography, the teachings, the collection of miracles of one particular person, that is, Jesus. We only have to recall that the Gospels were written twenty years after Paul. The event is not a teaching; Christ is not a master and he cannot have disciples. The pure event is reducible to this: that Jesus died on the cross and rose from the dead. This event is "grace" (*charis*). It is then neither a legacy, nor a tradition, nor a predication. It is supernumerary with respect to all that and is presented as pure donation. Our subjective constitution depends on this event: "You are not under law but under grace" (Rom 6:14).

The Way of Death and the Way of Life

What is the function of death in this affair? It is a question of knowing if we are within a dialectic. Is there a traversing of the negative that would be the path to an essential affirmation? Can we attain true life by traversing death? If it were the case, there would be a specifically redeeming function of suffering and death, the negation of which constitutes the life of the spirit. From this should follow the necessity to share this suffering. But the Paulinian scheme is non-dialectic, and the event is in no way on the side of death. Note that suffering plays no role in Paul's apologetics, not even in the death of Christ. The feeble and abject character of this death is certainly of importance to him, but he accords no function of redemption to suffering. Death must not be explored from the aspect of suffering, but from the aspect of the affirmative power of the new life. For Paul, we have the cross, but not the way of the cross: this will be my formula. No climbing to Calvary. No masochistic propaganda about suffering. For Paul, death is not the operation of salvation, because it is on the side of the flesh and the law. It has no sacred function, nor spiritual assignation. Death is in reality the name of the other way, the way that refuses to declare the event, even though this event includes death.

Paul says with respect to this: "For those who live according to the flesh set their minds on the things of the flesh; but those who live according to the Spirit set their minds on the things of the Spirit. To set the mind on the flesh is death, but to set the mind on the spirit is life and peace" (Rom 8:5–6). Death is a subjective determination, which is that of the flesh and so of the law. Life, on the contrary, is the subjectivity of the spirit. Death is not for Paul exclusively a question of dying or of biology, but a form of thinking. Death, which is thought in the sense of the flesh and the law, is Greek or Jewish. It cannot be constitutive of the Christ-event. So, what has death got to do with it? Why does Christ die? Death is the path by which we, human beings, become like unto God. That is its unique necessity; it is the means of attaining equality with God himself. By this thought of the flesh, the fact of being in the same element as God himself is dispensed to us by grace. Death names here an apparatus without transcendence. At some moment an end must be put to the separation from God. For, in the radical transcendence (the Father), the unique figure is, in the eyes of Paul, that of the law, an immobile structure. Paul perfectly understood that a doctrine of the real as event includes conditions of immanence, without which we remain in the domain of the miracle. The structure must be made immanent. This is what he designates in Romans 6:4–10:

> Therefore we have been buried with him by baptism into death so that just as Christ was raised from the dead by the glory of the Father, so we too might walk in newness of life.
>
> For if we have been united with him in a death like his, we will certainly be united with him in a resurrection like his. We know that our old self was crucified with him so that the body of sin might be destroyed and that we might no longer be enslaved to sin. For who has died is freed from sin. But if we have died with Christ, we believe that we shall also live with him. We know that Christ, being raised from the dead, will never die again; death no longer has dominion over him. The death he died, he died to sin, once for all: but the life he lives, he lives to God.

Death is not in itself an operation of salvation but an operation of equalization. We become like Christ for he becomes like us. Paul calls this a "reconciliation" (*katallagê*), which must be clearly distinguished from salvation (*sôteria*): "For if, while we were enemies, we were reconciled to God by the death of his Son, much more surely, having being reconciled, will we be saved by his life" (Rom 5:10). To understand the relation between *katallagê* and *sôteria,* the relation between life and death, is to understand that for Paul there is disjunction between the death of Christ and his resurrection. The resurrection is neither what comes after death nor what overcomes it, but something else. There is a separation between the function of death and the function of the resurrection, because death, including the death of Christ, is a notion of the flesh. Only one thing comes out of it: that God disengaged thought from the flesh. The event remains integrally affirmative. The operation is immanentist on the one hand, evental on the other. In a very Nietzschean sense, Paul writes, "For the Son of God, Jesus Christ, whom we proclaimed among you, Silvanus and Timothy and I, was not 'Yes' and 'No,' but in him it was always 'Yes'" (2 Cor 1:19).

Death is always what we have opted for. We could also say that the Christ-event, the fact that there was *this* son, outside the reach of death, retroactively denotes that death was a process and not a state of things. It is neither a destiny nor a destination, but a choice. So there is, rigorously, no

Being-for-death; there is never anything but a subject-for-death. A part of Paul's system is constantly scrutinizing this point: what can be said about death if it is construed as a process and not as a state of things? Paul ends up giving the name of law to death as a subjective figure. The law will become the operator of the identification of death as a subjective option. In short, we have four assertions:

The event is precisely named resurrection
It is radically singular as the resurrection of only one, of a son
Thus named, the event identifies death
This identification will be largely developed by
    Paul finally under the name of law

We can then articulate four points constitutive of Paul's theory of the subject.

1. Why is the way of the flesh as well as the way of death designated ultimately under the name of law? What is this knotting of flesh (*sarx*) and law, since the flesh, a figure of the subject, is the same thing as death, which falls under the name of the law? Three of Paul's texts can be evoked: "To set the mind on the flesh is death, but to set the mind on the spirit is life and peace" (Rom 8:6); "Christ redeemed us from the curse of the law by becoming a curse for us" (Gal 3:13); "For Christ is the end of the law so that there may be righteousness for every one who believes" (Rom 10:4). This last enunciation—if Christ is the pure event of the resurrection, the resurrection is what opens up to a way other than that of the flesh and death, that is to say, for Paul, life—establishes an essential correlation between law and death. The law is in effect what gives us access to the fact that death is effectively a subjective process and not the destiny of Being. It is only from the position of the law that the intelligence of desire is possible. Paul is the first thinker to state that law and desire are the same thing. The essence of the law is in effect to chain desire to an object. There must be law in order to indicate to desire the object that enchains it. It is not the subject that lives; it is desire that lives its own autonomous life. Sin is then a subjective structure at the heart of which we find the law of the object. Sin is correlated to the withdrawal of the will. For the subject to cease being connected to sin, there must be an event, for there is no law that comes as a successor to the law. There is no immanent successor. The resurrection is the possibility for a subject to be constituted within other dispositions than that of the law.

2. What exactly is the resurrection? It is an extraction from the process of death. But why does this radically singular event, that is to say, the resur-

rection of *this* son, have a universal effect? What in it has the power to level differences? Why does it follow that there is no longer either Greek, nor Jew, nor male, nor female, nor bondsman, nor freeman? It is because a link exists between the singular event and universality.

3. How does this event institute a new subject, since what counts is being a new creature? In other words: how can a subject be constituted along another path than that of death or the knotting of law to flesh? It is striking that this other subject is constituted with reference to an enunciation and not as the pure consequence of the pure event. The resurrection does not signify a power of direct constitution. What constitutes the subject is its being pronounced. If the resurrection had a power in itself, it might be assimilated to a miracle, and so to a sign. But the event is not a collection of testimonies and does not in itself have a power. The power comes from a subjective declaration, which will be called *pistis,* faith, or "conviction."

4. How can the subject persevere subsequent to subjectivation? What is this other way? What is the structure of life as life of the spirit? What is "true life," as Rimbaud calls it? This structure is love (*agapê*). It is not a matter of virtue, since Paul's fundamental conviction is that the contrary of sin is not virtue but faith. It is also a constitutive assertion of Kierkegaard's in the *Sickness unto Death.* "Virtue" senses its law and so its death. For faith, it is not so; faith unbinds the law from the literal. Paul takes the law, the law of Moses, and reduces it to "Love thy neighbor as thyself." The imperative is that the love of self be the norm or the measure of the love we are capable of. That supposes that the love of self be within a new era. The Christian subject has authentic reasons to love himself: he loves in himself the possibility of the way of life. He loves in himself the salvation of humanity.

These four points will weave the "Christian" discourse. What is it composed of? Its components are also four.

1. What causes a subject? An event. But the causality is not of a transitive order, for the event does not have of itself the power of causation. "One of us has been excepted from death": that is what causes the subject, but this cause is preserved from any objectivity. The object-cause has no objectivity. So it is absent; it has opened a hole in the world; it has defeated it. In this sense, there is an a-cosmic character to Paul's thinking.

2. The subject is constituted as divided with respect to its cause. There is a division constitutive of the subject with respect to its cause between the word and the intimate conviction, which Paul names conviction of the heart. The conviction of the heart alone does not make for salvation according to Paul: "The word is near you, on your lips and in your heart" (Rom 10:8). There is a

division instituted by speech itself between declaration and belief. Paul declares that, for salvation, it is the pronouncing that counts. A Christian subject is not a subject who believes in the event, but who declares he believes. The only Christians then are militant. Merely believing is not enough to inscribe the event within the world, for the only Being of the event is being declared, since it is a "having-taken-place" which has vanished. Belonging to this event requires taking heed of it, and so declaring it. The true subject bars his belief by the pronouncement. The faith, the *pistis,* is what is proclaimed and not simply what is nourished within subject interiority. The heart guarantees in this way a relation to what is just.

3. The insistence of the subject will convoke the Other as the place of love. Why is it love? This is what is left of the law when the letter has been extracted from it. For Paul, the relation to God is not to know but to be known by the Other, that is by God. The relation of salvation to God is to be known. Being known by the Other requires that knowledge be obliterated by love, which is truth in the place of the Other. What is important here is to obliterate the knowledge one has of the Other on behalf of the love we have for him. "Knowledge puffs up, but love builds up. Anyone who claims to know something does not yet have the necessary knowledge; but any one who loves God is known by him" (1 Cor 8:1–3).

4. The residue of any subjective configuration is the law. It is dead, mortal, obsolete. From the point of view of the subject, it is what is lost. A tentative definition of the Paulinian Christian subject might be: the subject is he who, declaring the event, finds himself immediately divided between an inaccessible intimacy and an enunciation that carries neither wisdom, nor sign. The truth will come to the place of the Other inasmuch as he insists on loving him. The law, which can be reciprocal with desire, is the dead remains of this love. Such a discourse on the subject can inspire us: not because we should believe in the resurrection of the dead, but because it is we ourselves who must resuscitate. Cornered between monetary abstraction and petty national, religious, or racial identities, we are no longer alive.

Translated by Thelma Sowley

Notes

1. In French *événementiel* is recent (1931) and is given in the dictionary as ill formed. In fact, well formed, it would have been *événemental.* The *Robert* defines it as meaning *de l'événement,* in English "relating to the event," "linked to the event," or

"belonging to the event." "Evental" is a neologism in English having the same structure as *événemental* in French. It is used by Oliver Felthman and Justin Clemens in their translation of Badiou under the title *Infinite Thought*. I know of two other translations of the term: "eventful" is certainly a contresens, and "event making," which is closer, is not really adequate, *une vérité événementielle* not being a truth that makes an event but a truth that is created by an event.

2. *Identitaire* is a neologism in French that has not yet found its place in *Grand Robert* (1991) but is commonly used in today's political and sociological discussions.

TWO

From Job to Christ: A Paulinian Reading of Chesterton

SLAVOJ ŽIŽEK

The standard notion that Paul created Christianity as we know it is fully justified: it was Paul who shifted the center from Christ's acts and teachings to the redemptive quality of his death. Today, two thousand years later, this death of God is still an enigma: how to read it outside the pagan-mythic topic of divine sacrifice or the legalistic topic of exchange (payment for sin)? What exactly dies on the cross? In the history of Christianity, it was Protestantism which was "Paulinian," focusing on the death of God, in contrast to "Johannine" Orthodoxy and "Petrine" Catholicism.

No wonder, then, that the most interesting moments in Catholic theology occur when it unexpectedly comes close to Protestantism. Such was the case with Jansenism, which gave a unique Catholic twist to the Protestant notion of predestination; and such is the case of Gilbert Keith Chesterton, who thought through the notion of the "death of God" to its radical conclusion: only in Christianity, God himself has to go through atheism. Chesterton first formulated this vision of the traumatic core of Christianity in his religious thriller *The Man Who Was Thursday,* the story of Gabriel Syme, a young Englishman who makes the archetypal Chestertonian discovery of how order is the greatest miracle and orthodoxy the greatest of all rebellions. The focal figure of the novel is not Syme himself, but a mysterious chief of a super-secret Scotland Yard department who is convinced that "a purely intellectual conspiracy would soon threaten the very existence of civilization":

> He is certain that the scientific and artistic worlds are silently bound in a crusade against the Family and the State. He has, therefore, formed a special corps of policemen, policemen who are also philosophers. It is their business to watch the beginnings of this conspiracy, not merely in a criminal but in a

controversial sense. . . . The work of the philosophical policeman . . . is at once bolder and more subtle than that of the ordinary detective. The ordinary detective goes to pot-houses to arrest thieves; we go to artistic tea-parties to detect pessimists. The ordinary detective discovers from a ledger or a diary that a crime has been committed. We discover from a book of sonnets that a crime will be committed. We have to trace the origin of those dreadful thoughts that drive men on at last to intellectual fanaticism and intellectual crime."[1]

As cultural conservatives would put it today, deconstructionist philosophers are much more dangerous than actual terrorists. While the latter want to undermine our politico-ethical order to impose their own religious-ethical order, deconstructionists want to undermine order as such.

We say that the most dangerous criminal now is the entirely lawless modern philosopher. Compared to him, burglars and bigamists are essentially moral men; my heart goes out to them. They accept the essential ideal of man; they merely seek it wrongly. Thieves respect property. They merely wish the property to become their property that they may more perfectly respect it. But philosophers dislike property as property; they wish to destroy the very idea of personal possession. Bigamists respect marriage, or they would not go through the highly ceremonial and even ritualistic formality of bigamy. But philosophers despise marriage as marriage. Murderers respect human life; they merely wish to attain a greater fullness of human life in themselves by the sacrifice of what seems to them to be lesser lives. But philosophers hate life itself, their own as much as other people's. . . . The common criminal is a bad man, but at least he is, as it were, a conditional good man. He says that if only a certain obstacle be removed—say a wealthy uncle—he is then prepared to accept the universe and to praise God. He is a reformer, but not an anarchist. He wishes to cleanse the edifice, but not to destroy it. But the evil philosopher is not trying to alter things, but to annihilate them.[2]

This provocative analysis demonstrates Chesteron's limitation, his not being Hegelian enough: what he doesn't get is that *universal(ized) crime is no longer a crime—it sublates (negates/overcomes) itself as crime and turns from transgression into a new order.* He is right to claim that, compared to the "entirely lawless" philosopher, burglars, bigamists, even murderers are essentially moral: a thief is a "conditionally good man." He doesn't deny property AS SUCH, he just wants more of it for himself and is then quite ready to respect it. However, the conclusion to be drawn from this is that CRIME IS AS SUCH "ESSENTIALLY MORAL," that it wants just a particular illegal reordering of the global moral order which should remain. And in a truly Hegelian spirit, one should bring this proposition (of the "essential morality" of the crime) to its immanent reversal: not only is crime "essentially moral" (in Hegelese: an

inherent moment of the deployment of the inner antagonisms and "contradictions" of the very notion of moral order, not something that disturbs moral
order from outside, as an accidental intrusion); but *morality itself is essentially
criminal*—again, not only in the sense that the universal moral order necessarily "negates itself" in particular crimes, but, more radically, in the sense that
*the way morality (in the case of theft, property) asserts itself is already in itself
a crime*—"property IS theft," as they used to say in the nineteenth century.
That is to say, one should pass from theft as a particular criminal violation of
the universal form of property to this form itself as a criminal violation: what
Chesterton fails to perceive is that the "universalized crime" that he projects
into "lawless modern philosophy" and its political equivalent, the anarchist
movement that aims at destroying the totality of civilized life, *is already realized in the guise of the existing rule of law,* so that the antagonism between
Law and crime reveals itself to be inherent to crime, the antagonism between
universal and particular crime.

However, when one continues to read the novel, it becomes clear that
Syme's position is only the starting point. At the novel's end, the message is
precisely the identity of crime and law, the fact that the highest crime is law
itself, that is, the novel's end *does* explicitly posit the identity between Law and
universalized/absolute crime—therein resides the final twist of Thursday, in
which "Sunday," the arch-criminal, anarchist's all-powerful leader, is revealed
as the mysterious chief of the super-secret police unit who mobilizes Syme into
the fight against anarchists (i.e., HIMSELF). After Syme is recruited by this mysterious chief reduced to a voice in darkness, his first duty is to penetrate the
seven-member Central Anarchist Council, the ruling body of a secret super-
powerful organization bent to destroy our civilization. In order to preserve
their secrecy, members are known to each other only by a name of the week;
through some deft manipulation, Syme gets elected as "Thursday."

At his first council's reunion, Syme meets "Sunday," the larger-than-life
president of the Central Anarchist Council, a big man of incredible authority, mocking irony, and jovial ruthlessness. In the ensuing series of adven-
tures, Syme discovers that the other five regular members of the council are
also secret agents, members of the same secret unit as himself, hired by the
same unseen chief whose voice they've heard. So they join their forces and
finally, at a lavish masked ball, confront Sunday. Here the novel passes from
mystery to metaphysical comedy: we discover two surprising things. First,
that Sunday, president of the Anarchist Council, is the same person as the
mysterious never-seen chief who hired Syme (and other elite detectives) to
fight the anarchists; second, that he is none other than God Himself. These

discoveries, of course, trigger a series of perplexed reflections in Syme and other agents. Syme's first reflection concerns the strange duality he noticed when he first met Sunday: seen from the back, he appears brutal and evil, while, seen from the front, face-to-face, he appears beautiful and good. So how are we to read this twosome nature of God, this unfathomable unity of Good and Evil in Him? Can one explain the bad side as just conditioned by our partial, limited, view, or—a horrible theological vision—is the back really His face, "an awful, eyeless face staring at me," whose deceptive mask is the good jovial face?

> When I first saw Sunday . . . I only saw his back; and when I saw his back, I knew he was the worst man in the world. His neck and shoulders were brutal, like those of some apish god. His head had a stoop that was hardly human, like the stoop of an ox. In fact, I had at once the revolting fancy that this was not a man at all, but a beast dressed up in men's clothes. . . . And then the queer thing happened. I had seen his back from the street, as he sat in the balcony. Then I entered the hotel, and coming round the other side of him, saw his face in the sunlight. His face frightened me, as it did everyone; but not because it was brutal, not because it was evil. On the contrary, it frightened me because it was so beautiful, because it was so good. . . . When I see the horrible back, I am sure the noble face is but a mask. When I see the face but for an instant, I know the back is only a jest. Bad is so bad, that we cannot but think good an accident; good is so good, that we feel certain that evil could be explained. I was suddenly possessed with the idea that the blind, blank back of his head really was his face—an awful, eyeless face staring at me! And I fancied that the figure running in front of me was really a figure running backwards, and dancing as he ran.[3]

If, however, the first, more comforting version is true, then "we have only known the back of the world." "We see everything from behind, and it looks brutal. That is not a tree, but the back of a tree. That is not a cloud, but the back of a cloud. Cannot you see that everything is stooping and hiding a face? If we could only get round in front—"[4]

However, things get even more complicated: God's essential goodness is held against him. When asked who he really is, and Sunday answers that he is the God of Sabbath, of peace, one of the enraged detectives reproaches him that "it is exactly that that I cannot forgive you. I know you are contentment, optimism, what do they call the thing, an ultimate reconciliation. Well, I am not reconciled. If you were the man in the dark room, why were you also Sunday, an offense to the sunlight? If you were from the first our father and our friend, why were you also our greatest enemy? We wept, we fled in terror; the iron entered into our souls—and you are the peace of God!

Oh, I can forgive God His anger, though it destroyed nations; but I cannot forgive Him His peace."[5]

As another detective notices in a terse English-style remark: "It seems so silly that you should have been on both sides and fought yourself."[6] If there ever was British Hegelianism, this is it—a literal transposition of Hegel's key thesis that, in fighting the alienated substance, the subject fights his own essence. The novel's hero, Syme, finally springs to his feet and, with mad excitement, spells out the mystery:

> I see everything, everything that there is. Why does each thing on the earth war against each other thing? Why does each small thing in the world have to fight against the world itself? Why does a fly have to fight the whole universe? Why does a dandelion have to fight the whole universe? For the same reason that I had to be alone in the dreadful Council of the Days. So that each thing that obeys law may have the glory and isolation of the anarchist. So that each man fighting for order may be as brave and good a man as the dynamiter. So that the real lie of Satan may be flung back in the face of this blasphemer, so that by tears and torture we may earn the right to say to this man, "You lie!" No agonies can be too great to buy the right to say to this accuser, "We also have suffered."[7]

This, then, is the formula provided: "So that each thing that obeys law may have the glory and isolation of the anarchist." So that Law is the greatest transgression, the defender of the Law the greatest rebel. However, where is the limit of this dialectic? DOES IT HOLD ALSO FOR GOD HIMSELF? Is He, the embodiment of cosmic order and harmony, ALSO the ultimate rebel, or is He a benign authority observing from a peaceful Above with bemused wisdom the follies of mortal men struggling against each other? Here is the reply of God when Syme turns to him and asks him: "Have you ever suffered?"

> As /Syme/ gazed, the great face grew to an awful size, grew larger than the colossal mask of Memnon, which had made him scream as a child. It grew larger and larger, filling the whole sky; then everything went black. Only in the blackness before it entirely destroyed his brain he seemed to hear a distant voice saying a commonplace text that he had heard somewhere, "Can ye drink of the cup that I drink of?"[8]

This final revelation—that God suffers even more than we mortals—brings us to the fundamental insight of *Orthodoxy,* Chesterton's theological masterpiece (which belongs to the same period; he published it a year later than *Thursday*), not only the insight into how orthodoxy is the greatest transgression, the most rebellious and adventurous thing, but a much darker insight into the central mystery of Christianity:

When the world shook and the sun was wiped out of heaven, it was not at the crucifixion, but at the cry from the cross: the cry which confessed that God was forsaken of God. And now let the revolutionists choose a creed from all the creeds and a god from all the gods of the world, carefully weighing all the gods of inevitable recurrence and of unalterable power. They will not find another god who has himself been in revolt. Nay (the matter grows too difficult for human speech), but let the atheists themselves choose a god. They will find only one divinity who ever uttered their isolation; only one religion in which God seemed for an instant to be an atheist.[9]

Because of this overlapping between man's isolation from God and God's isolation from Himself, Christianity is "terribly revolutionary. That a good man may have his back to the wall is no more than we knew already; but that God could have His back to the wall is a boast for all insurgents for ever. Christianity is the only religion on earth that has felt that omnipotence made God incomplete. Christianity alone has felt that God, to be wholly God, must have been a rebel as well as a king."[10] Chesterton is fully aware that we are thereby approaching "a matter more dark and awful than it is easy to discuss . . . a matter which the greatest saints and thinkers have justly feared to approach. But in that terrific tale of the Passion there is a distinct emotional suggestion that the author of all things (in some unthinkable way) went not only through agony, but through doubt."[11] In the standard form of atheism, God dies for men who stop believing in Him; in Christianity, God dies *for Himself.*[12]

Peter Sloterdijk was right to notice how every atheism bears the mark of the religion out of which it grew through its negation.[13] There is a specifically Jewish Enlightenment atheism practiced by great Jewish figures from Spinoza to Freud; there is the Protestant atheism of authentic responsibility and assuming one's fate through anxious awareness that there is no external guarantee of success (from Frederick the Great to Heidegger in *Sein und Zeit*); there is a Catholic atheism à la Maurras, there is a Muslim atheism (Muslims have a wonderful word for atheists: it means "those who believe in nothing"), and so on. Insofar as religions remain religions, there is no ecumenical peace between them—such a peace can only develop through their atheist doubles. However, Christianity is an exception here: it enacts the reflexive reversal of atheist doubt into God Himself. In his "Father, why have you abandoned me?" Christ commits what is for a Christian the ultimate sin: he wavers in his Faith. While in all other religions, there are people who do not believe in God, only in Christianity God does not believe in Himself. This "matter more dark and awful than it is easy to discuss" is narratively presented as the identity of the mysterious Scotland Yard chief and the president of the anarchists in *Thursday*.

The ultimate Chestertonian opposition thus concerns the locus of antagonism. Is God the "unity of the opposites" in the sense of the frame containing worldly antagonisms, guaranteeing their final reconciliation, so that, from the standpoint of the divine eternity, all struggles are moments of a higher Whole, their apparent cacophony a subordinate aspect of the all-encompassing harmony? In short, is God elevated above the confusion and struggles of the world in the way Goethe put it?

> And all our days of strife, all earthly toil
> Is peace eternal in God the Lord.[14]

Or is antagonism inscribed in the very heart of God, or is "Absolute" the name for a contradiction tearing apart the very unity of the All? In other words, when God appears simultaneously as the top policeman fighting the crime and the top criminal, does this division appear only to our finite perspective (and is God "in Himself" the absolute One without divisions)? Or is it, on the contrary, that the detectives are surprised to see the division in God because, from their finite perspective, they expect to see a pure One elevated above conflicts, while God in Himself *is* the absolute self-division? Following Chesterton, one should conceive such a notion of God, the God who says "Can ye drink of the cup that I drink of?" as the exemplary case of the properly *dialectical* relationship between the Universal and the Particular: the difference is not on the side of particular content (as the traditional *differentia specifica*), but on the side of the Universal. The Universal is not the encompassing container of the particular content, the peaceful medium-background of the conflict of particularities; the Universal "as such" is the site of an unbearable antagonism, self-contradiction, and (the multitude of) its particular species are ultimately nothing but so many attempts to obfuscate/reconcile/master this antagonism.

To put it even more pointedly: God is not only not the "unity of the opposites" in the (pagan) sense of maintaining the balance between the opposed cosmic principles, shifting the weight to the opposite sense when one pole gets too strong. God is not only not the "unity of the opposites" in the sense of one pole (the good One) encompassing its opposite, using evil, struggle, difference in general, as means to enhance the harmony and wealth of the All. It is also not enough to say that he is the "unity of the opposites" in the sense of being himself "torn" between the opposite forces. Hegel is talking about something much more radical: the "unity of the opposites" means that, in a self-reflexive short circuit, God falls into His own creation; that, like the proverbial snake, He in a way swallows/eats Himself by His own tail. In short, the "unity of the opposites" does not mean that God plays with Himself the game of (self-) alienation, allowing evil opposition in order to overcome it and thus assert its moral strength, and so on. It means that "God" is a mask (a travesty) of "Devil," that the difference between Good and Evil is internal to Evil.

What this Chestertonian identity of the good Lord and the anarchist Rebel enacts is the logic of the social *carnival* brought to the extreme of self-reflection: anarchist outbursts are not a transgression of the Law and Order. In our societies, anarchism already IS in power wearing the mask of Law and Order—our Justice is the travesty of Justice, the spectacle of Law and order is an obscene carnival—the point made clear by the arguably greatest political poem in English, "The Mask of Anarchy" by Percy Shelley, which describes the obscene parade of the figures of power:

> And many more Destructions played
> In this ghastly masquerade,
> All disguised, even to the eyes,
> Like Bishops, lawyers, peers, or spies.
>
> Last came Anarchy: he rode
> On a white horse, splashed with blood;
> He was pale even to the lips,
> Like Death in the Apocalypse.
>
> And he wore a kingly crown;
> And in his grasp a sceptre shone;
> On his brow this mark I saw—
> 'I AM GOD, AND KING, AND LAW!'

Today it is part of feminist politically correct rules to praise Mary, Percy's wife, as the one who gained a deeper insight than her husband into the destructive potential of modernity. In her *Frankenstein,* she stopped short of this radical identity of the opposites. Many interpreters of *Frankenstein* face a dilemma that concerns the obvious parallel between Victor and God on the one side and the monster and Adam on the other side: in both cases, we are dealing with a single parent creating a male progeny in a nonsexual way; in both cases, this is followed by the creation of a bride, a female partner. This parallel is clearly indicated in the novel's epigraph, Adam's complaint to God: "Did I request thee, Maker, from my clay / To mould Me man? Did I solicit thee / From darkness to promote me?" (*Paradise Lost* 10.743–45). It is easy to note the problematic nature of this parallel: if Victor is associated with God, how can he also be the Promethean rebel against God (recall the novel's subtitle: "The Modern Prometheus")? From Chesterton's perspective, the answer is simple: there is no problem here. Victor is "like God" precisely when he commits the ultimate criminal transgression and confronts the horror of its consequences, since *God IS also the greatest Rebel*—against Himself, ultimately. The King of the universe is the supreme criminal Anarchist. Like Victor, in creating man, God committed the supreme crime of aiming too high—of creating a creature "in his own image," new spiritual life, precisely like scientists today who dream of creating an artificially intelligent living being. No wonder that his own creature ran out of his control and turned against him. So what if the death of Christ (of himself) is the price God has to pay for his crime?

Mary Shelley withdrew from this identity of the opposites from a conservative position; more numerous are the cases of such a withdrawal from a "radical" leftist position. Exemplary here is *V for Vendetta,* a film which takes place in the near future when Britain is ruled by a totalitarian party called Norsefire; the film's main opponents are a masked vigilante known as "V" and Adam Sutler, the country's leader. Although *V for Vendetta* was praised (by Toni Negri, among others) and, even more, criticized for its radical—pro-terrorist, even— stance, it does not go to the end: it shirks from drawing the consequences from the parallels between V and Sutler. The Norsefire party is, we learn, the instigator of the terror it is fighting—but what about the further identity of Sutler and V? In both cases, we never see the live face (except the scared Sutler at the very end, when he is about to die). We see Sutler only on TV screens, and V is a specialist in manipulating the screen. Furthermore, V's dead body is placed on the train with the explosives, in a kind of Viking funeral strangely evoking the name of the ruling party: Norsefire. So when Evey—the young girl who joins V—is imprisoned and tortured by V in order to learn to overcome fear and be free, is this not parallel to what Sutler does to the entire English population, terrorizing them so that they get free and rebel? Since the model of V is Guy Fawkes (he wears Guy's mask), it is strange that the film refuses to draw the obvious Chestertonian lesson of its own plot: the ultimate *identity* between V and Sutler.[15] In other words, the missing scene in the film is the one in which, when Evey takes off the mask of the dying V, we see beneath the mask Sutler's face.

However, the attentive reader has already guessed that we do not have merely a duality, but a *trinity* of the features/faces of God: the whole point of the novel's final pages is that, to the opposition between the benevolent God of peace and cosmic harmony and the evil God of murderous rage, one should add a third figure, that of the *suffering* God. This is why Chesterton was right in dismissing *Thursday* as a basically *pre-Christian* book. The insight into the speculative identity of Good and Evil, the notion of God's two sides, peaceful harmony and destructive rage, the claim that, in fighting Evil, the good God is fighting himself (an internal struggle), is still the (highest) *pagan* insight. It is only the third feature, the suffering God, whose sudden emergence resolves this tension of God's two faces, that brings us to Christianity proper: what paganism cannot imagine is such a suffering God. This suffering, of course, brings us to the book of Job, praised by Chesterton, in his small, wonderful *Introduction to Book of Job,* as "the most interesting of ancient books. We may almost say of the book of Job that it is the most interesting of modern books."[16] What accounts for its "modernity" is the way in which the book of Job strikes a dissonant chord in the Old Testament:

> Everywhere else, then, the Old Testament positively rejoices in the obliteration of man in comparison with the divine purpose. The book of Job stands definitely alone because the book of Job definitely asks, "But what is the purpose of God? Is it worth the sacrifice even of our miserable humanity? Of course, it is easy enough to wipe out our own paltry wills for the sake of a will that is grander and kinder. But is it grander and kinder? Let God use His tools; let God break His tools. But what is He doing, and what are they being broken for?" It is because of this question that we have to attack as a philosophical riddle the riddle of the book of Job.

However, the true surprise is that, at the end, the book of Job does not provide a satisfying answer to this riddle:

> it does not end in a way that is conventionally satisfactory. Job is not told that his misfortunes were due to his sins or a part of any plan for his improvement. . . . God comes in at the end, not to answer riddles, but to propound them. And the "great surprise" is that the book of Job "makes Job suddenly satisfied with the mere presentation of something impenetrable. Verbally speaking the enigmas of Jehovah seem darker and more desolate than the enigmas of Job; yet Job was comfortless before the speech of Jehovah and is comforted after it. He has been told nothing, but he feels the terrible and tingling atmosphere of something which is too good to be told. The refusal of God to explain His design is itself a burning hint of His design. The riddles of God are more satisfying than the solutions of man."

In short, God performs here what Lacan calls a *point de capiton:* he resolves the riddle by supplanting it with an even more radical riddle, by redoubling the riddle, by transposing the riddle from Job's mind into the thing itself—he comes to share Job's astonishment at the chaotic madness of the created universe: "Job puts forward a note of interrogation; God answers with a note of exclamation. Instead of proving to Job that it is an explainable world, He insists that it is a much stranger world than Job ever thought it was." To answer the subject's interrogation with a note of exclamation, is this not the succinct definition of what the analyst should do during treatment? So, instead of providing answers from his total knowledge, God does a proper analytic intervention, adding a mere formal accent, a mark of articulation.

In this reading of Job, Chesterton overcomes his own dialectic of universality and its exception. One of Chesterton's great motifs is that Christianity aims to *save reason through sticking to its founding exception.* Deprived of it, reason degenerates into a blind self-destructive skepticism: into total *irrationalism*—or, as Chesterton liked to repeat: if you do not believe in God, you will soon be ready to believe anything, including the most superstitious nonsense about miracles. This was Chesterton's basic insight and conviction: that the irrationalism of the late nineteenth century was the necessary consequence of the Enlightenment rationalist attack on religion:

> The creeds and the crusades, the hierarchies and the horrible persecutions were not organized, as is ignorantly said, for the suppression of reason. They were organized for the difficult defense of reason. Man, by a blind instinct, knew that if once things were wildly questioned, reason could be questioned first. The authority of priests to absolve, the authority of popes to define the authority, even of inquisitors to terrify: these were all only dark defenses erected round one central authority, more undemonstrable, more supernatural than all—the authority of a man to think. . . . In so far as religion is gone, reason is going.[17]

Here, however, we encounter Chesterton's fateful limitation, which he himself overcomes when, in his text on the book of Job, he shows why God has to rebuke His own defenders, the "mechanical and supercilious comforters of Job":

> The mechanical optimist endeavors to justify the universe avowedly upon the ground that it is a rational and consecutive pattern. He points out that the fine thing about the world is that it can all be explained. That is the one point, if I may put it so, on which God, in return, is explicit to the point of violence. God says, in effect, that if there is one fine thing about the world, as far as men are concerned, it is that it cannot be explained. He insists on the inexplicableness of everything. "Hath the rain a father? . . . Out of whose womb came the ice?" (38:28f). He goes farther, and insists on the positive and palpable unreason of things; "Hast thou sent the rain upon the desert where no man is, and upon the wilderness wherein there is no man?" (38:26). . . . To startle man, God becomes for an instant a blasphemer; one might almost say that God becomes for an instant an atheist. He unrolls before Job a long panorama of created things, the horse, the eagle, the raven, the wild ass, the peacock, the ostrich, the crocodile. He so describes each of them that it sounds like a monster walking in the sun. The whole is a

sort of psalm or rhapsody of the sense of wonder. The maker of all things is astonished at the things he has Himself made.[18]

God is here no longer the miraculous exception which guarantees the normality of the universe, the unexplainable X who enables us to explain everything else. On the contrary, He Himself is overwhelmed by the overbrimming miracle of his creation. Upon a closer look, there is nothing normal in our universe—everything, every small thing that is, is a miraculous exception; viewed from a proper perspective, every normal thing is a monstrosity. We should not take horses as normal and the unicorn as a miraculous exception— even a horse, the most ordinary thing in the world, is a shattering miracle. *This* blasphemous God is the God of modern science, since modern science is sustained precisely by such an attitude of wondering at the most obvious. In short, modern science is on the side of "believing in anything." Is one of the lessons of the theory of relativity and quantum physics not that modern science undermines our most elementary natural attitudes and compels us to believe (accept) the most "nonsensical" things? To clarify this conundrum, Lacan's logic of the non-All can be of some help.[19] Chesterton obviously relies on the "masculine" side of universality and its constitutive exception: everything obeys natural causality—with the exception of God, the central Mystery. The logic of modern science is, on the contrary, "feminine." First, it is materialist, accepting the axiom that nothing escapes natural causality which can be accounted for by rational explanation; however, the other side of this materialist axiom is that "not all is rational, obeying natural laws"—not in the sense that "there is something irrational, something that escapes rational causality," but in the sense that it is the "totality" of rational causal order itself which is inconsistent, "irrational," non-All. Only this non-All guarantees the proper opening of the scientific discourse to surprises, to the emergencies of the "unthinkable." Who, in the nineteenth century, could have imagined things like relativity theory or quantum physics?

The ethical implications of God's reply are truly shattering. After Job is hit by calamities, his theological friends come, offering interpretations which render these calamities meaningful, and the greatness of Job is not so much to protest his innocence as to insist on the meaninglessness of his calamities (when God appears afterward, he gives right to Job against the theological defenders of faith). The structure is here exactly the same as that of Freud's dream of Irma's injection, which begins with a conversation between Freud and his patient Irma about the failure of her treatment due to a contaminated injection. In the course of the conversation, Freud gets closer to her, approaches her face and looks deep into her mouth, confronting the horrible sight of the live red flesh. At this point of unbearable horror, the tonality of the dream changes, and the horror all of a sudden passes into comedy: three doctors, Freud's friends, appear. In a ridiculous pseudo-professional jargon, they enumerate multiple (and mutually exclusive) reasons why Irma's poisoning by the injection was nobody's fault (there was no injection, the injection was clean . . .). So there is first a traumatic encounter (the sight of the raw flesh of Irma's throat), which is followed by the sudden change into comedy, into the exchange between three ridiculous doctors which enables the dreamer to avoid the encounter of the true trauma. The function of the three doctors is the same as that of the three theological friends in the story of Job: to obfuscate the impact of the trauma with a symbolic semblance. This resistance to meaning is crucial when we are confronting potential or actual catastrophes, from AIDS and ecological disasters to holocaust: they have no "deeper meaning." Therein resides the failure of the two Hollywood productions released to mark the fifth anniversary of 9/11: Paul Greengrass's *United 93* and Oliver Stone's *World Trade Center*. The first thing that strikes the eye is that both try to be as anti-Hollywood as possible: both focus on the courage of ordinary people, with no glamorous stars, no special effects, no grandiloquent heroic gestures, just a terse, realistic depiction of ordinary people in extraordinary circumstances. However, both films contain notable formal exceptions: moments which violate this basic realistic style. *United 93* starts with kidnappers in a motel room, praying, getting ready. They look austere, like angels of death—and the first shot after the title credits confirms this impression: it is a panoramic shot from high above Manhattan at night, accompanied by the sound of the kidnappers' prayers, as if the kidnappers stroll above the city, getting ready to descend on earth to take their harvest. Similarly, there are no direct shots of the planes hitting the towers in *WTC*; all that we see, seconds before the catastrophe, when one of the policemen is on a busy street in a crowd of people, is an ominous shadow quickly passing over them—the shadow of the first plane. (Plus, significantly, after the policemen heroes are caught in the rubble, the camera, in a Hitchcockian move, withdraws back into the air to a "God's view" of New York City.) This direct passage from the down-to-earth daily life to the view from above confers on both films a strange theological reverberation—as if the attacks were a kind of divine intervention. What is its meaning? Recall the first reaction of Jerry Falwell and Pat Robertson to the 9/11 bombings, perceiving them as a sign that God withdrew His protection from the United States because of Americans' sinfulness, putting the blame on hedonism, materialism, liberalism, and rampant sexuality, and claiming that America got what it deserved. The fact that the very same condemnation of the "liberal" America as the one from the Muslim Other came from the very heart of *l'Amerique profonde* should cause us to think. In a hidden way, *United 93* and *WTC* tend to do the opposite: to read the 9/11 catastrophe as a blessing in disguise, as a divine intervention from above to awaken us from moral slumber and to bring out the best in us. *WTC* ends with the off-screen words which spell out this message: terrible events like the Twin Towers destruction bring out in people the worst AND the best—courage, solidarity, sacrifice for community. People do things they would never imagine they could. And this utopian perspective is one of the undercurrents that sustain our fascination with catastrophe films: it is as if our societies need a major catastrophe in order to resuscitate the spirit of communal solidarity.

The legacy of Job prohibits us such a gesture of taking a refuge in the standard transcendent figure of God as a secret Master who knows the meaning of what appears to us as meaningless catastrophe, the God who sees the entire picture in which what we perceive as a stain contributes to global harmony. When confronted with an event like the Holocaust or the death of millions in Congo, is it not obscene to claim that these stains in some deeper sense contribute to the harmony of the Whole? Is there a Whole which can teleologically justify and thus redeem/sublate an event like the Holocaust? Christ's death on the cross thus means that one should drop the notion of God as a transcendent caretaker who guarantees the happy outcome of our acts, the guarantee of historical teleology—Christ's death on the cross is the death of *this* God, it repeats Job's stance, it refuses any "deeper meaning" that obfuscates the brutal real of historical catastrophes.

We need to consider a further complication here. Let us return to Freud's basic question: why do we dream at all? Freud's answer is deceptively simple: the ultimate function of the dream is to enable the dreamer to prolong his sleep. This is usually interpreted as bearing on the dreams we have just before awakening, when some external disturbance (noise) threatens to awaken us. In such a situation, the sleeper quickly imagines (in the guise of a dream) a situation which incorporates this external stimulus and thus succeeds in prolonging the sleep for a while. When the external signal becomes too strong, he finally awakens. However, are things really so straight? In another dream from *Interpretation of Dreams* about awakening, a tired father who spent the night watching at the coffin of his young son falls asleep and dreams that his son is approaching him all in flames, addressing at him the horrifying reproach: "Father, can't you see I am burning?" Soon father awakens and discovers that, due to the overturned candle, the cloth of his dead son's shroud effectively caught fire—the smoke that he smelled while asleep was incorporated into the dream of the burning son to prolong his sleep. So was it that father awoke when the external stimulus (smoke) became too strong to be contained within the dream scenario? Was it not rather the obverse: father first constructed the dream in order to prolong his sleep—to avoid the unpleasant awakening? However, what he encountered in the dream—literally the burning question, the creepy specter of his son making the reproach—was much more unbearable than external reality, so father awakened, escaped into external reality—why? To continue to dream, to avoid the unbearable trauma of his own guilt for the son's painful death.

In order to get the full weight of this paradox, we can compare this dream with the one about Irma's injection. In both dreams, there is a traumatic encounter (the sight of the raw flesh of Irma's throat; the vision of the burning son). However, in the second dream, the dreamer awakens at this point, while in the first dream, the horror is replaced by the inane spectacle of professional excuses. This parallel gives us the ultimate key to Freud's theory of dreams: the awakening in the second dream (father awakens into reality in order to escape the horror of the dream) has the same function as the sudden change into comedy, into the exchange between three ridiculous doctors; in the first dream our ordinary reality has precisely the structure of such an inane exchange which enables us to avoid the encounter of the true trauma.

From here, we should return to Christ: is Christ's "Father, why have you forsaken me?" not the Christian version of Freud's "Father, can't you see I am burning?" And is this not addressed precisely to God-Father who pulls the strings behind the stage and teleologically justifies (guarantees the meaning of) all our earthly vicissitudes? Taking upon himself (not the sins, but) the suffering of humanity, he confronts the Father with the meaninglessness of all of it.

The theological term for this identity of Job and Christ is double kenosis: God's self-alienation overlaps with the alienation from God of the human individual who experiences himself as alone in a godless world, abandoned by God who dwells in some inaccessible transcendent Beyond. For Hegel, the co-dependence of the two aspects of kenosis reaches its highest tension in Protestantism. Protestantism and the Enlightenment critique of religious superstition are the front and the obverse of the same coin. The starting point of this entire movement is the medieval Catholic thought of someone like Thomas Aquinas, for whom philosophy should be a handmaiden of faith. Faith and knowledge, theology and philosophy supplement each other as a harmonious, non-conflictual distinction within (under the predominance of) theology. Although God in itself remains an unfathomable mystery for our limited cognitive capacities, reason can also guide us toward Him by enabling us to recognize the traces of God in created reality—therein resides the premise of Aquinas's five versions of the proof of God (the rational observation of material reality as a texture of causes and effects leads us to the necessary insight into how there must be a primal Cause to it all, etc.). With Protestantism, this unity breaks apart. We have on the one side the godless universe, the proper object of our reason, and the unfathomable divine Beyond separated by a hiatus from it. When confronted with this break, we can either deny any meaning to an otherworldly Beyond, dismissing it as a superstitious illusion, or we can remain religious and exempt our faith from the domain of reason, conceiving it as an act of pure faith (authentic inner feeling, etc.). What interests Hegel is how this tension between philosophy (enlightened rational thought) and religion ends up in their "mutual debasement and bastardization." In a first move, Reason seems to be on the offensive and religion on the defensive, desperately trying to cut out a place for itself outside the domain under the control of Reason. Under the pressure of the Enlightenment critique and the advances of sciences, religion humbly retreats into the inner space of authentic feelings. However, the ultimate price is paid by the enlightened Reason itself: its defeat of religion ends up in its self-defeat, in its self-limitation, so that, at the conclusion of this entire movement, the gap between faith and knowledge reappears, but transposed into the field of knowledge (Reason) itself:

> After its battle with religion the best reason could manage was to take a look at itself and come to self-awareness. Reason, having in this way become mere intellect, acknowledges its own nothingness by placing that which is better than it in a faith outside and above itself, as a Beyond to be believed in. This is what has happened in the philosophies of Kant, Jacobi and Fichte. Philosophy has made itself the handmaiden of a faith once more.[20]

Both poles are thus debased: Reason becomes a mere "intellect," a tool for manipulating empirical objects, a mere pragmatic instrument of the human animal, and religion becomes an impotent inner feeling which can never be fully actualized, since the moment one tries to transpose it into external reality, one regresses to Catholic idolatry which fetishizes contingent natural objects. The epitome of this development is Kant's philosophy: Kant started as the great destroyer, with his ruthless critique of theology, and ended up with—as he himself put it—constraining the scope of Reason to create a space for faith. What he displays in a model way is how the Enlightenment's ruthless denigration and limitation of its external enemy (faith, which is denied any cognitive status—religion is a feeling with no cognitive truth value) inverts into Reason's self-denigration and self-limitation (Reason can only legitimately deal with the objects of phenomenal experience, true Reality is inaccessible to it). The Protestant insistence on faith alone, on how the true temples and altars to God should be built in the heart of the individual, not in external reality, is an indication of how the Enlightenment anti-religious attitude cannot resolve "its own problem, the problem of subjectivity gripped by absolute solitude."[21] The ultimate result of the Enlightenment is thus the absolute singularity of the subject dispossessed of all substantial content, reduced to the empty point of self-relating negativity, a subject totally alienated from the substantial content, including of its own content. For Hegel, the passage through this zero point is necessary, since the solution is not provided by any kind of renewed synthesis or reconciliation between Faith and Reason. With the advent of modernity, the magic of the enchanted universe is forever lost; reality is here to stay gray. The only solution is, as we have already seen, the very redoubling of alienation, the insight into how my alienation from the Absolute overlaps with the Absolute's self-alienation: I am "in" God in my very distance from Him.

The crucial problem is, How are we to think the link between these two "alienations," the one of the modern man from God (who is reduced to an unknowable In-itself, absent from the world subjected to mechanical laws), the other of God from Himself (in Christ, incarnation)? They are the same, although not symmetrically, but as subject and object. In order for (human) subjectivity to emerge out of the substantial personality of the human animal, cutting links with it and positing itself as the I = I dispossessed of all substantial content, as the self-relating negativity of an empty singularity, *God Himself*, the universal Substance, has to "humiliate" himself, to fall into its own creation, to "objectivize" himself, to appear as a singular miserable human individual in all its abjection—*abandoned by God*. The distance of man from God is thus the distance of God from Himself:

> The suffering of God and the suffering of human subjectivity deprived of God must be analysed as the recto and verso of the same event. There is a fundamental relationship between divine kenosis and the tendency of modern reason to posit a beyond which remains inaccessible. The *Encyclopaedia* makes this relation visible by presenting the Death of God at once as the Passion of the Son who "dies in the pain of negativity" and the human feeling that we can know nothing of God.[22]

This double kenosis is what the standard Marxist critique of religion as the self-alienation of humanity misses: "modern philosophy would not have its own *subject* if God's sacrifice had not occurred."[23] For the subjectivity to emerge—not as a mere epiphenomenon of the global substantial ontological order, but as essential to Substance itself—the split, negativity, particularization, self-alienation must be posited as something that takes place in the very heart of the divine Substance; that is, the move from Substance to Subject must occur within God himself. In short, man's alienation from God (the fact that God appears to him as an inaccessible In-itself, as a pure transcendent Beyond) must coincide with the alienation of God from Himself (whose most poignant expression is, of course, Christ's "Father, father, why have you forsaken me?" on the cross): finite human "consciousness only represents God because God re-presents itself; consciousness is only at a distance from God because God distances himself from himself."[24]

This is why the standard Marxist philosophy oscillates between the ontology of dialectical materialism, which reduces human subjectivity to a particular ontological sphere (no wonder that Georgi Plekhanov, the creator of the term "dialectical materialism," also designated Marxism as "dynamized Spinozism"), and the philosophy of praxis which, from young Georg Lukacs onward, takes as its starting point and horizon collective subjectivity which posits/mediates every objectivity, and is thus unable to think its genesis from the substantial order, the ontological explosion, "big bang," which gives rise to it. So if Christ's death is "at once the death of the God-man and the Death of the initial and immediate abstraction of the divine being which is not yet posited as a Self,"[25] this means that, as Hegel pointed out, *what dies on the cross is not only the terrestrial-finite representative of God, but God himself, the very transcendent God of beyond.* Both terms of the opposition, Father and Son, the substantial God as the Absolute In-itself and the God-for-us, revealed to us, die, are sublated in the Holy Spirit.

The standard reading of this sublation—Christ "dies" (is sublated) as the immediate representation of God, as God in the guise of a finite human person, in order to be reborn as the universal/atemporal Spirit—remains all too short. The point this reading misses is the ultimate lesson to be learned from the divine incarnation: the finite existence of mortal humans is the only site of the Spirit, the site where Spirit achieves its actuality. This means that in spite of all its grounding power, Spirit is a *virtual* entity in the sense that its status is that of a subjective presupposition: it exists only insofar as subjects *act as if it exists*. Its status is similar to that of an ideological cause like communism or nation: it is the substance of the individuals who recognize themselves in it, the ground of their entire existence, the point of reference which provides the ultimate horizon of meaning to their lives, something for which these individuals are ready to give their lives, yet the only thing that really exists are these individuals and their activity, so this substance is actual only insofar as individuals believe in it and act accordingly. The crucial mistake to be avoided is therefore to grasp the Hegelian Spirit as a kind of meta-Subject, a Mind, much larger than an individual human mind, aware of itself. Once we do this, Hegel has to appear as a ridiculous spiritualist obscurantist, claiming that there is a kind of mega-Spirit controlling our history. Against this cliché about the "Hegelian Spirit," one should emphasize how Hegel is fully aware that "it is in the finite consciousness that the process of knowing spirit's essence takes place and that the divine self-consciousness thus arises. Out of the foaming ferment of finitude, spirit rises up fragrantly."[26] This holds especially for the Holy Spirit: our awareness, the (self-)consciousness of finite humans, is its only actual site; the Holy Spirit also rises up "out of the foaming ferment of finitude." Badillon says in Claudel's *L'otage*, "*Dieu ne peut rien sans nous.* God can do nothing without us." This is what Hegel has in mind here: although God is the substance of our (human) entire being, he is impotent without us, he acts only in and through us, he is posited through our activity as its presupposition. This is why Christ is impassive, ethereal, fragile: a pure sympathizing observer, impotent in himself.

We can see apropos this case how sublation (*Aufhebung*) is not directly the sublation of the otherness, its return into the same, its recuperation by the One (so that, in this case, finite/mortal individuals are reunited with God, return to his embrace). With Christ's incarnation, the externalization/self-alienation of divinity, the passage from the transcendent God to finite/mortal individuals is a *fait accompli*. There is no way back; all there is, all that "really exists" is from now on individuals; there are no Platonic Ideas or Substances whose existence is somehow "more real." What is sublated in the move from the Son to Holy Spirit is thus God Himself: after crucifixion, the death of the incarnated God, the universal God returns as a Spirit of the community of believers, that is, HE is the one who passes from being a transcendent substantial Reality to a virtual/ideal entity which exists only as the "presupposition" of acting individuals. The standard perception of Hegel as an organicist holist who thinks that really existing individuals are just "predicates" of some "higher" substantial Whole, epiphenomena of the Spirit as a mega-Subject who effectively runs the show, totally misses this crucial point.

What, then, is sublated in the case of Christianity? It is not the finite reality which is sublated (negated—maintained—elevated) into a moment of ideal totality. *It is, on the contrary, the divine Substance itself (God as a Thing-in-itself) which is sublated: negated (what dies on the cross is the sub-*

stantial figure of the transcendent God) but simultaneously maintained in the transubstantiated form of Holy Ghost, the community of believers which exists only as the virtual presupposition of the activity of finite individuals.

Notes

1. G. K. Chesterton, *The Man Who Was Thursday* (Harmondsworth, U.K.: Penguin, 1986), 44–45.

2. Chesterton, *Man Who Was Thursday*, 45–46.

3. Chesterton, *Man Who Was Thursday*, 168–70.

4. Chesterton, *Man Who Was Thursday*, 170.

5. Chesterton, *Man Who Was Thursday*, 180.

6. Chesterton, *Man Who Was Thursday*, 180.

7. Chesterton, *Man Who Was Thursday*, 182–83.

8. Chesterton, *Man Who Was Thursday*, 183.

9. G. K. Chesterton, *Orthodoxy* (San Francisco: Ignatius, 1995), 145.

10. Chesterton, *Orthodoxy*, 145.

11. Chesterton, *Orthodoxy*, 145.

12. For a more detailed analysis of the philosophical implications of Chesterton's *Orthodoxy*, see chapters 2–3 of Slavoj Žižek, *The Puppet and the Dwarf* (Cambridge, Mass.: MIT Press, 2003).

13. See Alain Finkelkraut and Peter Sloterdijk, *Les battements du monde* (Paris: Fayard, 2003), 131.

14. "Und alles Draengen, alles Ringen / Ist ewig Ruh' im Gott den Herrn."

15. There is a brief hint in this direction in the middle of the film; however, it remains unexploited.

16. G. K. Chesterton, "Introduction to Book of Job," www.chesterton.org/gkc/theologian/job.htm.

17. Chesterton, *Orthodoxy*, 39.

18. Chesterton, "Introduction."

19. For the logic of non-All, see Jacques Lacan, *Seminar, Book XX: Encore* (New York: Norton, 1998).

20. G. W. F. Hegel, *Faith and Knowledge* (Albany: SUNY Press, 1977), 55–56.

21. Catherine Malabou, *The Future of Hegel* (New York: Routledge, 2005), 110.

22. Malabou, *Future of Hegel*, 103.

23. Malabou, *Future of Hegel*, 111.

24. Malabou, *Future of Hegel*, 112.

25. Malabou, *Future of Hegel*, 107.

26. Hegel, *Lectures on the Philosophy of Religion* (Berkeley: University of California Press, 1984–1987), 233.

PART TWO

Paul between Jews and Christians

THREE

Historical Integrity, Interpretive Freedom: The Philosopher's Paul and the Problem of Anachronism

PAULA FREDRIKSEN

In 1583, Matteo Ricci entered China. Trained in philology, philosophy, and rhetoric by Jesuits in Rome, gifted at languages, Ricci was uniquely suited to his mission: to bring the heathen Chinese into the Church. Once he finally held in his hands the religious literature of this foreign culture, however, he made a surprising discovery. Ricci saw (though the Chinese had not) that the ancient scriptures of Buddhism and Taoism revealed the clear imprint of the Christian Trinity.

I thought of Matteo Ricci as I made my way through Professor Badiou's essay on Paul and universalism. Postmodern Paris is no less far from Paul's Mediterranean than Renaissance Rome was from Ming dynasty China. And Badiou's sense of discovery and recognition when reading the Pauline epistles, which he communicates with excitement and conviction in his book, echoes what I imagine would have been Matteo's experience of Taoist Trinitarianism. Such recognition opens interpretive possibilities and closes cultural gaps. And indeed, in the title of his opening chapter, Badiou proclaims the erasure precisely of this gap between Paris and Philippi, between the present and the past. "Paul," states that chapter's title, is "our contemporary."

Such a position is a hard sell to historians. (We are "the heathen" in my analogy.) It is true that, like philosophers, historians look for meaning in texts (as also in other kinds of data). And it is true that, like philosophers, historians through their interpretations of those data seek to generate meaning, to render the evidence intelligible.

But the frame of reference for historical interpretation is not and cannot be the present. To do history requires acknowledging difference between us and the objects of our inquiry. Historical interpretation proceeds by acceding to the priority of the *ancient* context. Our frame of reference is the *past.* In our particular instance, this morning, for example, my question is not, What *does* Paul mean? that is, to us. Rather, I ask, What *did* Paul mean? that is, to his first-century contemporaries—sympathizers, admirers, opponents, enemies. They, not we, were the audience of his message. He was obliged to be intelligible not to us but to them.

This intelligibility can be alarmingly elusive. Consistency does not rank among Paul's strong suits. In fairness, this impression may be due to the nature of our evidence. We have only seven authentic letters composed, it seems, fifteen to twenty years after Paul joined this new messianic movement. They are real letters addressed to particular communities, occasioned by specific incidents: our grasp of their context is often conjectural. The texts of these letters have certainly altered over time. Thanks to generations of copyists, we no longer have the letters as they left Paul's mouth. And the literary integrity of individual letters is uncertain. Scholars have argued that our present versions of Philippians, 2 Corinthians, and Romans represent various epistles edited together. All this means that, in terms of Paul's "thought," coherence often has to be distilled or imposed.

The deutero-Pauline letters, also preserved in the New Testament collection, make this same point from a different direction: 2 Thessalonians, Ephesians, Colossians, 1 and 2 Timothy, and Titus came from other Christians in the generation following Paul's who saw themselves as standing in a tradition that he had established. They accordingly authorized their own statements by writing in his name. The positions taken by this second group of authors vary significantly among themselves and differ markedly from some of Paul's. That Paul was so widely interpreted by those who stood so close to him should caution us about the difficulties of construing his thought. Put succinctly, often Paul shoots from the lip.

How, then, shall we define and identify Paul's ideas on universalism? And how shall we understand them? In light of the messiness of the primary evidence, I propose that we approach this question obliquely. Before turning to Paul himself, let's see what happened to him once he strayed among the philosophers—not modern ones but ancient ones.

I will begin this investigation not with Paul, then, but with two of his greatest ancient interpreters. Each of these later readers of Paul expended great effort to render Paul a coherent universalist, and they worked philosophically no less than exegetically in order to do this. These two later readers disagreed sharply with each other, even though they constructed their respective positions by appeal to precisely the same passages in Paul.

According to Origen of Alexandria (187–254 CE), our first interpreter, Paul's message was that all would be saved. According to Augustine of Hippo (354–430 CE), our second interpreter, Paul's message was that all should be damned. According to Origen, every rational being has free will; according to Augustine, humanity can only sin. According to both Origen and Augustine, God's two great characteristics are justice and mercy. But Origen's God expresses these attributes simultaneously: he is both just and merciful. Augustine's God expresses these attributes serially and selectively: he is *either* just *or* merciful. For Augustine, even babies, if unbaptized, go to hell. For Origen, even Satan will at last attain redemption, for God wants nothing less.

Paul's discussion in Romans 9 clinches both arguments, for both men. Let's see what each of them had to shape in Paul in order to get where he wanted to go. What these two great Christian theologians reject or finesse, I will argue, can provide us with a glimpse of what our mid-first-century itinerant Jewish visionary was actually talking about.

But first, a little more context. Both Origen and Augustine were driven to Paul not only because of Paul's prominence in the canon, but also because of Paul's prominence with their opposition. Other Christian churches had formulated their theologies through strong misreadings of the apostle. As Origen makes his constructive arguments, then, he does so against the challenge of Valentinian Gnostics and the followers of Marcion. And at Augustine's back stand the Manichees.

These three heretical communities, though distinct, shared several points of principle. They all repudiated the god of the Old Testament as well as his book. They repudiated matter and flesh as his particular medium. They read the charged pairs of Pauline rhetoric—flesh and spirit, circumcision and baptism, law and gospel, Jew and gentile—as polar opposites, and they constructed their own vision of Christianity uniquely around what they saw as the positive pole. They held that Christ had not actually had a fleshly body, but that he had appeared, as Paul proclaimed, "in the likeness of man" and "in the form of a slave" (Phil 2:6). And they held, accordingly, that as Christ was not raised in a fleshly body, neither would the redeemed believer be. Instead, salvation meant redemption *from* the material cosmos, this world of flesh. The individual soul, fallen into this lower universe, would slip back up through the material cosmos of the lower god to the realm of spirit and life and light, the kingdom of Christ's father. Flesh would remain where it belonged, in the realm below the moon. As Paul had said, "Flesh and blood cannot inherit the kingdom of God, nor can the perishable put on the imperishable" (1 Cor 15:50). And who were the saved?

Those "spiritual men" (*pneumatikoi*) or "perfect men" (*teleioi*) to whom Paul disclosed "secret and hidden wisdom" (1 Cor 2:6–7). Unspiritual men ("soulish," *psychikoi*) cannot understand a spiritual message (v. 14). People, in short, were saved in accordance with their intrinsic nature. Will was moot.

We come, then, to Origen. In his great work of systematic theology, the *Peri Archôn* or *On First Principles,* Origen presented a vast vision of "true" Christianity, coordinating, in four books, his understanding of God (Book I), the cosmos (Book II), free will (Book III), and scripture (Book IV). Through allegorical interpretation, spiritual understanding, stated Origen, the Jewish Bible could be revealed to be a book of Christian witness: its god is the father of Christ. Obscure passages of scripture, whether in the Old Testament or in the New, were placed there by divine providence in order to stimulate diligent believers to seek out the hidden wisdom of *lectio divina.* This was so because the nature and structure of scripture, Origen explained, recapitulated that of the time-bound human being. "For just as man consists of body, soul and spirit," he says, "so in the same way do the scriptures, which have been prepared by God for man's salvation" (IV.2.4). The body of the text corresponds to its simple narrative, and perhaps to its historical meaning. The eye of flesh can see this level, the uneducated can understand it. The soul of the text is those teachings that edify one's own soul. But the spirit of the text is its deepest or highest significance. This meaning can be understood only with mental effort, the striving of the mind; and it is on this level of spiritual meaning that the exegete attains an understanding of the mind of God.

In this schema as elsewhere, Origen asserts the priority of spirit over matter. Its priority is ontological, and therefore moral as well: spirit is "good." As an ancient thinker, and specifically as a Middle Platonist, Origen could hardly have thought otherwise. The ultimate source of everything, however, is *purely* spirit, God himself. Origen identifies this god as Trinity: Father, Son, and Holy Spirit. Again, as a member of the third-century "true Church," he could hardly do otherwise. Despite this three-ness, however, the Christian god exhibits the characteristics of the high god of pagan *paideia:* he is self-existing, where everything else is contingent. He is perfect, which means he is changeless. And he is absolutely without any kind of body. *Only* God is *asomaton* (I.1.6). Everything that is not-god has body of some sort.

Given this god's radical changelessness, how can he be a "creator"? Origen answers ingeniously with his doctrine of double creation. Before time existed—which is to say, before matter existed—God presided over a universe of eternally generated rational beings. These rational beings, since not-god, did have bodies, but they were (as Paul says in 1 Cor 15) "spiritual bodies." "Body" here serves as a principle of individuation: in the spiritual, eternal realm, it distinguishes one rational being from another. These beings were "made" in "the image of God" through God's perfect image, his Son. The meaning of this divine image of the Divine Image is spiritual and moral. These creatures had an absolutely unimpeded capacity to choose between good and evil. Put differently—and in the idiom of Greek moral philosophy rather than in the biblical idiom of Origen's theology—free will is constitutive of rational being.

Again, only God is, by nature, changeless. Not-god, since contingent, will have an innate tendency to change. Since it is innate, this tendency is not culpable. But in the world before time, this natural tendency had consequences.

To explain how we got from a timeless spiritual creation to everything else, Origen evokes the idea of souls (or their love) "cooling." (This idea refers *psyche* "soul" to *psychesthai*, "to cool," Plato's famous wordplay in the *Timeaus*.) Origen explains that all but one of these rational beings wavered in its affectionate concentration on their Maker. That one more constant being, through the free exercise of its own will, loved God with such ardor that it fused with its "object," the Logos (II.6.3): the soul of Jesus thus merged with the godhead of Christ. All the other rational beings slipped away—some, like Satan, to the maximum degree imaginable. But this slippage, since "natural," was *not* culpable: God could not with justice "punish" his creatures for not being him, or for being not-him. What was culpable, however, was that these rational beings failed to brake their decline, to move their will in order to arrest their turn from God. Different beings "stopped" at various "distances" from God. Then God, both just and merciful, "acted" to affect their redemption: out of absolutely nothing, he called matter into being (II.1.1–4).

"Now since the world is so very varied and comprises so great a diversity of rational beings," observes Origen, "what else can we assign to the cause of its existence except the diversity in the fall of those who declined from unity in dissimilar ways?" (II.1.1). The diversity of circumstances and of material bodies expresses the diversity of moral responses that these souls made to their decline from God and the good. God in his mercy and justice, in other words, arranged the wonderfully plastic medium of matter, or "flesh," to accommodate all these different ethical levels of accomplishment or failure. God places the rational being into a particular historical material body in order to assist it on its way back to God.

The entire material universe, in other words, is a temporary and providential order, a school for souls. And every soul began life in exactly the same way: Jesus' soul, your soul, my soul, Satan's soul, the souls of the sun and the moon and the stars. All of our different kinds of bodies register the moral trajectory of our freely willed decisions. If all souls had not begun from a condition of exact equality, God would not be just, whether as creator or as judge.

God in his mercy and justice placed the soul of each fallen rational being into precisely the sort of material circumstance that it needed in order to freely choose to do the right thing, and eventually (re)turn toward God. God is patient and infinitely resourceful. His providence micromanages the material universe; he has all the time in the world. (And since rational beings are eternal, so do they.) The material body, in other words, is a temporary and propaedeutic device. Once every rational being has finally learned what it needs to learn in order to freely choose to love God, matter will sink back into the nothing whence it came. Ethnicity, gender, social station: all the contingencies of historical existence drop away at redemption (cf. Gal 3:28). The "saints" will rise in their "spiritual bodies." Even Satan and his minions will come round: anything else would represent a failure on God's part. But God cannot fail. And he loves all his creatures equally. God throws no one away.

To prove the reasonableness of all these propositions—that the Bible must be understood spiritually; that the soul has a long history of ethical choices before it appears in a historical, fleshly body; that God providentially cares for all his creatures; that if God is just (and he is), then the choice of the will must be free—Origen, in Book III, turns particularly to Paul. "Let us see how Paul reasons with us as being men of free will and ourselves responsible for our destruction or salvation" (III.1.6). Origen then attends to Romans 9. There Paul refers to three biblical passages notoriously hard to reconcile with a strong idea of moral freedom: the hardening of Pharaoh's heart, the choice of Jacob over Esau, and God's forming persons as a potter forms clay pots, some as vessels of honor and some as vessels of dishonor. "These passages," Origen observes, "are in themselves sufficient to disturb ordinary people with the thought that man is not a free agent, but that it is God who saves and who destroys whomever he will" (III.1.7).

First, to Pharaoh. Obviously he did not sin by nature, because then God would not have needed to harden his heart to ensure his disobedience. God's hardening Pharaoh proves just the opposite: that it was within Pharaoh's power to choose to obey. So why does a good and just God intervene in Pharaoh's decision by "hardening" him (III.1.9–10)? The phrase, explains Origen, is a scriptural *façon de parler*. Just as a kind master will say to his servant who has been spoiled through the master's forbearance, "It was I who made you wicked," or "I am to blame for these offenses," so the Bible speaks of Pharaoh's heart being hardened: the fleshly level of the Exodus story presents God's forbearance as a kind of complicity in Pharaoh's sin. But in reality—seen from the perspective of eternity—God "allows" Pharaoh his freedom because Pharaoh *is* free. And God, master of providence, also knows that by Pharaoh's obstinacy other souls became obedient (like those of the Egyptians who chose to leave Egypt with Moses). Finally, God also knows how, through plagues and the drowning in the sea, "he is leading even Pharaoh" (III.1.14).

But God works with Pharaoh well beyond the borders of the Exodus story. "God deals with souls not in view of the fifty years of our life here," says Origen, "but in view of the endless world. He has made our intellectual nature immortal and akin to himself, and the rational soul is not shut out from healing, as if this life were all" (III.1.13). Behind these biblical episodes, as behind this life itself, stands the endless shining plain of Origen's cosmology and soteriology. And behind both of these stands Origen's ethics (if we want to look at this philosophically) or rather his commitment to the god of the Bible (if we want to look at this religiously): God is both just and merciful. He loves all his creatures. He wants all his creatures to turn back to him, and he arranges matter, thus history, to facilitate his purpose: the education of the rational soul to freely chose the Good.

Origen's cosmology nullifies the need for theodicy. In light of eternity, there is no evil, only various learning situations. Thus any difficulty with Jacob and Esau disappears: "The reasons why Jacob was loved and Esau hated," he explains, "lie with Jacob before he came into the body and with Esau before he entered Rebecca's womb" (III.1.22). ("Hate" of course is another scriptural *façon de parler*.) Humans do not exhaust the category of intelligent life. People, stars, and demons also make themselves, through their uncoerced choices, into vessels of honor or dishonor. But God himself is the impartial lover of souls, swaying considerate scales. The image of the potter, from the prophets via Romans, is actually a statement of God's scrupulous fairness. "Every soul in God's hands," urges Origen, "is of one nature, and all rational beings come, if I may say so, from one lump," the *phurama* of Romans 9:21.

Origen was born in 187 in Alexandria. He died in Caesarea in 254, a belated victim of the Decian persecution. His language was Greek, his philosophical education superlative. It helped, of course, that he was a genius. Trained in rhetoric and philology, he worked with rabbis on the Hebrew text behind the Septuagint.[1] He was comfortable with interpretive ambiguities, frequently proffering multiple opinions on non-doctrinal issues and inviting his hearer to choose whichever one struck her as more reasonable. He was a lay teacher and a charismatic lifelong celibate. (Indeed, so untroubled was his asceticism that two posthumous rumors arose to account for it, one that Origen's serenity was achieved by drugs [Epiphanius], the other, by the knife

[Eusebius, on Mt 19:12].)[2] His circumstances and his temperament could not have been more different from Augustine's.

I will spend less time on Augustine because his theology is so much more familiar. Origen's represents the road not taken. We still live with the consequences of Augustine's theology, and of Augustine's Paul.

Augustine was North African, born in 354, well after the imperialization of the Christian denomination favored by Constantine. His only language was Latin. Augustine could not read Greek, and so he was limited to scripture in translation not only for the Old Testament but also for the New. His knowledge of Greek philosophy and of the rich tradition of Greek patristic commentary, Origen's included, was also limited to what he could get in translation.[3] It helped, of course, that he too was a genius, although (to quote Gibbon) "his learning is too often borrowed, his arguments too often his own."

But, more to the point, Augustine was not a lay professor. He was a bishop of the imperial church. This meant that he had political and institutional incentives to be clearer on doctrine than Origen the layperson ever had to be. For one thing, by Augustine's day, doctrine translated socially into policy. By the fourth century, heretics were persecuted by the Christian state. Augustine was one of the theological architects of this policy of coercion.[4]

Finally, Augustine came of age theologically just as the storm clouds of the Origenist controversy, turbulent and highly charged, gathered and blackened the ecclesiastical landscape of the West.[5] Theories of the soul's preexistence suddenly seemed uncomfortably close to dualist heresy. And as souls became more incarnate, so too did history. Eternity fell away as the meaningful arena of God's saving action shifted to this world. The faithful recited creeds asserting their belief in the resurrection, not of the body, but of the *flesh*. The eternal fires of hell burned too attractively to be renounced or explained away. And nobody wanted Satan to be saved.

Different context, different interpreter, different temperament, different theology—and accordingly, a different Paul. Between 392 and 396, Augustine produced a steady stream of commentaries, short think pieces, and essays on Paul's epistles. He returned repeatedly, especially to Romans, as he tried to find his feet. Finally, in the months before he wrote his early masterwork, The *Confessions,* Augustine arrived at a reading of Romans 9 from which he never wandered.[6] He won the war of exegesis against Manichees, against Donatists, and against the philosophical theology of his own conversion eleven years before. The queen gambit in this match was the freedom of the will.

Contemplating the figure of Pharaoh, Augustine concluded that God did harden Pharaoh's heart because God was justly punishing him for his sins. So too with the election of Jacob over Esau: God did choose Jacob and reject Esau before either was born—and before either had done anything good or evil. (For Augustine, the soul begins its life with and in the fleshly body.) Why then were Pharaoh and Esau rejected? "Is there injustice with God? God forbid" (Rom 9:14; *ad Simpl.* 1.2.16). But then how did God judge between them? Answered Augustine: God only knows. Piety demands that the believer assert that God must have had good reason, but those reasons are known only to him: they are *occultissimi,* "most hidden." *Aequitate occultissima et ab humanis sensibus remotissima iudicat:* "He judges by a standard of justice most hidden and distant from human measure" (*ad Simpl.* 1.2.16). We can never know why God does what he does.

Not that God need do anything, Augustine insists. After the sin of Adam, the entire species became a *massa luti* or *massa perditionis* or *massa peccati.* All these images refer to Paul's *phurama* in Romans 9:21, the clay from which the divine potter shapes his pots. After Adam, says Augustine, all humanity is literally a lump of sin. Condemnation is all anyone deserves. God in his justice leaves most people in that condition, and they have no right to complain, since they were "in Adam." "Who are you, O man, to answer back to God?" But in his gracious mercy, God mysteriously does elect a few to salvation. Why? On what grounds? Augustine again answers with Paul: Who has known the mind of God, or who has been his councilor? His judgments are unsearchable, his ways past finding out (Rom 11:33; *ad Simpl.* 1.2.22). Humans should be grateful that God has, for some mysteriously chosen individuals, relaxed his righteous wrath.

For both Origen and Augustine, then, the clay of Romans 9 is an image of the equality of all souls. But Origen's souls are all equal in nature, which means that they all have free will. Further, in emphasizing that God works this clay, Origen reiterates through Romans 9 that God is, so to speak, the parent of the souls. He loves his creation. Ultimately he will ensure that all are redeemed. Augustine's souls, by contrast, are all equal in sin. His potter is a judge, and a seemingly arbitrary one at that. (Piety demands that we censor the thought.)

How can a just god condemn men who cannot help but sin? On this question Augustine expends enormous forensic finesse. Man cannot help but sin, but that does not mean that his will is not free. It is simply divided, lacking willpower, in punishment for the sin of Adam. *But nothing outside the will forces the will to sin: the will, uncoerced, sins because it chooses to sin.* It cannot choose other, but its choice is still, in this sense, free (*ad Simpl.* 1.2.21).

Augustine projects this understanding of the divided will back onto his reading of Romans chapter 7. The divided "I" of Romans 7—wanting to do good

but able only to do evil, delighting inwardly in the law of God but captive out-
wardly to the law of sin—had been understood to be a rhetorical presentation
called *prosopopeia*, "speaking in character."[7] With a kind of rhetorical ventrilo-
quism, Paul throws his voice into that of the sinner who is not yet "in Christ."[8]
But Augustine eventually insists that Paul here speaks of a man who is already
"in Christ," under grace, because only such a man could rejoice in God's law, if
only inwardly. Despite the reception of grace, this man is still a sinner.

So said Augustine in 396. Decades after he made this argument, facing
off against the Pelagians in the 420s, Augustine will later insist that the I of
Romans 7 was none other than Paul himself (*de praed. sanct.* 1.4.8). Thanks
to Luther, this reading still has some cachet: Badiou proclaims that Paul is
here "manifestly speaking about himself, almost in the style of Augustine's
Confessions" (p. 81).

Paul himself, I'd wager, would disagree. (I certainly do.) After all, as he
wrote in Philippians, "If any man thinks that he has reason for confidence in
the flesh, I have more: circumcised on the eighth day, of the people of Israel, of
the tribe of Benjamin, a Hebrew born of Hebrews, as to the law a Pharisee, as to
zeal a persecutor of the community, as to righteousness under the law blameless" (Phil 3:4–6). If ideological consistency is not Paul's strong suit, neither is
anguished introspection. He is no Origenist, and no Augustinian either.[9]

I examine both Origen and Augustine on Paul at such length to make
my point about philosophical interpretation and anachronism. We have
seen how both theologians interpreted Paul within their respective systems.
Their reliance on philosophy, the intellectual framework of their theologies,
helped each of them to produce a more consistent apostle. What could not
be accommodated to their respective models through reinterpretation they
either drop or ignore. Badiou, of course, though committed to a very different philosophical framework, performs similarly. All three appropriate from
Paul what each finds usable. All three translate via reinterpretation what
can be used in service of articulating the newer system (Origenist universal
salvation, Augustinian universal condemnation, or Badiou's universal post-
Marxism). And all three insist that it is the apostle, not they, who speaks.

Our three different readers drop different things. But what all three
drop is Paul's apocalyptic. Origen's eternity is so vast that even his vision of
the End lasts forever. The sweep of eschatological excitement in the finale
of Paul's letter to the Romans is to the tempo of the *Peri Archôn* what the
Seventh Symphony is to *Bolero*.

Augustine de-eschatologizes Paul in another way. His theology is osten-
sibly more historical. (Your fleshly body, for example, really is in Augustine's

view a part of who you are, not just something into which you've been tem-
porarily dipped.)[10] But by relocating the hermeneutical center of gravity in
Romans from 11–15 (the letter's eschatological finale) to Romans 7, Augustine
retrained our way of looking at Paul. His Paul speaks of existential conflict,
not of cosmic redemption. For Augustine, the second coming of Christ in
his resurrected body has already occurred, at Pentecost, with the establishment of his body, the Church. Augustine, the fourth-century bishop of the
imperial Church, is not staying up late at night waiting for Jesus to come
back; neither, consequently, is his Paul.

Badiou de-eschatologizes Paul by concentrating so resolutely on the resurrection as a contextless "event." It's just *there*, punctiliar, isolated, dominating
everything. An event (as the older German theologians used to say) in the
history of consciousness. But Christ's resurrection is *not* that for the historical
Paul. Paul was a mid-first-century visionary Jew, not an early-twenty-first-
century postmodern Parisian. The significance of Christ's resurrection for
Paul is that it indicates what time it is on God's clock. It's the end of history,
and the hour of the establishment of God's kingdom. The form of this world is
passing away (1 Cor 7:31). Salvation is nearer to us that when we first believed;
the night is far gone, the day is at hand (Rom 13:11–12). Christ is the firstfruits of
the general resurrection (1 Cor 15:20). His rising means that the transformation
of history is imminent (1 Thess 4:13–17). Further, the god who will bring about
that transformation is an ethnic god, the god of Jewish scripture, the god of
Abraham, Isaac, and Jacob. Gentiles may have been added in, but it's the god
of Israel who has done all the heavy lifting, just as he had promised the (Jewish) patriarchs (Rom 15). Paul's universalism is both heavily mythological and
specifically ethnic.

Millenarian movements always succeed as their major prophecy fails.
The kingdom of God arrived neither in Jesus' lifetime, nor in Paul's—nor
in Mark's, nor in the lifetime of John of Patmos. Grass has grown through
Akiva's cheekbones, and still the Messiah has not come, or come again. That
is simply an observation. But it need not represent a theological problem.

Theological readings of foundational religious texts are intrinsically
anachronistic. Their categories of meaning come from outside and well after
the categories native to the authors of the foundational texts. To read such
texts theologically means to read them philosophically (theology is a subset
of philosophy) and thus systematically (hence the – *logy* of these endeavors).
Badiou gives us a post-Lacanian example of such a systematic and systematizing project: God may be missing, but nothing else is. Systematic rereading is how these ancient Jewish eschatological texts that are Paul's letters

retain—or, rather, *obtain*—contemporary meaning. There is no dishonor in this. It is theology's project.

But in view of its inevitable anachronism—its falseness to the messiness, the opacity, the stubborn independence, the sheer otherness of the past that is the context of foundational texts, such as Paul's—such a reading can only be false to the original author. I wish that practitioners of such projects would say, "I interpret Paul this way, this is what Paul means to me," a hermeneutical claim, rather than "this is what Paul means," a historical claim. As a historical claim, such assertions can only be anachronistic; and an anachronistic historical claim can *only* be false, whatever ideological merit it might otherwise display.

"The historian meets the gap between himself and others at its most sharp and uncompromising," Peter Brown once observed. "The dead are irreducible."[11] They are certainly freed of any obligation to make sense to us. If we as historians seek to understand how people in the distant past made sense to each other, then we have to work hard to reconstruct their world, not to project upon them concerns from ours. The ancient dead stand with their backs toward us, their faces turned to their own generation. The dead are not our contemporaries, and if we think they are, we are not listening to them, but talking to ourselves.[12]

I am making an epistemological claim here, namely, that only a historical interpretation of such texts can give us at least an approximation of what the ancient subject thought. Ancient humans, like their modern counterparts, are gloriously inconsistent intellectually and morally, and affected by their immediate social and cultural environment in ways that are both profound and, occasionally, obvious. For this reason, I think that any application of any systematic or systematizing interpretive theory will distort the lived messiness that the primary evidence attests to. "Methodology" is no less distorting to historical reconstruction than is theology (or, in Badiou's case, atheology). Origen's Paul tells us not about Paul but about Origen; Augustine's Paul, about Augustine. Thus, to respond finally to Badiou's characterization of Paul posed in his first chapter heading—Paul: Our Contemporary—I would have to say, Yes. Badiou's Paul is our contemporary. And that is precisely how we know that Badiou, in giving us his fresh reading of the apostle's letters, has presented us not with a study of Paul and his concerns, but with an oblique self-portrait, and an investigation of concerns and ideas that are irreducibly Badiou's.

Notes

1. See N. deLange, *Origen and the Jews* (Cambridge, 1976).

2. Eusebius, *Ecclesiastical History* vi.8; Epiphanius, *Panarion* 64.3.11–12; see discussion in H. Chadwick, *Early Christian Thought and the Classical Tradition* (Oxford, 1966), 67f.

3. He felt the lack of the commentaries more acutely and asked Jerome to stop bothering with his biblical translations and to concentrate instead on patristic writings, most especially Origen's; *Ep.* 28.2.2.

4. See J. J. O'Donnell, *Augustine: A New Biography* (New York, 2005), chap. 8, "The Augustinian Putsch in Africa."

5. Elizabeth A. Clark, *The Origenist Controversy* (Princeton, N.J., 1992), 159–250.

6. That is, through the argument of his essay on Romans 9 in the *ad Simplicianum*, written in 396, shortly before the *Confessions*. For a review of how he gets to his new position, see P. Fredriksen, "Beyond the Body/Soul Dichotomy," *Recherches augustiniennes* 23 (1988): 87–114.

7. The classic study is W. Kümmel, *Römer 7 und das Bild des Menschen im Neuen Testament* (1929; Munich 1974); see too E. P. Sanders, *Paul, the Law, and the Jewish People* (Philadelphia, 1983). For the way Augustine's later reading affected Romans 7, see P. Fredriksen, "Paul and Augustine: Conversion Narratives, Orthodox Traditions, and the Retrospective Self," *Journal of Theological Studies* 37 (1986): 3–34.

8. I owe this happy phrasing to Professor Andrew Jacobs.

9. K. Stendahl, "Paul and the Introspective Conscience of the West," in *Paul among the Jews and Gentiles* (Philadelphia, 1976).

10. For his most programmatic statement of this conviction, *de civitate Dei* 22.4–5; 17, women will be raised in their female bodies; 19, fat people will not be raised in an overweight body; and 20, amputees will have limbs restored.

11. *Religion and Society in the Age of S. Augustine* (London, 1972), 20f.

12. For the way such thinking affects the quest for the historical Jesus, see P. Fredriksen, *Jesus of Nazareth, King of the Jews* (New York, 1999), 261–70.

FOUR

Paul between Judaism and Hellenism

E. P. SANDERS

The Question of Context

The problem of interpretation is in part the problem of context: in the light of what views, events, and social structures shall we read X? The historian begins with the basic commitment either to read X in light of X's own day or to determine how X was understood during some subsequent period. But even when the context is limited, the interpreter still faces problems, since people live simultaneously in multiple contexts. Some are large, some small, some remote, some close at hand. Our contexts shape us: when we live, what our parents were like, where we live, where we used to live, with whom we live, where we study, where we work, what books we read—and so on almost forever—determine much of who we are. This has always been true, and the modern historian who studies ancient people and events cannot pick one of the contexts and know that it is the best one for the interpretation of X. Study of context requires a lot of people studying all sorts of contexts.

In the case of Paul, a Greek-speaking Jew of the first century, there has always been a major question of whether to read his letters primarily in the context of Greco-Roman culture or that of Judaism. But there is no single entity called Greco-Roman culture. It was diverse. Judaism was also diverse. If one reads Paul against the backdrop of Philo and ancient Jewish symbols and art, for example, one discovers *a* Paul: the one discussed by Erwin Goodenough and Samuel Sandmel. W. D. Davies wrote about Paul as a Rabbinic Jew, which led to *a* Paul who was noticeably different from the Paul of Goodenough and Sandmel—though both Pauls are Jewish.[1]

Limitations on scholarly time and ability are important in considering what people think about Paul's context. Once upon a time it was at least conceivable to be well-educated in Greek, Latin, and Hebrew literature. This depended principally on learning classical languages and literature before entering university. It also helped that the primary sources were smaller in extent than they are now. Writing on Paul in the light of both cultures has become almost impossible because fewer people learn Greek and Latin early in life, because source material has increased in quantity (e.g., the Dead Sea Scrolls and inscriptions from the Greco-Roman world), and because the secondary literature has grown enormously. Now most of us can manage only a part of one of these two vast cultures.

We tend to compare and contrast Paul with what we know. How could it be otherwise? We learn by comparison and contrast, and the brain automatically conducts these activities. Thus everyone reads Paul in the light of what he or she knows. The historian self-consciously chooses one or more ancient contexts to compare with Paul. But the world still awaits—and will probably continue to await—the master work on Paul's context.

I myself have never written about the *source* of Paul's ideas. Lots of people think that I have and that somewhere in the pages of *Paul and Palestinian Judaism* there is a claim that Paul must be discussed only in the light of Jewish sources of Palestinian origin.[2] There is no such claim: I merely compared him with the material that I had spent ten years studying. I thought that I had lots of ten-year periods left to study something else. But time has passed, and I am out of ten-year periods. Although I could now add Greek-speaking Judaism, I am still incompetent to study Paul in the light of any significant aspect of the gentile culture in which he lived.

In thinking about the subject of the conference, however, I thought of a way of combining one of its themes—universalism—with a very modest exploration of Paul's cultural and social context. In this chapter I shall explain how I would *start* if I *were* ever to try to situate Paul more precisely in the enormous world that he inhabited. I called this chapter "Paul between Judaism and Hellenism," but I could add, "and the question of universalism." After discussing two topics on Judaism and Hellenism in Paul's letters, I shall apply the effort to what Paul wrote about universalism.

Paul as a Man of Two Cultures

The mere fact that Paul was a Greek-speaking Jew, probably from Asia Minor, tells us that he relates both to Judaism and to Greco-Roman culture in some way. Even if he opposes aspects of one or the other, he still relates to it. Context shapes people, whether they accept what is going on around them or not, and we are affected by what we oppose as well as by what we accept.

What we do not know at the outset is *how deeply* he was embedded in each culture. Surface familiarity is not in dispute. What is surface familiarity? Consider the following modern analogy. Only a small percentage of the populace of Europe and North America have read the works of Sigmund Freud. Yet more or less everyone knows Freudian concepts, and many people use them routinely. For example, the idea that we have an "unconscious" mind that is *active,* despite the fact that we are not aware of it, was unknown in the eighteenth century. Now, however, we all suppose that we have both a conscious and an unconscious mind and that the unconscious mind is continuously active. It sometimes produces "Freudian slips," causing us to blurt out something that our conscious mind wants to conceal. I know about Freudianism at this level, as do the readers of this chapter. Does this prove that we all had the same education and that it included the works of Freud? A reader who mentally replies no to this rhetorical question gets an A for the day: we all have some surface familiarity with aspects of Freud's work, but we did not all receive the same education, nor have we all read Freud.

It is easy to spot what we may call "Greekisms" in Paul that show some knowledge of Hellenistic or Roman thought. I shall quote two of my favorites: "We look not at what can be seen but at what cannot be seen; for what can be seen is temporary, but what cannot be seen is eternal" (2 Cor 4:18). This sounds highly Platonic: the *real* world is eternal and invisible. What is *seen,* the world of sense perception, is transient, and what is transient cannot be *real.*[3] This view is highly Greek. It was not the view of many ancient Jews (Philo is an important exception). It is also foreign to the modern world.

The second passage is Philippians 4:11–12:

> Not that I am referring to being in need; for I have learned to be content with whatever I have. I know what it is to have little, and I know what it is to have plenty. In any and all circumstances I have learned the secret of being well-fed and of going hungry, of having plenty and of being in need.

In the phrase "I have learned to be content," the word translated "content" is *autarkês,* better translated "self-sufficient." The word and the concept were common to many strands of Greco-Roman philosophy, but were especially characteristic of the Stoics and Cynics. Almost any Stoic or Cynic philosopher could have written the two sentences in Philippians 4:11–12.[4]

Scholars who wish to connect Paul primarily to Stoicism or other forms of Greek thought, of course, must and *do* probe much deeper than such surface similarities.[5] I cite these two passages only to illustrate the fact that there is no doubt that Paul knew, at some level or other, many strands of Greco-Roman culture and thought. It was, after all, the world he lived and traveled in. He did not spend his life in an isolated Jewish ghetto, nor was he blind and deaf to the world around him.

Quotations and Education

One of the best ways to get deeper into the topic would be to describe Paul's education, and this is the first thing that I would try to reconstruct if I were to explore the sources of his thought. The book of Acts tells us that Paul was "brought up in this city [Jerusalem] at the feet of Gamaliel, educated strictly according to [his] ancestral law" (Acts 22:3). It would take too long to show in detail that this is highly improbable as a precise description of Paul's education. Briefly, he seldom shows knowledge of the Hebrew text of the Bible where it differs from the Greek translation, and he shows no knowledge of specifically Pharisaic modes of biblical interpretation. He did share some views with Palestinian Pharisees, such as belief in the resurrection, the combination of free will with predestination, and reliance on tradition as well as on the written text of the Bible.[6] But many Jews shared these views.[7] The three items show only that Paul was not a Palestinian Sadducee; they do not prove that he was a Palestinian Pharisee. He was, of course, a Pharisee, since he says that of himself (Phil 3:5). That probably means only that he believed in the resurrection and in some specific nonbiblical traditions. There are *no signs of a distinctively Palestinian Pharisaic education.* And so, along with most Pauline scholars, I reject the view that Paul as a small child moved to Jerusalem and was brought up and educated within Palestinian Pharisaism.

In this case, we might seem to have no knowledge of Paul's education. But we do. We know that when he wanted to prove a point by appealing to another text, he quoted the Jewish scripture in the Greek translation of what Christians call the Old Testament. This translation is frequently called the Septuagint (abbreviated LXX).

Ancient education was based on memorization: when students studied texts, they memorized them.[8] One of the points of being a learned Roman, for example, was being able to produce a telling quotation at the right moment; and to this end a lot of material, especially from Homer and the later poets (including dramatists), was memorized.[9] Literary works, such as Homer and the Jewish Bible, were on scrolls and were divided only into "books," with no chapter, paragraph, or verse numbers. And there were no indexes. Finding a quotation in a scroll was extremely time-consuming and tedious. It was much simpler and easier for children to memorize than it was for adults to look things up.

This has been forgotten, or was never known, by most people today. The view that one does not need to carry information in one's head was introduced into the American educational system a long time ago. I first heard it, with a feeling of dismay and disagreement, when, at age ten, I had just memorized Longfellow's "The Midnight Ride of Paul Revere" in honor of my birthday, which is the eighteenth of April. On that day, April 18, 1947, my teacher told the class that we did not need to memorize, but rather to know how to look things up—implying that we would spend our lives with large reference books ready at hand; I envisaged them strapped to my back or hanging around my neck. Before the twentieth century, however, which brought the heinous and destructive view that people do not need habitual knowledge carried securely in their heads, children memorized. Bright children, who started at the age of seven or earlier and studied until around fifteen or sixteen, could memorize a lot of Homer, the Bible, or any other long works.

The Greek or Roman child had to cope with an enormous amount of literature. In the Greek language, the two most important authors to study were Homer and Euripides, but students also had to pay attention to the other great dramatists, poets, and historians.[10] In Rome, this led to emphasis on the memorization of many, many *sententiae*—lines that were "praiseworthy quite apart from [their] original context."[11] The quantity of great literature meant that memorization of anthologies was very common and began in primary school. In secondary school, students memorized longer continuous texts, as well as more anthologies.[12] If Paul had a standard Greco-Roman education, he would have memorized substantial parts of Homer, Greek tragedy (especially Euripides), and other classics as well.

Stanley Stowers has proposed that "Paul's Greek educational level roughly equals that of someone who had primary instruction with a *grammaticus,* or teacher of letters, and then had studied letter writing and some elementary rhetorical exercises."[13] The words "primary" and "elementary" indicate that Paul did not reach the higher levels of education in Greek. This judgment, I assume, rests in part on the quality of Paul's Greek prose (accurate *koinê* or "common" Greek, by no means as sophisticated as the Greek of the wealthy and the aristocrats), in part on the rhetorical forms that Stowers finds in Paul's letters. I have no difficulty with this evaluation (assuming that it refers to Paul's level of Greek and his knowledge of some rhetorical forms). We shall return to this below.

If Paul had a Palestinian Pharisaic education, he would have memorized the Bible in Hebrew,[14] and possibly a lot of the Pharisaic discussions of various legal topics as well. Education in Hebrew rested on precise knowledge of the only really important literature—the Hebrew Bible—which is much shorter than the total of classical Greek literature. After Paul's day, Rabbinic discussions assume memorization of the Hebrew Bible.

Since I think that Paul was a Diaspora Pharisee instead of a Palestinian Pharisee, however, I do not use our knowledge of Palestinian Pharisees or Rabbis as proof about Paul. But I note this point in order to indicate that memorizing a work as long as the Bible was a task that was within the capacity of a reasonably gifted and diligent student. Paul was more than diligent. His self-description was this: "I advanced in Judaism beyond many of my own age among my people, so extremely zealous was I for the traditions of my fathers" (Gal 1:14). We cannot know the range of traditions Paul learned, but it was certainly traditionally Jewish to learn the Bible. And advancing beyond those of his own age sounds like a boast about what an excellent student he had been. Precise knowledge of the Bible must be at least part of this claim in Galatians.

If Paul had an education that was largely Jewish in content but modeled on Hellenistic education and conducted in Greek, he presumably started by memorizing easier parts of the Greek translation of the Bible at around six or seven years of age, and then moved forward to memorize whole books. It is quite possible that he memorized it all; that would have been simple and in some ways convenient for an industrious, super-bright Jewish boy. I think it likely that this is precisely what Paul did, though we cannot exclude the possibility that he memorized only the Law and the Prophets, while also spending a lot of time on the Psalms. His quotations do not include every biblical book; on the other hand we have only seven surviving letters, and so we cannot limit his knowledge of the Bible to just those parts that he quoted in the letters we have.

I am proposing, then, that Paul was well-educated in the Bible but had a mediocre education in the Greek language and probably not much instruction in classical Greek literature. I doubt that he knew much Greek literature because he shows no inclination to quote it. The two passages cited above as revealing knowledge of Greek philosophy (2 Cor 4:18; Phil 4:11–12) might have led to pithy quotations from Plato or one of the Stoics, but this is precisely what is missing from Paul's letters in general. There is a Greek aphorism in 1 Corinthians 15:33 ("Bad company ruins good morals"), but according to C. K. Barrett this "is the only quotation from a non-biblical source in the genuine Pauline literature."[15] There are many points in Paul's letters that might have attracted an appropriate saying from gentile literature, but his quotations are in fact from the Bible.

Besides having precise and detailed knowledge of the text of the Greek translation of Hebrew scripture, he was also, as we shall see more fully below, a world-class expert in biblical argumentation. Consequently I am willing to guess that his education included the elements of Greek grammar, syntax, vocabulary, and some modes of argumentation in a school that took most of its examples—which children and youths studied and memorized—from the Septuagint. Alternatively, one could propose a very basic education in Greek language and literature followed by further education in a Greek-speaking Jewish school. I merely wonder whether or not these two were combined: a Jewish school that taught in Greek and made extensive use of the Greek translation of the Bible, with very little Greek literature in the curriculum.

In any case, *what* he frequently quotes—the Greek translation of Hebrew scripture—surely tells us a lot about his education. Since education was based on memorization, and since quoting from scrolls was so difficult, what Paul quotes must reveal at least some of what he memorized as a child and youth.

We shall appreciate Paul's knowledge of scripture better if I explain three things about it.

1. He could write without quoting his scripture explicitly, and he probably routinely preached to gentiles without overtly referring to the Bible. In Philemon, 1 Thessalonians, Philippians, and 2 Corinthians 10–13, there is not a single explicit quotation from Jewish scripture: no instance in which Paul used "as it is written," or a similar phrase, before a quotation.

2. Nevertheless, in all these cases except Philemon, the language of the Greek Bible is clearly evident at several places. I shall take only three examples: one from 1 Thessalonians, one from Philippians, and one from 2 Corinthians 10–13.

    a. 1 Thessalonians 4:8, which states that God gives his Spirit to people, called "you," is a combination of two verses from Ezekiel, 36:27 and 37:14.

    b. The words "blemish" and "crooked and perverse generation" in Philippians 2:15 are taken from Deuteronomy 32:5.[16]

    c. "Let the one who boasts boast in the Lord" (2 Cor 10:17) is taken from LXX 1 Kingdoms [1 Samuel] 2:10[17] and Jeremiah 9:22–23.[18]

It is worth noting that the quotations in Philippians 2:15 and 2 Corinthians 10:17 agree with the Greek translation of the Bible where it differs from the Hebrew version (see notes 16 and 17).[19]

The casual, incidental way in which these and many other quotations crop up in Paul's diction clearly points to memorization. Imagining that on his journeys he carried with him the twenty or so large scrolls necessary to contain the Bible, and that before writing each letter he turned the scrolls and found suitable phrases, is, in my judgment, wrongheaded. That is not what Greek or Latin orators and authors did; there is no reason to attribute such a laborious activity to Paul. His letters would have taken weeks to write.

The constant conflation of two or more biblical passages into one sentence (as in the three examples cited above) also points to memorization. Once he thought of a word, he thought of sentences—usually more than one—where the word appears in the Bible. His mind was impregnated with the words of scripture. A quotation simply appears, sometimes unheralded and unannounced, in connection with numerous key words in his letters.

3. When he appeals explicitly to the Bible, he reveals a remarkably precise and detailed knowledge of it. For example, in Galatia, rival Jewish Christian missionaries were trying to persuade Paul's gentile converts to accept circumcision and the Law of Moses. Their argument was, I believe, clear, simple, and persuasive to many. They could claim that Genesis 17 shows that males who follow the God of Israel must be circumcised:

> God said to Abraham: "As for you, you shall keep my covenant, you and your offspring after you throughout their generations. This is my covenant, which you shall keep, between me and you and your offspring after you: Every male among you shall be circumcised. . . . Any uncircumcised male who is not circumcised in the flesh of his foreskin shall be cut off from his people; he has broken my covenant." (Gen 17:9–14)

Paul replies with his usual dash and vigor. In Galatians 3–4 he develops three different arguments from the Abraham story to prove, despite Genesis 17, that the Bible does not require circumcision for gentile converts. These three arguments are very complicated, and explaining how they work would take far too much space. Here I want only to point out some facts about the scriptural quotations in one of these arguments, Galatians 3:6–14. In these nine verses, Paul quotes scripture six times. Two of the quotations are the *only* passages in the Greek translation of the Hebrew scripture that combine the words for "righteousness" and "faith" in the same sentence, and one is the *only* passage that combines "law" and "curse" in the same sentence.[20] It is, of course, the memory that produces this result. It would take forever and a day to find the only examples of certain word combinations by turning scrolls.

I conclude from this and other virtuoso performances (e.g., 1 Cor 10:1–13) that Paul was highly, highly, highly expert in Jewish scripture and in arguments based on it. It is impossible to demonstrate this level of familiarity with anything else. He knew his scripture at least as well as the most expert students of Homer knew the *Iliad* and the *Odyssey*. In fact, from reading the letters one of the few things that we know for sure about his education is that he knew the Greek translation of Hebrew scripture cold: backward and forward.

This does not prove a negative of any kind. It does not prove that Paul had not memorized the Bible in Hebrew; we cannot know that he had not studied Homer, or Epicurus, or Zeno; and it certainly does not prove that Stoic or Cynic modes of teaching were unknown to him.[21] We can be certain, however, that Paul had absorbed the heart of Judaism, the Bible. Paul's older Jewish contemporary, Philo of Alexandria, shows that this absorption could be combined with a deep knowledge of Greek philosophy and mythology; but for Paul, I think that the case still needs to be made. I expect that the substantial numbers of New Testament scholars who are well-versed in Greco-Roman sources will continue to toil at this, and I wish them all success. Paul was a complicated individual, and there is no reason to suppose that he knew only one sort of thing. I wish to emphasize, however, that what we *know* about the content of his education is that he could write everyday Greek accurately and that he had studied the Bible with great care and precision. He also knew how to argue, and he was especially expert in the argumentative use of the Bible.

History and Eschatology

The second topic that I would investigate if I were to examine Paul's sources—his full context—would be his view of time and history. This topic is important because Jews and Greeks had quite different views of history. The common Greek opinion was that history is cyclical. It is quite easy to get into very deep waters in considering Greek views of time and history; three strides would put me in over my head, and so I shall merely quote J. M. Rist on two of the leading Stoics, Cleanthes (331–232 BCE) and Chrysippus (c. 280–207 BCE):

> According to Diogenes Laertius, Cleanthes thought that all human souls survive until the destruction of the world by fire at the end of each particular world-cycle, while Chrysippus held that only the souls of the wise survive

so long; the others presumably outlive the body but do not last until the *ekpúrôsis* [conflagration].[22]

That is, "history" runs in cycles, each ending in a great conflagration, which is followed by a new beginning.

The Jewish view was that history runs only once—from creation to a grand climax. The idea of a decisive future event is at least as early as Amos (eighth century BCE), but it was further developed during the Persian period, which began in 538 BCE and lasted until the conquests of Alexander the Great between about 333 and 323 BCE. From the Persians, many Jews adopted the idea of a climactic showdown between good and evil, which would be won by the good God. At that time the bodies of the righteous would be raised from the dead.[23]

On this topic, Paul shows himself to be profoundly Jewish. He thought that the grand climax had begun; the resurrection of Jesus was the beginning of the final days of ordinary history: the raised Jesus was the "first-fruits" of the many who would be raised (1 Cor 15:20, 23). Moreover, Jesus would return to be greeted by dead and living Christians. The dead would come out of their graves to meet him in the air (1 Thess 4:13–17). Christ would reign until the end of history, when he would turn the kingdom over to God, who would then be "all in all" (1 Cor 15:28). In his debate with the Corinthians over these last events, Paul shows more than a little influence of Greek thought, including the view that God would be "all in all," which sounds highly Stoic.[24] It is impossible to explore here the shifts in Paul's thinking about the afterlife from 1 Corinthians 15 (which is, on the whole, traditionally Jewish) to 2 Corinthians 3–5 (where he incorporates more Greek views). But these chapters reveal his versatility and flexibility when locked in a serious theological argument with intelligent gentiles, who disagreed with some of his traditional Jewish views about the afterlife, especially the bodily resurrection. It was not at all difficult for Greek-speakers to accept the immortality of the soul, but the resurrection of the body was difficult, as 1 Corinthians 15 shows.

Despite numerous strongly Greek touches, especially in 2 Corinthians 5:2, the main thrust of Paul's thought on the resurrection of Jesus, the return of the Lord, and the future new life of Christians is distinctly Jewish. There is no world cycle; history is running in a straight line from the first Adam to the second Adam, Christ (1 Cor 15:42–50), whose return will be the culmination of ordinary history—not the end of the world, but the end of history as we know it.

Universalism

It is in the context of this discussion about the future that universalism appears in Paul's thought. In his long chapter on the resurrection in 1 Corinthians 15, we read, "For as all die in Adam, so *all* will be made alive in Christ" (1 Cor 15:22, my emphasis). The reader who stops with 1 Corinthians will puzzle over the significance of the statement that death, which applies to all people, will be countered in Christ by equally universal life. It is just one sentence: perhaps it is only a neatly turned phrase. Possibly he got carried away by rhetoric and said too much. *Surely* he thought that only those who are in Christ will live in the new age.

Certainly he wrote often enough about the coming destruction of those who do not have faith in Christ:

> The word of the cross is foolishness to "those
>   who are perishing" (1 Cor 1:18).
> "For we are the aroma of Christ to God among those who are being
>   saved and among those who are perishing" (2 Cor 2:15).
> The gospel is "veiled to those who are perishing" (2 Cor 4:3).
> God "has endured with much patience the objects of wrath
>   that are made for destruction" (Rom 9:22).

Most fully:

> For many live as enemies of the cross of Christ; I have often told you of them, and now I tell you even with tears. Their end is destruction; their god is the belly; and their glory is in their shame; their minds are set on earthly things. But our citizenship is in heaven, and it is from there that we are expecting a Savior, the Lord Jesus Christ. He will transform the body of our humiliation that it may be conformed to the body of his glory. (Phil 3:18–21)

In these passages, and others, Paul appears as a Christological exclusivist: someone who holds the view that only those who put their faith in Jesus as the Christ will be saved, while the others will be destroyed. (They will not go to hell. There is no hint in Paul's letters of hell as a place of eternal torment. The unconverted, rather, merely perish forever.)

In Paul's letters, however, there is another view, as we have seen, namely, that just as Adam brought universal death, so Christ brought universal life (1 Cor 15:22). Although we would not know the significance of this statement if we had only 1 Corinthians, Paul returns to it in Romans:

So that you may not claim to be wiser than you are, brothers and sisters, I want you to understand this mystery: a hardening has come upon part of Israel, until the full number of the Gentiles has come in. And so all Israel will be saved; as it is written,

Out of Zion will come the Deliverer; he will banish ungodliness from Jacob. And this is my covenant with them [Isa 59:20–21], *when I take away their sins* [Isa 27:9].

As regards the gospel they [the Jews] are enemies of God for your [gentile Christians'] sake; but as regards election they are beloved, for the sake of their ancestors; for the gifts and the calling of God are irrevocable. Just as you [Gentiles] were once disobedient to God but have now received mercy because of their [the Jews'] disobedience, so they [the Jews] have now been disobedient in order that, by the mercy shown to you [gentiles], they [the Jews] too may now receive mercy. For God has imprisoned all people in disobedience so that he may be merciful to all. O the depth of the riches and wisdom and knowledge of God! How unsearchable are his judgments and how inscrutable his ways!

For who has known the mind of the Lord? Or who has been his counselor? [Isa 40:13] (Rom 11:25–34)

In this passage, we see a conflict in Paul's mind. His Christological exclusivism—that *only* those in Christ will be saved—would result in the destruction of most Jews. He clearly states that result in Romans 9 and the earlier verses of Romans 11. But how could that be? God chose Israel and made promises to the descendants of Abraham (Gen 12:1–18:21). Would he now go back on his word? Paul desperately seeks a way to provide for the salvation of Israel. He first proposes that they will be included because of jealousy. When they see the streams of gentiles whom Paul has converted joining the people of God, the Jews will become jealous and will then put their faith in Christ. That is the view of Romans 11:14. Yet what if that does not work? Paul finally states, as we see in Romans 11:26–29 (quoted above), that God will figure out a way to save all Israel.

Yet Paul cannot see how *only* all Israel will be saved. Paul believed in the essential equality of Jew and gentile before God (Rom 3:29–30, quoted below). At the time of writing, most Jews *and* most Gentiles seemed to Paul to be among the disobedient. How can God save only one bunch of the disobedient—the Jews—and destroy the rest? And so he finally concludes that this too is impossible. God consigned all people to disobedience, in order that he could have mercy on them all equally. The clear import of Romans 11:32 is that God will manage to save everyone.

It is important to note the setting of Romans 11:26–32 in the unfolding of events as Paul sees them. The time when all Israel will be forgiven, and presumably all gentiles as well, will be when the Deliverer comes from Mount Zion (quoting Isaiah). In Paul's mind, this will be when Jesus returns, an event that he thought lay in the immediate future. Thus in the very last moments of history, when the Deliverer comes, God will have mercy on everyone.

Let me explain this in another way. When Paul is considering his own missionary work and that of the other apostles of Christ, he naturally sees destruction as the fate of those who refuse the Christian gospel. It is as if he said, "You reject me? God will destroy you!" That is the view that he takes in the passages on destruction, such as Philippians 3:18–21. But when he thinks of the actual end of history, when God brings down the curtain and concludes ordinary history, he cannot imagine that God will fail in his intention to save everyone. God, for Paul, created the world and rules it. Well, he does not rule all of it at the present time—meaning Paul's present time—since much of the world is under the domain of Satan, who is active during the period of Paul's own ministry (e.g., 1 Thess 2:18; 2 Cor 11:14). Paul probably has Satan in mind when he speaks of the evil "god of this eon," who has blinded the unbelievers (2 Cor 4:4).

But one of the major points of Jewish expectation of the climax of history was that the good God would win. Satan cannot prevail in the end times. How can God win if most people are destroyed? What kind of victory would that be? God created people, and he loves them. His intention toward them, that they be saved, will finally be fulfilled. When the redeemer comes from Mount Zion, all the disobedient, Jew and Gentile alike, will be saved.

Just how God will do it is a mystery. That is the meaning of the final exclamation in Romans 11:33, quoted above: "O the depth of the riches and wisdom and knowledge of God! How unsearchable are his judgments and how inscrutable his ways!" God, who can do anything, will finally do what the apostles cannot. He will redeem the entire creation, both the physical cosmos, as Paul says in Romans 8:19–21, and the really difficult part of the created order, disobedient humans.

The home of Paul's prediction of universal salvation at the end of Romans 11 is Jewish eschatology: Jewish thought about the end of history. Judaism supplied the principal categories of Paul's brain when he thought about time and history.

I should emphasize, however, that Greco-Roman thought about human equality contained important resources for universalism. The unity of all things and all people was basic to Stoic monism (belief in the unity of all things), and this implies human equality, at least in principle. Everyone granted that there were social distinctions, which should not, however, entirely override nature: one should remember that "no one is a slave by nature."[25] We see the assertion of equality, for example, in Cicero:

> [Some] men are claiming that there is no law or compact which they share for the common welfare with their fellow-citizens. Such an attitude is destructive of all fellowship in the body-politic. As for those who argue that we must take sympathetic account of fellow-citizens but not of outsiders, they are destroying the fellowship common to the human race, and once this is removed, kindness, generosity, goodness and justice are wholly excluded.[26]

Cicero was one of the ancient authors who were most closely studied in the seventeenth and eighteenth centuries. When John Locke wrote that "all Men by Nature are equal,"[27] he was standing in a tradition that was influenced by Greek and Roman philosophical thought as well as by the story of the creation in Genesis. Locke frequently quoted the Bible, since he was arguing against the theological defense of the divine right of kings, which was opposed to human equality; but one cannot say that his main principles were biblical.[28] Thomas Jefferson, who was strongly influenced by Locke, cast the idea in terms of creation ("that all men are created equal; that they are endowed by their creator with certain inalienable rights").[29] Human equality was in fact one of the two main points on which the Enlightenment thinkers could find agreement between the Bible and the writings of ancient Greeks and Romans, though it was the latter that largely shaped their opinions. (The other main point of agreement between the two ancient sources was ethical behavior.)

Was Paul (like Locke) influenced not only by his view of the God of Israel as creator and ruler of the world but also by Greco-Roman thought on the question of human equality? This is quite possible. The existence of the Greek-speaking culture that Paul knew, which contained both Jew and gentile, may partly explain his insistence on gentile equality in the people of God. But despite this possibility, we must note that his appeals are to God: "Is God the God of Jews only? Is he not the God of Gentiles also? Yes, of Gentiles also, since God is one" (Rom 3:29–30). Paul's first reference to universal salvation is set in the context of the creation ("For as in Adam all die, so also in Christ shall all be made alive," 1 Cor. 15:22), and Romans 11:32 is equally theological ("For God has consigned all people to disobedience, that he may have mercy upon all"). The best I can do here is to suggest that Greek and Roman thought about human equality forms part of the deep background of Paul's bursts of universalism.[30] In the foreground we see his view of God the creator and ruler of the universe.

The result of our short study of Paul's view of history is the same as the result of considering his quotations: despite some "Greek" phrases and agreement with Greco-Roman thought on human equality, the main line of his view of history and its outcome was Jewish.

I realize that people want Paul to have only one thought on such an important theological topic as exclusivism and universalism: the salvation of some versus the salvation of all. Alas! he had two thoughts. Those who want to make Paul a perfectly consistent thinker, whose words can be used to construct a perfect system of Christian theology, are doomed to lives of frustration and disappointment. So I hope that the reader does not want that too much. Paul was, instead, an embattled apostle who knew of fighting without and fears within (2 Cor 7:5); his hopes and exclamations cannot all be contained within our little theologies. Personally, I am very proud of and very pleased with the man who wrote the end of Romans 11, who rose above the negative feelings that he had about those who rejected his message and who envisaged a God who could know no defeat. "Is it not good to have passionate hopes and commitments which cannot all be reduced" to a simple, catechetical scheme?[31]

Notes

1. Erwin R. Goodenough with A. Thomas Kraabel, "Paul and the Hellenization of Christianity," in *Religions in Antiquity: Essays in Memory of Erwin Ramsdell Goodenough,* Studies in the History of Religions 14 (Leiden: Brill, 1968), 23–68; Samuel Sandmel, *The Genius of Paul: A Study in History,* 2nd ed. (New York: Schocken, 1970); W. D. Davies, *Paul and Rabbinic Judaism,* 5th ed. (1948; Mifflintown, Pa.: Sigler, 1998).

2. E. P. Sanders, *Paul and Palestinian Judaism* (London: SCM; Philadelphia: Fortress, 1977).

3. See, for example, Plato, *Symposium* 210a–212a, in which the priestess Diotima addresses Socrates and some of his male students. She leads them from physical beauty to the beauties of the soul, institutions, the sciences, and so on, ending with the goal: the vision of Beauty itself. All of its physical manifestations will pass away, but Beauty, which is true and good, is eternal and thus real. It is visible only to the eye of the mind.

4. For remarks on *autarkeia,* "self-sufficiency," see J. M. Rist, *Stoic Philosophy* (Cambridge: Cambridge University Press, 1969), 58–63. Malherbe points out that self-sufficiency was common to "philosophers of different persuasion": Abraham Malherbe, *Moral Exhortation: A Greco-Roman Sourcebook,* Library of Early Christianity (Philadelphia: Westminster, 1986), 12–13; for illustrations, see especially 112–14, 120.

5. Two recent books stand out in my mind as excellent large-scale efforts to read Paul primarily in light of his gentile or Greco-Roman environment: Stanley Stowers, *A Rereading of Romans: Justice, Jews, and Gentiles* (New Haven, Conn.: Yale University Press, 1994); and Troels Engberg-Pedersen, *Paul and the Stoics* (Edinburgh: T&T Clark; Louisville: Westminster/John Knox, 2000). Neither compiles lists of parallels of the sort that would show surface similarity. Stowers employs Greco-Roman rhetorical and

literary forms to illuminate what Paul argues and how he argues it in Romans. Engberg-Pedersen focuses on the mode of argument (which he calls a model) in Paul's letters and Stoic sources, especially the discussions of anthropology and ethics. Dale Martin has made excellent use of Greco-Roman sources on a more limited topic, the body: *The Corinthian Body* (New Haven, Conn.: Yale University Press, 1995). These three books contain references to other leading works in the field, which are too numerous to list here.

6. Resurrection: 1 Corinthians 15; predestination: Romans 8.29–30; 9.22; free will: Romans 10.5–17; tradition: Galatians 1.14. On these topics in Pharisaism, see Sanders, *Judaism: Practice and Belief 63 BCE–66 CE* (London: SCM; Philadelphia: Trinity, 1992), 416, 421, 418–19, 421–24.

7. On fate and free will, see *Practice and Belief,* 250–51, 287, 373–76; on life after death, see 42–43, 284, 298–303, 333, 369–70; on tradition, see 333–36.

8. See Henri Marrou, *A History of Education in Antiquity* (London: Sheed & Ward, 1956), 154, 166; Stanley F. Bonner, *Education in Ancient Rome from the Elder Cato to the Younger Pliny* (London: Methuen, 1977), 39, 111, 144, 307.

9. Bonner, *Education in Ancient Rome,* 248; cf. 81, 219.

10. For the basic curriculum, see Marrou, *History of Education,* 162–64.

11. Bonner, *Education in Ancient Rome,* 248.

12. See Marrou, *History of Education,* 154 (primary schools); 166 (secondary schools).

13. Stowers, *Rereading of Romans,* 17.

14. Saul Lieberman, *Hellenism in Jewish Palestine: Studies in the Literary Transmission, Beliefs, and Manners of Palestine in the I Century B.C.E.–IV Century C.E.* (New York: Jewish Theological Seminary of America, 5722-1962), 52.

15. C. K. Barrett, *A Commentary on The First Epistle to the Corinthians,* Harper's New Testament Commentaries (New York: Harper & Row, 1968), 367. Barrett traces the quotation to Menander's lost comedy *Thais.* He proposes that Paul knew the phrase because it had become proverbial. Related points are found elsewhere in Greek literature, but they are expressed less economically. See Hans Conzelmann, *I Corinthians,* Hermeneia (Philadelphia: Fortress, 1975), 279 n. 141.

16. The Hebrew and English of Deuteronomy 32:5 do not include the word "blemish," which appears in the Greek translation of Deuteronomy and in Paul's quotation of it.

17. The verse that Paul partially quotes is in the Greek translation of the Bible but does not appear in Hebrew or English.

18. The verse numbers are 22–23 in the Greek and Hebrew, 23–24 in the English translation.

19. This issue is very complicated, since we know neither that the Greek Bible which Paul studied is the same as the Septuagint (LXX) as we now have it, nor that the Hebrew text of his day was the same as the Massoretic (Hebrew) text that is in use today. I assume, however, that there is some continuity in both cases. Paul so often agrees with the Septuagint (as reconstructed by modern scholars) against the Massoretic text that it is likely that his disagreements with the Massoretic text result from the fact that the Greek text as he learned it in his childhood and youth was close to the Septuagint as we know it. There are, to be sure, counterexamples, in which Paul's quotation is closer to the Massoretic text than to the LXX (e.g., the quotation of Job 41:3 in Rom 11:35).

20. Galatians 3:6 quotes Genesis 1:6; Galatians 3:11 quotes Habakkuk 2:4 (righteousness and faith); Galatians 3:10 quotes Deuteronomy 27:26 (law and curse).

21. See n. 5 on Troels Engberg-Pedersen.

22. Rist, *Stoic Philosophy,* 93. See also the quotation from Diogenes Laertius, n. 24 below.

23. See Shaul Shaked, "Iranian Influence on Judaism: First Century BCE to Second Century CE," *The Cambridge History of Judaism,* vol. 1, ed. W. D. Davies and Louis Finkelstein (Cambridge: Cambridge University Press, 1984), 308–25.

24. The Stoics held that God and Nature are the same, and so either God or Nature could be "all in all." See Marcus Aurelius, *Meditations* 4.23 ("O Nature: from you are all things, in you are all things, to you all things return"); Seneca, *Letters* 92 ("the totality in which we are contained is one, and it is god; and we are his partners and his members"). According to Diogenes Laertius, one of the meanings of "world" in Stoic thought is "God," "who at stated periods of time absorbs into himself the whole reality and again creates it from himself." J. von Arnim, *Stoicorum veterum fragmenta,* 4 vols. (Leipzig, 1905–24), 2:526), quoted in Jason L. Saunders, *Greek and Roman Philosophy after Aristotle* (London: Collier-Macmillan, 1966), 90. Copleston illustrates the dominant Stoic view by quoting Pope: "All are but parts of one stupendous whole,/Whose body Nature is and God the soul." See Alexander Pope, "Essay on Man," I.9.267, quoted in Frederick Copleston, *A History of Philosophy,* vol. 1, *Greece and Rome* (Westminster, Md.: Newman, 1959), 388.

25. Seneca, quoted in Saunders, 127. See also Seneca's *Letter* 47, "Slaves."

26. Cicero, *On Obligations* III.28. P. G. Walsh, *Oxford World's Classics* (Oxford: Oxford University Press, 2000), 93; cf. I.51 (p. 19); I.85, 88 (pp. 30–31).

27. John Locke, *The Second Treatise of Government* §54, referring back to §4. See *Locke: Two Treatises of Government,* ed. Peter Laslett (1960; Cambridge: Cambridge University Press, 2003), 304, 269. The *Treatises* were originally published in 1689.

28. On the position that Locke opposed, see Locke, *Treatise* I §1–§4 (Laslett, 141–43). For biblical arguments, see, e.g., I §61 (pp. 184–86); I §112–§118 (pp. 222–27); II §6 ("For Men being all the Workmanship of one Omnipotent, and infinitely wise Maker; All the Servants of one Sovereign Master," p. 271). In *Treatise* I, which is against a theological argument that supported the divine right of kings, the argument is thickly exegetical, and Locke shows his customary biblical expertise. In *Treatise* II, the constructive argument, there is still some exegesis and appeal to equality of creation (as in II §6, just quoted), but the main principles of his argument are Reason and the Law of Nature: "The *State of Nature* has a Law of Nature to govern it, which obliges every one: And Reason, which is that Law, teaches all Mankind, who will but consult it, that being all equal and independent, no one ought to harm another in his Life, Health, Liberty, or Possessions" (II §6). This statement immediately precedes the (secondary) appeal to creation in the same paragraph.

29. Thomas Jefferson, "A Declaration by the Representatives of the United States of America, in General Congress Assembled," in *Writings,* Library of America (New York: Literary Classics of the United States, 1984), 19.

30. There is a difference between "universal salvation" (as in Rom 11:32) and "human equality" (as in Cicero), since Greco-Roman philosophy did not focus on salvation but rather on human behavior in this world. Equality and universal salvation, however, seem to me to be intimately related, and each can support the other.

31. E. P. Sanders, *Paul* (1991; Oxford: Oxford University Press, 2001), 149.

FIVE

The Promise of Teleology, the Constraints of Epistemology, and Universal Vision in Paul

DALE B. MARTIN

After all these years of running from The Universal, should we now be embracing it? After learning so well to deconstruct so many statements claiming to represent Universal Truth, should we be putting other universal truths in their place? It has been shown, at least to the satisfaction of many of us, that all statements of universal truth actually represent local points of view, particular statements of truth true in particular situations. Claims made for the universal—statements of truth that claim to escape the contingency and limit of locality—are after all locative indeed. Even the statement "two plus two is four" can be shown to be *not* "universally true" *as* a "statement." But is it now time to leave behind the critique of universalistic claims, indeed, the suspicion of the universal, and begin again the search for universal values, universal truth?

I do not mean to imply that the argument is over and the universal lost. Just recently a letter writer in the *New York Times Review of Books* complained that "human rights" and "human dignity" should not be attributed to the influence of Christianity but to "universal human values."[1] But how does he know that? Although Alain Badiou seems to be looking for universals, he simultaneously appears suspicious of the claims of human "rights," or at least he seems to want to appropriate for his own program the *absence* of any notion of "rights" in the Apostle Paul.[2] Where is the valuable universal here? Is the value of human rights—not to mention specifically delineated, particular rights—a universal value or not? And what does that mean? That all rational, thinking human beings of goodwill necessarily will agree that all human beings possess the same delineated rights?

The fracturing of "culturalisms" and "identity politics" that so disturbs Žižek and Badiou certainly seems to suggest some need for the universal.[3]

And even if we do not propose universal values, others certainly will. The U.S. government constantly dispenses propaganda touting universal values of democracy and human rights, though that is really just a mask for the values the United States truly desires to promote throughout the world, whether through merely coercive methods or actual violence and warfare. I refer to the U.S. government's truly valued values of state-sponsored multinational business interests and the promotion of American power and imperialism, the goal of which is turbo-capitalism. That in itself is a dominant universalism. Žižek brilliantly begins one of his meditations with this quotation:

> All old-established national industries have been destroyed or are daily being destroyed. They are dislodged by new industries, whose introduction becomes a life and death question for all civilized nations, by industries that no longer work up indigenous raw material, but raw material drawn from the remotest zones; industries whose products are consumed, not only at home, but in every quarter of the globe. In place of the old wants, satisfied by the productions of the country, we find new wants, requiring for their satisfaction the products of distant lands and climes. In place of the old local and national seclusion and self-sufficiency, we have intercourse in every direction, universal inter-dependence of nations. And as in material, so also in intellectual production. The intellectual creations of individual nations become common property. National one-sidedness and narrow-mindedness becomes more and more impossible, and from the numerous national and local literatures, there arises a world literature.[4]

Though these words are from *The Communist Manifesto,* published over 150 years ago, they seem more true now than then. The global universalism of turbo-capitalism is being promoted with great energy as the one true universal, though under the guise of democracy, human rights, or nationalism. Perhaps we must come up with *some* universal, if for nothing else than as an alternative to the obvious universalism of the false prophets of American politics.

And so Badiou and Žižek, among others, have proposed Paul as one source for thinking the universal, along with the "event" and the "subject," terms not easy to define or nail down in their work. As Žižek puts it, Paul "elevate[d] Christianity from a Jewish sect into a universal religion (religion of universality)."[5] Or elsewhere, "The key dimension of Paul's gesture is thus his break with any form of communitarianism: his universe is no longer that of the multitude of groups that want to 'find their voice,' and assert their particular identity, their 'way of life,' but that of a fighting collective grounded in the reference to an unconditional universalism."[6]

Or in Badiou's words, "For him who considers that the real is pure event, Jewish and Greek discourses no longer present, as they continue to do in the work of Levinas, the paradigm of a major difference for thought. This is the driving force behind Paul's universalist conviction: that 'ethnic' or cultural difference, of which the opposition between Greek and Jew is in his time, and in the empire as a whole, the prototype, is no longer significant with regard to the real, or to the new object that sets out a new discourse. No real distinguishes the first two discourses any longer, and their distinction collapses into rhetoric. As Paul declares, defying the evidence: 'There is no distinction between Jew and Greek' (Rom. 10:12)."[7] I will later challenge this reading of Paul as unproblematically universal, but there can be no doubt that throughout Christian history—though especially in the modern world—Paul has been read as a great universalizer, and there is much in his letters to commend the reading.[8]

Moreover, what universal there is in Paul must be read in relation to his monotheism (though exactly what monotheism means in Christianity, as in any religious system, is highly debatable and variable). Again, as Badiou puts it, "That there is but a single God must be understood not as a philosophical speculation concerning substance or the supreme being, but on the basis of a structure of address. The One is that which inscribes no difference in the subjects to which it addresses itself. The One is only insofar as it is for all: such is the maxim of universality when it has its root in the event. Monotheism can be understood only by taking into consideration the whole of humanity. Unless addressed to all, the One crumbles and disappears."[9]

The famous Pauline notion of "grace" is also central for his universalism. "There is for Paul," Badiou writes, "an essential link between the 'for all' of the universal and the 'without cause.' There is an address for all only according to that which is without cause. Only what is absolutely gratuitous can be addressed to all. Only charisma and grace measure up to a universal problem."[10] I believe Badiou is also on target in his understanding that hell or, as he puts it, "distributive justice" has little place in Paul.[11] Paul is not interested in limiting the reach of hope. The centrality of both hope and love in Paul's thought means that "universality mediates identity." "The One is inaccessible without the 'for all.'"[12]

For Badiou reading Paul, and here we get to the heart of Badiou's critique of identity politics and solely communitarian ethics, differences may be acknowledged—in fact *must* be acknowledged—but that acknowledgment must take the form of *indifference*. "In order for people to become gripped by truth, it is imperative that universality not present itself under the aspect of a particularity. Differences can be transcended only if benevolence with regard to customs and opinions presents itself as *an indifference that tolerates differences,* one whose sole material test lies, as Paul says, in being able and knowing how to practice them oneself."[13] "Differences, like instrumental tones, provide us with the recognizable univocity that makes up the melody of the True."[14]

To what extent is this portrait of Paul true? I find these readings of Paul strong, insightful, and generally on target even from the ascetic point of view of modern historical criticism. One of the remarkable parallels I see between the work of Žižek and Badiou on the one hand and Paul's ideas on the other is the fact that in both there is definitely truth, even a universal truth, but it is a truth remarkably without content. To make this clear, I must provide a lengthy quotation from Badiou's work:

> Paul's general procedure is the following: if there has been an event and if truth consists in declaring it and then in being faithful to this declaration, two consequences ensue. First, since truth is eventual, or of the order of what occurs, it is singular. It is neither structural, nor axiomatic, nor legal. No available generality can account for it, nor structure the subject who claims to follow in its wake. Consequently, there cannot be a law of truth. Second, truth being inscribed on the basis of a declaration that is in essence subjective, no preconstituted subset can support it; nothing communitarian or historically established can lend its substance to the process of truth. Truth is diagonal relative to every communitarian subset; it neither claims authority from, nor (this is obviously the most delicate point) constitutes any identity. It is offered to all, or addressed to everyone, without a condition of belonging being able to limit this offer, or this address.[15]

I take this to mean that this truth cannot be translated completely, commensurably, without remainder into some other statement of truth. Truth sets no structure or law outside the event itself. And it cannot be identified with any particular community.[16]

Note, however, how this tells us much of what truth is *not* but little of what it *is*. It doesn't tell us what truth actually says in a propositional manner. Truth in this sense cannot be defined. Indeed, it seems that it cannot even be "said" apart from repeating the narrative of the event itself.[17] As Badiou says, "If a truth is to surge forth eventally, it must be nondenumerable, unpredictable, uncontrollable. This is precisely what Paul calls grace: that which occurs without being couched in any predicate." Or elsewhere, "Truth for Paul is never anything but 'faith working through love' (Gal. 5:6)."[18]

I believe this is an insightful and accurate reading of Paul. Sure, we can agree that Paul adhered to Jewish monotheism, at least of a sort. So we can say that Paul did believe it necessary to believe "that" (i.e., to agree with the proposition) God is one, that there is only one true, living God. But what else about that God one must believe is seldom spelled out by Paul. Paul is content to know nothing but "Jesus Christ crucified" (1 Cor 1:23; 2:2). Truth for Paul is contained in the undistillable narrative that "God was in Jesus Christ reconciling the world to himself" (2 Cor 5:19). The Thessalonian disciples seem basically satisfied with a gospel whose content is little more than the fact that they have, as Paul says, "turned to God from images to serve a living and true God and to await his son from the skies, whom he raised from among the corpses, Jesus, the one rescuing us from the coming anger" (1 Thess 1:9–10).[19]

Paul is not really a theologian. He is not at all concerned with abstract proposals about the nature of God; he is certainly ignorant of the doctrine of the Trinity; he is not concerned to define carefully the nature of Christ, even to the point that he says things about Christ that strike us as contradictory and heretical, separated as we are from Paul by the church's councils and carefully worded creeds.[20] For example, at times Paul sounds like an innocent subordinationist, depicting Christ as subordinate to God the Father, an idea later labeled as heresy.[21] It would be anachronistic to accuse Paul of heresy, though, precisely because Paul is unconcerned with the careful statements of doctrine and propositions of truth that later come to make up orthodoxy. Paul doesn't exactly contradict orthodoxy as much as precede it: Paul is concerned with the event and what it will mean in the lives of people, nations, and the cosmos, but not with identifying the truth content of the gospel in any philosophical or propositional sense. And in that case, the writings of Badiou and Žižek and Paul himself are notably similar in the *absence* of content to their truth. They proclaim a truth without content.

Paul's truth looks so contentless partly because he has an ambiguous relationship to knowledge itself. Paul seldom makes direct claims to certain knowledge about God, a point as well known to biblical scholars as it is surprising to most people, who think of Paul as the first dogmatist of Christianity.[22] Paul, on the contrary, asks, quoting Isaiah, "Who has known the mind of God?" (Rom 11:34; Isa 40:13), with the implied answer, "No one!" What we do know, according to Paul, we know only "in part" (1 Cor 13:9, 12). Elsewhere Paul says, "Anyone claiming to know does not yet know; but whoever loves God *is known by him*" (1 Cor 8:2–3). Paul shifts knowledge into the passive voice. To the Galatians, Paul starts off sounding as if he will make a positive claim about knowledge of God, but then he reverses himself from active to passive: "Now that you have come to know God," he first says, but then corrects himself, "or rather *to be known by God*" (Gal 4:9).[23] For Paul, epistemology is constrained. Knowledge is partial, limited, through a glass darkly—or translated better into contemporary English: seen only as in a smoky, faulty, obscuring mirror, like trying to put on makeup while looking into a dirty chrome hubcap (1 Cor 13:12). Paul's epistemological reservation—the constraints of knowledge that come with our present, natural existence—limit what we can say about God and truth to little more than repeating the proclamation that in the death, burial, and resurrection of Jesus we have hope as long as we entrust ourselves to that event. The constraints on epistemology assumed by Paul render his truth relatively without content and unpredictable.

The other aspect of Paul's thought that severely restricts what can be said positively about truth is his eschatology, which has been curiously ignored or rejected by most contemporary philosophical interpreters.[24] Paul was, as almost all biblical scholars will now admit, an apocalypticist.[25] Scholars of Paul have long recognized what most people, perhaps especially most Christians, do not: that although justification is a past and present experience for those who trust Christ—we *have been* justified—*salvation*, according to Paul, is something no one possesses and everyone must await.[26] Romans 6 teaches that although we have been crucified and buried with Christ in baptism, we *will be* resurrected with him, presumably only in the Parousia, the coming of Christ that includes the resurrection at the end (esp. Rom 6:4, 5, 8; see also 8:11). The creation is far from already redeemed according to Paul; rather, it "groans" in labor pains as it awaits its redemption (Rom 8:19–22). Unlike modern popular Christianity, which asks people if they "have been saved" by Jesus their "Lord and Personal Savior," Paul seldom attributes any past or current salvation to the activity of Jesus.[27] Rather, he refers to Jesus as our savior from "the coming anger" (1 Thess 1:10). We await the Parousia of Jesus. "Parousia" may denote "presence," but in Paul, when it is used of Jesus and not of Paul or other "normal" people, it never refers to the current presence of Jesus but to his future appearing.[28] It is *at that time* and not before, Paul implies, that his followers will be found "blameless" (1 Thess 3:13; 4:15; 5:23). Paul's apocalypticism promises salvation and clarity *in the future;* but at the same time his apocalypticism consigns current human existence to a waiting—in the assurance of hope, to be sure, but still a waiting. So one of the reasons we now know so little is because the full apocalypse, the unveiling of truth, has not yet been completed. In fact it has scarcely begun.

Paul again opposes the philosophers. Paul's eschatology is of course a certain kind of teleology. As a "logic of the end," teleology is not the sole preserve of the philosophers. True, in their hands, teleology has most often been completely conservative or even reactionary. Aristotle, for example, used teleology to argue that nature *as it is currently constituted* is the best possible way it could be. All things exist for a purpose, a *telos*. The "end" of all things, their *telos,* can be seen in their proper function. The reason for their existence can be seen in how they fulfill their "purpose," their "goal" (*telos*). In his famous argument supporting slavery, the conservatism of Aristotle's teleology is clear: some human beings are *made for the purpose of being* slaves and others of being masters.[29] Human beings find their true destiny, their purpose, their *telos* when they serve the purpose for which they were brought into existence by Nature. These notions, and their ideological conservatism, are more obvious in, say, Galen, the second-century medical writer, but Galen is correct to read them out of Aristotle's philosophy.[30] Aristotle's philosophy is deeply teleological, and its teleology, by focusing on "the way things should be" simply as a defense of "the way things are," works against any revolution or social reform.

Aristotle's philosophical teleology has had profoundly negative effects on Western civilization, philosophy, and politics ever since. We find an equally disastrous teleology in the late ancient Christian writer Eusebius, that apologist for Constantine and Christian empire. Writing at the beginning of the fourth century, after the triumph of Constantine over rival emperors and of Christianity over the Greek and Roman worlds, Eusebius rejected the apocalypticism of Jesus, Paul, and John the author of Revelation and substituted in its place a "realized eschatology" in which one need not await Jerusalem to descend from heaven in the future because the heavenly Jerusalem already existed in Christian Constantinople.[31] One need not await, with groaning and travail, the redemption of creation by the coming Christ because Christians experienced salvation already in the victories and protection of the *present* monarch of Christ, Constantine. The fulfillment of teleology for Eusebius existed in the person of Constantine, the monarchical representative, indeed embodiment, of Christ in the present. The future kingdom of Paul's hopes, the announced kingdom of Jesus of Nazareth, the prophesied kingdom of John the Seer on Patmos were all brushed aside by Eusebius, court preacher of Christian imperialism, in celebration of the already accomplished victory of Christianity in the Emperor Constantine and in the establishment of the kingdom of God, indeed the Empire of God, on earth in the fourth century after the birth of the Lord.

A survey of teleologies, especially philosophical teleologies, would reveal, I wager, that they are almost always conservative, teaching the impossibility of radical change due to the relative perfection of existing reality. We could mention, for instance, the teleology of Hegelian historiography, which saw at least the theretofore highest level of *Geist* in the purified Hegelian

Protestantism of nineteenth-century German thought, as Kierkegaard never tired of mocking.[32] But my purpose in bringing up comparative teleology is to highlight just how different Paul's is from these. Paul's teleology, *his* "logic of the end," steadfastly reserves perfection and even salvation for a future coming. Thus we "know in part" only (1 Cor 13:9, 12). We experience our future salvation only in promise and hope. Therefore, no existing human community or knowledge can claim to *be* the kingdom of God. That is in the future. Paul's teleology is full of promise, not presence. Paul's teleology insists not on current fulfillment of purpose, as one would find in Aristotle, Galen, Eusebius, or Hegel. Paul's teleology, rather, points out just how the current social and political situation needs radical redemption and revolution. It is a teleology not of fulfillment but of promise. Not of certainty but of hope.

Once we see this, we can also begin to see that so many of Paul's current philosophical readers get him wrong on one very important point: their desire to see in him the founder of a new people, a new ethnicity, a new religion. For not only is Paul constrained by his eschatology from announcing the establishment of the kingdom of God in the Church, he is also prohibited from proclaiming a new people or a new religion because of his faithfulness to Israel and the God of Israel. Žižek has written, "Saint Paul conceives of the Christian community as the new incarnation of the chosen people: it is Christians who are the true 'children of Abraham.' ... God kept his promise of redemption to the Jewish people, but, in the process itself, he changed the identity of the chosen people."[33] Badiou says that "the new universality bears no privileged relation to the Jewish community."[34] Both claims, as claims for Paul, seem to me transparently false.[35] It is true, as Badiou suggests, that Paul will not allow any ethnic group to *possess* the truth to the exclusion of others: "Paul's unprecedented gesture consists in subtracting truth from the communitarian grasp, be it that of a people, a city, an empire, a territory, or a social class."[36] This is true in the sense that Paul does not allow the *ethnos* of the Jews to grasp the truth for its sole possession, but it seriously ignores the continuing centrality of Israel for Paul and the privileging, at least in some sense, of Israel forever.[37]

Even when Paul insists that his gospel is for all people, he nonetheless repeats more than once that the blessings of the gospel are "to the Jew first" and only *then* to the Greek (Rom 1:16; 2:9–10). To his own rhetorical question of whether there is any advantage for the Jew, Paul responds, "Much in every way!" (Rom 3:1–2).

But the most telling signs that Paul has no interest in forming a new people, or even more outrageously a new religion, come from noting how he actually uses the terms "Israel" and "gentile." Even writing to those *we* would certainly call "gentiles," Paul almost never addresses them *as* gentiles. In fact, he does so only once, when reminding the Roman believers that he, as the apostle to the gentiles, has been addressing them as gentiles in order to convince them of the irrevocable faithfulness of God to the Jews (Rom 11:13). Instead, Paul regularly uses the term *ethnê* (gentiles or "the nations") to refer only to those *outside* the Church. To the Corinthians, he speaks of a time "when you *were* gentiles," as if they are no longer (1 Cor 12:2). He complains that someone in the Corinthian church has been sleeping with his stepmother, an offense, he says, "not even found among the gentiles" (1 Cor 5:1). In this case, the word is used so clearly to refer only to those outside the Church that modern translations often render it as "pagans" in order to *preclude* reference to the Corinthian recipients of the letter, in spite of the fact that the translators know perfectly well that those recipients were ethnically gentiles.

But if Paul's converts are no longer gentiles, what are they? He most commonly calls them brothers (*adelphoi*) or holy ones ("saints," *hagioi*), both terms that were in his time regular designations by Jews for other Jews. He insists that they are children of Abraham, which in common Jewish discourse would have designated them again as Jews.[38] He even seems to include them among the descendants of the Israelites who wandered with Moses in the wilderness. It is admittedly a matter of interpretation, but I think he is including his readers in 1 Corinthians 10:1 when he says, "Our fathers were all under the cloud and all passed through the sea." His inclusion of these Corinthians among the descendants of Israel becomes even likelier later in the chapter when he then designates *unbelieving* Jews as "Israel *kata sarka*," Israel "according to the flesh" (1 Cor 10:18). This is the *one* place Paul uses the term "Israel" to refer to those Jews who are not believers in Jesus Christ, and thus he modifies the term with the limitation *kata sarka*, "according to the flesh," thus implying that the unadorned "Israel" must refer to something else.

Paul is not inventing all this. His notion that only *part* of Israel is truly Israel is a not-uncommon theme in the Jewish scriptures. Several of the prophets spoke in terms of a remnant of the people, and Paul appropriates this very old remnant theology to support his own interpretation. "Not all those from Israel are Israel . . . not all the seed of Abraham are truly children" (Rom 9:6–7). Paul himself is like Elijah, representing a "remnant according to election" from the whole number of those who think of themselves as Israel (Rom 11:1–5). The flip side of this remnant theology is the inclusion of the other nations into Israel, which is also a theme of Jewish scripture Paul is eager to adopt for his own mission. Hosea had already quoted the God of Israel as proclaiming "I will call the 'not-my-people' 'my people' (*laon mou*), and the 'not-beloved' 'beloved'" (Hos 2:23, quoted in Rom 9:25–26). In fact, the places Paul quotes Jewish scriptures in densest concentrations are precisely those where he is arguing for the inclusion of the "nations" among God's people. In those sections of Romans in which he is arguing for the inclusion of the gentiles, Paul quotes at least sixteen passages from Jewish scripture to support his own message. Thus two linchpins of Paul's message are both taken directly from Jewish scripture: his argument that only a remnant of Israel is in his time among the faithful, and his argument that foreigners must be included among Israel.

This leads up to what many of us would see as the climax of Paul's argument and the crux of the letter to the Romans, where Paul compares the gentile believers to wild olive branches now grafted into the cultivated stalk of Israel:

> Now if some of the branches were cut off, while you, a wild-olive shoot, were grafted in among them and you became sharers of the root of the richness of the olive, do not boast over the branches. If you boast—well, you do not bear the root, but the root bears you. So you say, "Branches were cut off so that I might be grafted in." Sure. In unbelief they were cut off, while you stand in belief. Do not be arrogant, but afraid. For if God did not spare the natural branches, he will not spare you. Therefore, note both the kindness and the severity of God: severity toward those who have fallen, and kindness toward you, if you remain in the kindness, since also you may be cut off. And those, if they do not remain in unbelief, will be grafted in. For God is able again to graft them in. For if you were cut off from the wild-olive which was yours by nature and grafted into the cultivated olive contrary to nature [*para physin*], by how much more will the natural branches be grafted into their own olive tree? For I do not want you to be unaware, brothers, of this mystery, in order that you may not think too highly of yourself: a partial hardening has happened to Israel until the full number of the nations enters in, and thus all Israel will be saved. (Rom 11:17–26a)

I want to emphasize two aspects of this remarkable quotation usually ignored by Christians and philosophers alike. First, we must wonder how seriously or literally to take Paul's last statement here, but I tend to take him exactly at his word: "all Israel will be saved." None of us is saved right now since the apocalypse has not yet occurred. But Paul seems to be saying, really, that he expects the salvation of *all* Israel, and I believe he means here the future salvation of *all Jews*. Paul seems to me a universalist at least to the extent that he believes in the eventual salvation of the entire people of Israel, all the Jews.

Second, Paul conceives of the inclusion of non-Jews not by the creation of a new people, not by the supersession of Israel by some other, new nation or even non-nation. Rather, Paul envisions the grafting of the nations *into the people of Israel.* Again, this is not the cosmopolitanism of the philosophers—the idea that the truly philosophical person will be a *politês* (citizen) of the *kosmos* (the world). Paul seems to be calling all other peoples to become citizens of *Israel.* The gentiles are brought into the *nation of Israel* and *not* made to constitute a new nation, people, or, to cite an even more egregious misreading of Paul, new "religion." As remarkable as it is, given the past two thousand years of European and world history, Paul promises the adoption of the gentiles into Israel, not the rejection of Israel in favor of a new people, nor even the creation of a new, nonethnic universal people. This is not "natural," as Paul admits. In fact, this is God acting "contrary to nature," "against nature" (*para physin;* 11:24). This is the queer God who defies "natural law," goes against nature, and grafts the wild peoples of the world into the root of the Jews, making them in the process part of Israel, the people of God.[39]

These realizations should convince us to admit finally that there is no "Christianity" in Paul; there are no "Christians" in Paul's letters or his vision.[40] We should push this realization further than a note about mere terminology. Indeed, the words "Christian" or "Christianity" never occur in Paul's letters, but their absence is not a matter of mere words. Paul does not have a word for Christians or Christianity because he *couldn't;* such notions would destroy his vision entirely. The creation of a new people or a new religion would mean, in Paul's thought, that God has been proven unfaithful to his first promises and to his people. Paul is concerned with the faithfulness of Christ and the faithfulness of believers, to be sure. But Paul is much more concerned with the justice and faithfulness of *God,* and that would be destroyed with the rejection of the history and people of Israel in favor of a new people, a new faith, a new religion.[41] The letter to the Romans does have as one of its themes a universal vision of the inclusion of all peoples as people of God, but its even more central theme is the faithfulness of God to God's promise and people. And that necessitates that we see Paul working not to establish a new people but to graft the gentiles into the ongoing and eternal Israel of God. There is no Christianity in Paul; there are no Christians in Paul's letters; there is no absence of ethnicity in Paul's thought: there is the faithfulness of God to Israel that has finally necessitated the grafting of all the peoples through faith into the stock of Israel. The theme of Romans, put in Latin, would not be *extra ecclesiam nulla salus* (no salvation outside the church), but, and this is what so many Christians refuse to recognize when they read Romans, *extra Israel nulla salus:* "there is no salvation outside Israel."

I thus agree that Paul may provide an interesting resource for thinking about the universal, the event, and the subject. It might be more interesting, and would certainly be truer to Paul, to attempt to think about that universal without the exclusion of ethnicity entirely, since Paul never threw out ethnicity but rather concentrated on the nature of that ethnicity. What would it mean to think of grafting our ethnicities into those of others? And which others? And how?

But I wish to return now to the point I made above about the "truth without content" I discern in Žižek and Badiou on one side and in Paul on the other. With Paul's eschatological reservation (which also means the constraints of his epistemology since we cannot now know what we will know), and with his particular teleology (which is one of *promise* not *presence*), one may think of Paul as advocating a universal truth, but it is one, as is that of Badiou and Žižek, with a "content" that is difficult if not impossible to define or delineate.[42] This may not be bad. We may, for instance, think of a universal that refers more to an openness than to foundationalist philosophical propositions. We may compare such a universal to the empiricism advocated by Bas van Fraassen, a philosopher of science.

Bas van Fraassen, especially in his book *The Empirical Stance,* admits that "old-fashioned" foundationalist philosophies of empiricism can no longer withstand the scrutiny of skepticism. The older idea that we may arrive at secure, eternal, objective truths about, say, nature if we just look carefully enough and without prejudice seems now naive and insupportable. As van Fraassen explains, "The search for a rock-solid foundation for knowledge was precisely the rock on which empiricism foundered."[43]

Van Fraassen advocates not an empiricism that would promote foundationalist and eternal propositions about nature, reality, or truth, but a more modest and open-ended point of view: a stance. We should simply remind ourselves continually that we must be open to surprises of our world, that we must test our notions by constant critical comparison with "facts" (realizing that those are socially manufactured) and the readings of others. As van Fraassen puts it, "Stances do involve beliefs and are indeed inconceivable in separation from beliefs and opinion. The important point is simply that a stance will involve a good deal more, will not be identifiable through the beliefs involved, and can persist through changes of belief. . . . All our factual beliefs are to be given over as hostages to fortune, to the fortunes of future empirical evidence, and given up when they fail, without succumbing to despair, cynicism, or debilitating relativism."[44]

I would suggest, taking my lead here from Paul and van Fraassen, that we remain open to a vision of the universal redemption of all humankind. We may not know what shape that universal will take. We may not have specific answers from that vision that we may apply even politically with complete assurance, much less scientifically or philosophically. But that need not prohibit us from insisting, sometimes to others but mostly to ourselves, that we be open to the universal if it overtakes us. Thus, in place of a universalism of truth in the form of propositional statements of ethics, politics, or philosophy, we may advocate, again for others but mostly for ourselves, a "universal stance."

But that makes me ask, Is this a "universal" that is *enough*? When we get into debates about headscarves, scriptures, ten commandments, warfare, social justice, democracy, capitalism, abortion, death, will a "universal stance"—as opposed to universal propositions of translatable or paraphrasable truths—be enough to save us from ethnic solipsism, from mere communitarianism, from identity politics and in-group privileging? I really don't know. Can "truth without content" actually serve the needs which previous generations sought to meet by means of Universal Truth? I tend to doubt it. Do we need more? Perhaps.

But I also wonder, especially after reading Paul, Žižek, and Badiou, whether we need the universal again after all. If our needs can be met by a universal stance rather than The Universal Truth, can we really say we need a universal after all? Perhaps in the end we don't need so much to stand *on* something in particular as to stand *for* particular things and *against* other particular things. Perhaps, as subjects shaped and continuing to shape ourselves by an event, we could learn to live with the constraints of epistemology and the promise of apocalyptic teleology even in the absence of the universal.

Notes

I would like to thank the graduate students and colleagues at Yale who participated with me in a group that read works of Žižek, Badiou, and Jacob Taubes. For explicit suggestions toward the improvement of this paper, I thank Diana Swancutt, Joshua Garroway, Timothy Marquis, Brent Nongbri, and Michael Peppard.

1. Letter by John S. Koppel, *New York Times Book Review*, April 3, 2005, 6.

2. Alain Badiou, *Saint Paul: The Foundation of Universalism* (Stanford, Calif.: Stanford University Press, 2003), 77.

3. For the rejection of communitarianism, see, e.g., Slavoj Žižek, *The Puppet and the Dwarf: The Perverse Core of Christianity* (Cambridge, Mass.: MIT Press, 2003), 130; Žižek, *The Fragile Absolute—or Why Is the Christian Legacy Worth Fighting For?* (London: Verso, 2000), 10–11; Badiou, *Saint Paul*, 5, 6, 9, 10–11, passim; Badiou, *Ethics: An Essay on the Understanding of Evil* (London: Verso, 2001), 76.

4. Karl Marx and Friedrich Engels, *The Communist Manifesto* (Harmondsworth, U.K.: Penguin, 1985), 83–84, quoted in Žižek, *Fragile Absolute*, 13.

5. Žižek, *Puppet and the Dwarf*, 10. See also Žižek, *The Ticklish Subject: The Absent Centre of Political Ontology* (London: Verso, 1999), 157–58, 226.

6. Žižek, *Puppet and the Dwarf*, 130.

7. Badiou, *Saint Paul*, 57. "To declare the nondifference between Jew and Greek establishes Christianity's potential universality; to found the subject as division, rather than as perpetuation of a tradition, renders the subjective element adequate to this universality by terminating the predicative particularity of cultural subjects" (p. 57). "There is no doubt that universalism, and hence the existence of any truth whatsoever, requires the destitution of established differences and the initiation of a subject divided in itself by the challenge of having nothing but the vanished event to face up to" (p. 58).

8. The most familiar classic version of Paul as the great "universalizer" of Christianity was that promoted by the Tübingen School of German scholarship in the early and mid-nineteenth century led by Ferdinand Christian Baur. See, for example, Baur, *Paul the Apostle of Jesus Christ, His Life and Work, His Epistles and His Doctrine*, 2 vols., 2nd ed. (London: Williams & Norgate, 1876), originally published in German in 1831; and Baur, *The Church History of the First Three Centuries*, 3rd ed. (London: Williams & Norgate, 1878), esp. 1:47. The portrait became ubiquitous in the nineteenth and twentieth centuries. For another famous expression of the "universalizing Paul" who freed Christianity from the particularities of Judaism, see Adolf von Harnack, *What Is Christianity?* (Philadelphia: Fortress, 1986), originally published in 1900 as *Das Wesen des Christentums*. Though admitting that before Paul some Hellenistic Jewish disciples first pressed the universalism of Christianity (174), Harnack insisted that it was Paul "who delivered the Christian religion from Judaism" and transformed the gospel "into the universal religion" (180; see 175–89 for Harnack's account of Paul at length). A more recent example of this reading of Paul is the famous and influential work by Martin Hengel, *Judaism and Hellenism* (Philadelphia: Fortress, 1981), originally published as *Judentum und Hellenismus: Studien zu ihrer Begegnung unter besonderer Berücksichtigung Palästinas bis zur Mitte des 2. Jh. v. Chr.*, WUNT 10 (Tübingen: Mohr-Siebeck, 1969). For a very different sort of universalizing interpretation of Paul, see Daniel Boyarin, *A Radical Jew: Paul and the Politics of Identity* (Berkeley: University of California Press, 1994). For historical contextualization of this earlier consensus of scholarship and critique, see Wayne A. Meeks, "Judaism, Hellenism, and the Birth of Christianity," and Dale B. Martin, "Paul and the Judaism/Hellenism Dichotomy: Toward a Social History of the Question," both in *Paul Beyond the Judaism/Hellenism Divide*, ed. Troels Engberg-Pedersen (Louisville: Westminster/John Knox, 2001), 17–27; 29–61. See also Shawn Kelley, *Racializing Jesus: Race, Ideology, and the Formation of Modern Biblical Scholarship* (London: Routledge, 2002), especially 75–82 for Paul as universalizer in F. C. Baur's Hegelian scheme and the Tübingen School.

9. Badiou, *Saint Paul*, 76.

10. Badiou, *Saint Paul*, 77.

11. Badiou, *Saint Paul*, 95.

12. Badiou, *Saint Paul*, 96–97, esp. 97. See also the insightful readings of the centrality of love in Paul from another philosopher, in lectures delivered at Heidelberg in 1987: Jacob Taubes, *The Political Theology of Paul* (Stanford, Calif.: Stanford University Press, 2004), esp. 52–55.

13. Badiou, *Saint Paul*, 99 (emphasis in original).

14. Badiou, *Saint Paul*, 106.

15. Badiou, *Saint Paul*, 14.

16. See also Badiou, *Ethics,* x, 70.

17. For biblical scholars, this all sounds like the role played by the notion of the early Christian *kerygma* (preached message; "kernel" of the Christian message) in the thought of Rudolf Bultmann and his disciples. For Bultmann, kerygma is "the proclamation of the decisive act of God in Christ" which, contrary to the attempts by Harnack and other "liberal" theologians, cannot be reduced "to a few basic principles of religion and ethics." Hans Werner Bartsch, ed., *Kerygma and Myth: A Theological Debate* (London: SPCK, 1960), 1:13. According to Bultmann, though, the kerygma is not to be equated with the myth that accompanies it. Bultmann was controversial, but later largely followed, also in his insistence that the beginning of Christianity was not in the message Jesus himself preached, but the message the disciples later preached *about* Jesus: "the proclaimer" became "the proclaimed." Christian faith lies not in some abstraction of Jesus' own message but in existential faith in the significance for the human individual of the *event* of God's act in Jesus. It is the stark proclaiming of that *event* which constitutes the kerygma, not its mythological packaging or its doctrinal or theological interpretation. Bultmann both began and concluded his *Theology of the New Testament* with these points about the kerygma (New York: Scribner's, 1951), 1:3; 2:239–41.

Scholars may also note that Badiou's use of "event" sounds something like the function of "story" or "realistic event" in narrative theology, exemplified by Hans W. Frei's use of terms such as "realistic story" or "narrative depiction." See, for instance, *The Eclipse of Biblical Narrative: A Study of Eighteenth and Nineteenth Century Hermeneutics* (New Haven, Conn.: Yale University Press, 1974), 13–15. For Frei, the meaning of the gospel proclamation cannot be simply distilled from the telling of the gospel itself, which is a narrative about an event, even if the event is not a historical one. See also Frei, *The Identity of Jesus Christ: The Hermeneutical Bases of Dogmatic Theology* (Philadelphia: Fortress, 1975), xiii–xiv: "Whether or not the Gospels are other things besides realistic stories, what they tell us is a fruit of the stories themselves. We cannot have what they are about (the 'subject matter') without the stories themselves. They are history-like precisely because like history-writing and the traditional novel and unlike myths and allegories they literally mean what they say. There is no gap between the representation and what is represented by it."

18. Žižek can also speak of the "empty Universal"; see, for example, *Ticklish Subject,* 101.

19. As usual, I provide my own Greek translations, unless otherwise noted. My translations may sometimes sound a bit odd, even awkward, but I provide them in order to emphasize some aspect of the text that may go unnoticed when quoting more traditional or published translations.

20. One still occasionally comes across a biblical scholar attempting to make Paul a Trinitarian. But even a conservative Christian scholar such as Gordon D. Fee confesses, when challenged, that Paul has only a "latent Trinitarianism." In the absence of an actual doctrine of the Trinity in Paul, we can nonetheless discern that Paul "experienced" God as triune. See "Paul and the Trinity: The Experience of Christ and the Spirit for Paul's Understanding of God," in *The Trinity: An Interdisciplinary Symposium on the Trinity,* ed. Stephen T. Davis et al. (Oxford: Oxford University Press, 1999), 49–72. Even in these more careful contexts, Fee pushes Paul's language in ways that are usually unconvincing to less conservative scholars. Most contemporary critical scholars of Paul avoid reading the doctrine of the Trinity back into Paul's day, much less into his letters.

21. See 1 Corinthians 11:3; 15:24–28; and Dale B. Martin, *The Corinthian Body* (New Haven, Conn.: Yale University Press, 1995), 232, 296 n. 18.

22. See, for example, J. Louis Martyn, "Epistemology at the Turn of the Ages," in *Theological Issues in the Letters of Paul* (Nashville, Tenn.: Abingdon, 1997), esp. 107–10.

23. My own thinking on these verses was first stirred by a comment made by Abraham J. Malherbe when I was a student of his in graduate school.

24. Žižek ignores the eschatological reservation that runs throughout Paul's own letters, instead suggesting that for Paul the Messiah has already arrived. See Žižek, *Puppet and the Dwarf,* 135–36, 141. This is true only in a very tenuous sense for Paul, for the future coming of the Messiah is more significant in Paul's thought when considering the blessings and accomplishments promised by the gospel. Paul's emphasis on apocalyptic keeps the blessings of the eschaton in the future, not the present.

Badiou admits the presence of apocalyptic in Paul's letters but downplays too much, in my opinion, its significance for Paul's thought. See *Saint Paul,* 95. Badiou's nod in the direction of Paul's apocalyptic sometimes suggests that apocalyptic does play some kind of role in Badiou's appropriation of Paul, but not explicitly. The end of the book has some interesting remarks that suggest this point. Badiou writes, "But if everything depends on an event, must we wait? Certainly not. Many events, even very distant ones, still require us to be faithful to them. Thought does not wait. . . . Besides, waiting is pointless, for it is of the essence of the event not to be preceded by any sign, and to catch us unawares with its grace, regardless of our vigilance" (*Saint Paul,* 111). I believe Badiou's points about hope, waiting, the unexpected nature of the coming, and faithfulness even to an unseen future event all reflect something of a structure of apocalyptic even if it is not claimed explicitly or even consciously.

25. Early, classic treatments of Paul's apocalypticism are found in two books by Albert Schweitzer: *Paul and His Interpreters: A Critical History* (London: Adam and Charles Black, 1912) and *The Mysticism of Paul the Apostle* (1930; Baltimore: Johns Hopkins University Press, 1998). See also two more recent and influential books by J. Christiaan Beker, *Paul the Apostle: The Triumph of God in Life and Thought* (Philadelphia: Fortress, 1980) and *Paul's Apocalyptic Gospel: The Coming Triumph of God* (Philadelphia: Fortress, 1982). The overwhelming consensus among scholars today is that Paul's thought is definitely eschatological (and apocalyptic if one wishes to differentiate the two, though I do not); insofar as debate continues, it is only about the extent to which apocalyptic pervades and determines Paul's thought.

26. Romans 5:1, 9; 8:30; 1 Corinthians 6:11.

27. Not to imply that all modern Christians use such language. As one joke has it, when Episcopalians are asked if they have accepted Jesus as their "Lord and Personal Savior," the likely response would be, "Isn't that a bit selfish?"

28. *Parousia* as referring to someone's presence (or that as a possible reading): 1 Cor 16:17; 2 Cor 7:6–7; 10:10; Phil 1:26; 2:12. As the future coming of Christ: 1 Cor 15:23; 1 Thess 2:19; 3:13; 4:15; 5:23.

29. Aristotle, *Politics* 1.2.8; see Dale B. Martin, *Inventing Superstition: from the Hippocratics to the Christians* (Cambridge, Mass.: Harvard University Press, 2004), 72–78.

30. On Galen's teleology, see Martin, *Inventing Superstition,* 118–24.

31. Martin, *Inventing Superstition,* 223–24.

32. This is not to say that teleologies are always conservative. One could see teleology of a different sort, perhaps, in classical Marxism—or, say, in Walter Benjamin's

"messianic" philosophy—that could serve revolutionary purposes. For another anti-conservative attempt at eschatology, and here in direct connection with Paul, see also Giorgio Agamben, *Il tempo che resta: Un commento alla Lettura ai Romani* (Turin: Bollati Boringhieri, 2000), which deserves a treatment in its own right, more than I can adequately provide at this time. My point here is just that teleology has almost always served politically and ideologically conservative ends in Western philosophy.

33. Žižek, *The Puppet and the Dwarf,* 130.

34. Badiou, *Saint Paul,* 23.

35. Again, I am not alone or even innovative. The tendency among scholars of Paul for the past ten to fifteen years has been to read Paul as emphasizing the continuity of Israel, not the supersession of Israel by some kind of nonethnic identity. See, for example (among the many works that could be cited—and one must keep in mind that these scholars may disagree with one another on separate significant issues), John G. Gager, *Reinventing Paul* (Oxford: Oxford University Press, 2000); Mark D. Nanos, *The Mystery of Romans: The Jewish Context of Paul's Letter* (Minneapolis: Fortress, 1996); Nanos, *The Irony of Galatians: Paul's Letters in First-Century Context* (Minneapolis: Fortress, 2002); Stanley K. Stowers, *A Rereading of Romans: Justice, Jews, and Gentiles* (New Haven, Conn.: Yale University Press, 1994); Denise Kimber Buell and Caroline Johnson Hodge, "The Politics of Interpretation: The Rhetoric of Race and Ethnicity in Paul," *Journal of Biblical Literature* 123 (2004): 235–51; Diana Swancutt, *Pax Christi: Empire, Identity, and Protreptic Rhetoric in Paul's Letter to the Romans* (forthcoming). For a study of issues of ethnicity, race, and identity in early Christianity more widely, see Denise Kimber Buell, *Why This New Race: Ethnic Reasoning in Early Christianity* (New York: Columbia University Press, 2005).

36. Badiou, *Saint Paul,* 5.

37. The Greek word *ethnos* is proving increasingly difficult for scholars of early Christianity to translate, mainly because our own notions of race, ethnicity, and identity are in a state of flux. The translation "nation" can sometimes do the job, but it misleadingly may invoke notions of the modern nation-state, which the ancient term did not necessarily mean. The Greek does refer to what we would call an ethnic group, with its own customs, native language, perhaps religious practices, and so on. Scholars today generally avoid the term "race" as hopelessly misleading and anachronistic. An additional problem occurs because the English word "gentiles" is the normal biblical translation of *ethnê* (the plural form), yet that word made sense only in opposition to "the Jews" (similarly to the way "barbarian" could refer to anyone not Greek), and of course other people in the ancient world did not consider that humanity was so divided into only two significant groups: "Jews" and "everyone else" ("gentiles"). Thus, though it is not felicitous, we biblical scholars increasingly find ourselves using the transliteration *ethnos* and then explaining, as best we can, the problem. The reader must keep in mind, though, that *ethnos* could be used to refer to *any* "ethnic" group or nation but that in the writings of the New Testament it was also used in the sense of "gentiles." For a good discussion of the problems of race and ethnicity, both in translating ancient Greek today and in the history of scholarship, see Buell, *Why This New Race,* esp. x–xii, 5–21. I am not convinced by Buell's arguments that ethnicity is as problematic as race. My own opinion remains, in spite of Buell's arguments to the contrary, that "race" is a more misleading term when used of the Greco-Roman world than is ethnicity, though obviously neither modern term completely captures what we would consider the corresponding ancient categories. I would still maintain

that people in the Greco-Roman Mediterranean did think of themselves as members of groups that correspond in significant ways to what we mean by particular ethnic groups (Greek, Roman, Jew, Egyptian, Persian, Syrian, Gaul, German, etc.) but did not think of themselves in terms of the larger, global terms that we moderns have used as racial categories (black, white, Asian, in the wide way we use the term often to include anyone in all of, at least, East Asia, or to use earlier terms, Aryan or Semitic). This is not to say that modern notions of ethnicity are either unambiguous or that modern notions fit ancient categories perfectly. But in my opinion, "ethnicity" is much less misleading than "race."

38. Galatians 3:7, 29; and children of Sarah: Galatians 4:31; see also Romans 4:11–12, 16–17.

39. In Romans 1:26 Paul condemned the gentile world for disrupting the gender hierarchy of male-female sexual relations by calling such behavior "contrary to nature" (*para physin*). It is interesting, perhaps ironic—and ignored by modern conservatives who wish to appropriate Paul's language about sex acts "contrary to nature" to condemn modern homosexuality—that Paul in Romans 11:24 uses the same terms, "contrary to nature," to describe the saving action of God. But why should anyone be surprised that God is queer? On this connection, see Eugene F. Rogers Jr., *Sexuality and the Christian Body: Their Way into the Triune God* (Oxford: Blackwell, 1999), 64.

40. This is not an original thought on my part, nor am I being particularly innovative. There is a growing trend among scholars of Paul to agree that the use of the term "Christian" for the people of his churches is anachronistic, even if we are not sure what term to substitute in its place—and even if some of us find nothing wrong with anachronism as long as it is being practiced advisedly. See, for example, Dieter Georgi, "The Early Church: Internal Jewish Migration or New Religion?" *Harvard Theological Review* 88 (1995): 35–68; John G. Gager, *Reinventing Paul*, 23–25; Mark D. Nanos, *Mystery of Romans*, esp. 21 n. 1; Nanos, *Irony of Galatians*, esp. 20; Philip F. Esler, *Conflict and Identity in Romans: The Social Setting of Paul's Letter* (Minneapolis: Fortress, 2003), 12–13; Judith M. Lieu, *Christian Identity in the Jewish and Graeco-Roman World* (New York: Oxford University Press, 2004); Diana Swancutt, "Pax Christi: Romans as Protrepsis to Live as Kings" (Ph.D. diss.; Duke University, 2001), 4 n. 5.

41. For example, Romans 1:17; 3:3, 21, 25–26; 11:29; 15:8. Recall that the Greek term usually translated "righteousness" in these contexts may also, and perhaps should instead, be translated "justice."

42. For Paul "the gospel" is basically a statement about the saving act of God in Christ, which cannot predictably or simply be translated into a particular proposition either about doctrine (e.g., that Christ is fully equal with God the Father or, on the contrary, subordinate, or that the nature of God is triune) or about ethics. We may say, for instance, that the most central ethical value for Paul is love, but moving from that to ethical particulars in any direct and predictable way is impossible (is it more loving to allow abortion or not? to forbid homosexual relations or allow them or encourage them? to be pacifist or allow the use of violence in certain situations?). We cannot distill from Paul's gospel propositional answers to such questions, even though we may use his gospel for inspiration in creating doctrinal and ethical answers.

43. Bas C. van Fraassen, *The Empirical Stance* (New Haven, Conn.: Yale University Press, 2002), 117.

44. Van Fraassen, *Empirical Stance*, 62–63.

SIX

Paul among the Antiphilosophers; or, Saul among the Sophists

DANIEL BOYARIN

For Jonathan on his return

Is Saul among the prophets?

1 SAMUEL 10:12

The conditions of philosophy are transversal. They are uniform procedures recognizable from afar, whose relation to thought is relatively invariant. The *name* of this invariance is clear: it is the name "truth."[1]

To mock philosophy is to philosophize truly.[2]

In his recent book, John David Dawson has written of an earlier theoretically minded reader of Paul's letters:

> Any Christian claim that Boyarin has misconstrued Paul's intention runs the considerable risk of simply repeating Paul's indictment against his own Jewish contemporaries—that they cannot understand Paul because they refuse to entertain as a real possibility the very conclusion that his argument advances.[3] In the counterreadings I offer in order to highlight the presuppositions of Boyarin's reading, I point out ways in which Boyarin's approach to Paul does systematically deny one possible conclusion to Paul's argument. As a consequence, by reading Paul at his theoretically most accessible, Boyarin fails to read him at his theologically strongest.[4]

This is not the place (nor do I wish) to defend my reading of Paul.[5] Of course, Dawson is exactly right: my project is to read Paul at his theoretically most accessible and thus make sense of the implications of his texts for those who "refuse to entertain as a real possibility the very conclusion that [Paul's] argument advances." My question, and the question of all non-Christian thinkers who read Paul seriously, is, What can we learn from Paul if we *don't* believe Christian theological claims per se; don't accept the adoption of Jesus as son, the resurrection, nor even, for some of us, the apparent abrogation of Torah law? On my reading, "texts and meanings" and the ethics of group identity formation exercise this ancient converted reader, at least as much as the intelligibility of divine performances. His thoughts on texts and mean- ings, as well as his textual practice, have much to teach us when read at their most theoretically accessible points. Much is lost when we don't read Paul at his theologically strongest points, tantamount to those points which are entirely contained within a believing Christian's discourse. But even more is lost when we read them only that way. In other words, if we are to consider the value or interest of a Pauline contribution to theory—one way, at least, of understanding "Paul among the philosophers"—it will be precisely by bracketing or even denying the theological claims of his text.[6] And so, it seems, thinks Alain Badiou, as well. I share with Badiou the sense of Paul as a radical thinker but differ significantly on what that means. For both of us Paul is a radical. For me, however, he is a radical Jew in a particular time and historical clime, the first Bolshevik indeed, but only metaphorically so.[7] For Badiou, after his operations of subtraction, Paul is simply an instantiation of the Idea of the radical, the militant per se, almost literally Lenin himself.

Badiou's Truth

At the very outset of his book, Badiou stakes out what might be taken as the exact contrary of Dawson's position: "Basically, I have never really connected Paul with religion. It is not according to this register, or to bear witness to any sort of faith, or even antifaith, that I have, for a long time, been interested in him."[8] Badiou goes further, however, than merely stating his own lack of interest in Paul's specific religious commitments and methods; he actually characterizes them as irrelevant, as so much noise along with everything else that renders Saul/Paul a particular historical individual: "Anyway, the crucible in which what will become a work of art and thought burns is brimful with nameless impurities; it comprises obsessions, beliefs, infantile puzzles, various perversions, undivulgeable memories, haphazard reading, and quite a few idiosyncracies and chimeras. Analyzing this alchemy is of little use."[9] For Badiou, Paul is a "subjective figure of primary importance," not a Jew (or even a Christian) but pure subject. We need to pay attention to the particular sense that "subject" has in Badiou's thought: "For Badiou, the question of agency is not so much a question of how a subject can *initiate* an action in an autonomous manner but rather how a subject *emerges* through an autonomous chain of actions within a changing situation. That is, it is not everyday actions or decisions that provide evidence of agency for Badiou. It is rather those extraordinary decisions and actions which *isolate* an actor from their [*sic*] context, those actions which show that a human can actually be a free agent that supports *new* chains of actions and reactions. For this reason, not every human being is always a subject, yet some human beings *become* subjects; those who act in *fidelity* to a chance encounter with an *event* which disrupts the *situation* they find themselves in."[10] Not only is Paul a subject entirely abstracted from the "accidents" of specific religious ideas and sociocultural, historical entanglements, this abstracted or subtracted subjectivity is a kind of incarnation of a Platonic idea, the idea of the militant: "For me, Paul is a poet-thinker of the event, as well as one who practices and states the *invariant traits* of what can be called the militant figure. He brings forth the entirely human connection, whose destiny fascinates me, between the general idea of a rupture, an overturning, and that of a thought-practice that is this rupture's subjective materiality."[11]

Materiality in its most common acceptation is, however, of no interest finally to Badiou, remaining so much "alchemy," unworthy of analysis, just as for Paul (my formulation) the accident of Jewishness and its particular practices of kinship, community, and custom are *adiaphora*. It is hard for me to conceive of a more radically Platonic basis for a philosophy of the subject (or of any other part of philosophy) than this one in which a Form—not beauty but militancy—is so embodied in the figure of an erstwhile human being that contemplation of that human being, nay that subject, can lead thought beyond to the very idea of militancy itself. As Clemens and Feltham state, "So, what is the general result of Badiou's adoption of set theory as the language of being? Quite simply that it has nothing to say about beings themselves—this is the province of other discourses such as physics, anthropology and literature. This is one reason why Badiou terms set theory as *subtractive* ontology: it speaks of beings without reference to their attributes or their identity; it is as if the beings ontology speaks of have had all their qualities subtracted from them. As a result, unlike Plato and Aristotle's ontologies, there is neither cosmos nor phenomena, neither cause nor substance."[12] Nonetheless, there seems to be a very Platonic moment in this ontology, precisely in its ascription of "invariant traits" to a "general idea of rupture," an ontological insistence, as it were, on the possibility of truth.[13] Indeed, as Badiou himself asserts, "the philosophical gesture that I propose is Platonic."[14]

For Badiou, Paul's great contribution is epistemological, that is, to a theory of truth, and the epistemology of his contribution is precisely homologous with Paul's own subjective figuration as articulated by Badiou: "Paul's unprecedented gesture consists in subtracting truth from the communitarian grasp, be it that of a people, a city, an empire, a territory, or a social class."[15] For Badiou this term "subtraction" is a term of art. What sutures any given situation to being is subtractive in a double sense.[16] "The first is that it is subtracted from presentation and, second, it does not participate in any of the qualities of the situation—although it is proper to the situation, it is as if all of the particularities of the situation are removed or subtracted from it."[17] That is, Paul does not participate in any of the qualities of the situation that he is in and he calls for a new People, equally subjective figures as a People, who also will not/do not participate in any of the qualities of their situation, as if all these particularities of their situation are subtracted from it.

It needs to be said, contra a certain mood or tendency among Paul scholars, that Badiou is frequently enough a very good and close reader of Paul, even though he does not perform the close reading before our eyes. Badiou's language of event and militance captures something about Paul's texts (and especially the crucial Galatians) that more properly theological language misses. The notion of fidelity to the newness of the event and the absolute rupture that it occasions, out of history but a total reconfiguration of history, seems to me to gloss Paul's language of fidelity to the cross and the total betrayal of that were one to continue to observe the law better than any I've seen.[18] Indeed, while Badiou is accused (as we all are) of making a Paul in the image of his own thought, I am tempted, against Badiou's own declarations, to imagine Badiou's thought being formed by Paul, so fine is this fit in my eyes.

Badiou, I repeat, captures something vital about Paul that even the most uncompromising theological interpretations miss. This can be exemplified by a close look at the crucial passage at the end of Galatians 2, where Paul argues most forcefully that keeping the law at all renders the death of Christ δωρεὰν, of no avail. I will quote the passage in the familiar RSV translation:

> We ourselves, who are Jews by birth and not Gentile sinners, yet who know that a man is not justified by works of the law but through faith in Jesus Christ, even we have believed in Christ Jesus, in order to be justified by faith in Christ, and not by works of the law, because by works of the law shall no one be justified. But if, in our endeavor to be justified in Christ, we ourselves were found to be sinners, is Christ then an agent of sin (ἁμαρτίας διάκονος)?

Certainly not! But if I build up again those things which I tore down, then I prove myself a transgressor. . . . I do not nullify the grace of God, for if justification were through the law, then Christ died to no purpose.

A Badiouish reading of this passage makes sense of it in a way that nothing else can, in my view. There are deep flaws in Paul's logic here, for there is nothing in what he says that disqualifies the Jacobean—so-called Judeo-Christian, what an unfortunate choice of terminology in this context—idea that faith in Christ comes to add to the law and not to subtract it, that when Jesus says (as, to be sure, he will only say a generation after Paul) that he comes to fulfill the law, he means just that, to supply its meaning and fulfillment, to complete it, not to abrogate it. Keeping the law and having faith in Jesus Christ would not be, on that account, in any way contradictory, and, I repeat, there is nothing in Paul's argument as it is usually understood that disproves such a theology. Badiou's Paul, however, makes sense of this passage. Faith here does not mean believing in Christ, or even trusting in his faithfulness to us, in any conventional sense, but fidelity to the event of the absolute newness that has entered the world with the crucifixion. (By the way, I find that Badiou's reading of Paul strangely de-emphasizes the cross for the resurrection, but it *is* the death here to which Paul appeals, not the resurrection. In the crucial passage for Badiou of 1 Corinthians, Paul preaches Christ and him crucified, not and him resurrected!)[19] In that sense, anything suggesting that the world has not been entirely transformed through this event will precisely make it not be an event at all; Christ will have died for nothing. Badiou's thought makes clear the Paulinian claim that the event is such only by virtue of the militant subject-ive response. Without that fidelity, nothing will have taken place; the world will not have changed at all. The faith of which Paul speaks here is militant fidelity to the event. Anything less than militance does not compromise the event; it disqualifies it entirely as event, throws us back into the situation. Yes, Badiou has read Paul well, even brilliantly here, if I may make so audacious as to say so; insofar as Paul is a theologian, something like this reading seems imperative to me. Badiou's language gives us language that makes theological sense of Paul, paradoxically traditionalist sense—according to one sort of Pauline tradition. It is Badiou's reading, then, that I would adduce against Dawson as showing that at least sometimes precisely when we don't read Paul theologically, we read him at his strongest and not his weakest as Dawson would have it.

There is, however, another reading lurking (actually standing on the sidelines, waving a red flag and hollering, Look at me!). But in order to see it, we have to put back all of the "nameless impurities" into the crucible. Speaking in literary terms, there are, in a sense, two characters named "Paul" in this piece of the text. There is Paul the author of the epistle who is telling us a story about Paul and in which Paul the apostle is a character. (Indeed, much of the argument of Galatians proceeds as a kind of autobiography.) There is Paul inside the story of the incident at Antioch and Paul outside the story and telling it to us. They are not necessarily saying the same thing, or if they are, they are not necessarily making the point in precisely the same way. The argument of Paul the character is a simple and highly pointed political and rhetorical one, not philosophical at all.[20] Paul the narrator relates that Paul and Peter had been together in Antioch among the Christian community there. They, together with the other Jewish members of the community, have been eating with the gentile members (presumably this means eating nonkosher food). But when "men from James" come to Antioch from Jerusalem, Peter, afraid of being condemned as a sinner, separates from commensality with the gentiles, as do all the other Jews in the community including Barnabas, naturally infuriating the militant, Paul. Given these conditions, we can understand Paul's logic quite straightforwardly and in a worldly manner: he attacks Peter's alleged hypocrisy and weakness.[21] We (I and you, Peter), albeit born to the law, have shown through our previous actions of violating the law that we know that it is powerless to save. If now you go back on your previous behavior, you are, as it were, confessing that you have been a sinner till now and that, therefore, the gospel with which you have acted in accordance is a message of sin, and Christ an agent of sin. If you confess that with your behavior, then indeed the game is lost. No one will believe again that salvation is through faith, and Christ will have been crucified in vain.[22] Badiou characterizes Paul's discourse "knowing how, armed only with the conviction that declares the Christ-event, one is to tackle the Greek intellectual milieu, whose essential category is that of wisdom (*sophia*), and whose instrument is that of rhetorical superiority (*huperokhē logou*)."[23] Yet the situation of Paul's own logos with respect to the Antioch event is one of rhetorical superiority.

The philosophical reading gleaned from Badiou and the rhetorical/political reading of Paul's logic in these verses that I have just proposed thus correspond to these two levels in the text. As addressed to Peter and Barnabas and their fellows, Paul's utterances are precisely in "persuasive words" and, if not wisdom, certainly powerful rhetoric. It is in that context that the worldly meaning of his words functions most powerfully. On the other hand, Paul's quotation of them now makes that historical instance, his report of what happened at Antioch, into a paradigm with which to persuade the present-day Galatians of something, as well: you too, if you now, having once accepted Christ on the terms with which I presented him to you—saving through faith alone—now in fear of the same sort of men whom Peter feared, accept the law on yourselves, you too will be confessing Christ as agent of sin. In the case of the Galatians, however, it is not the practical, political effect that their activities will have on others that is at issue but rather their own fidelity to the event or alternatively their acting in a way that will discredit the event qua event and render them themselves non-subjects. It is thus this level which can be translated into Badiou's terms of fidelity to the event, while the first one, the narrative within the narrative, is political speech and rhetoric par excellence. Paul produces here a virtual allegory, in which the earlier incident at Antioch is type for the antitype in Galatia.

The key passage to support Badiou's epistemological reading is the beginning of 1 Corinthians, to which he alludes several times and discusses at some length:

> Has not God made foolish the wisdom of the world? For since, in the wisdom of God, the world did not know God through wisdom, it pleased God through the folly of what we preach to save those who believe. For Jews demand signs and Greeks seek wisdom, but we preach Christ crucified, a stumbling block to Jews and folly to Gentiles, but to those who are called, both Jews and Greeks, Christ the power of God and the wisdom of God. For the foolishness of God is wiser than men, and the weakness of God is stronger than men. (1 Cor 1–20b–25)

The climax of Badiou's gloss on this statement is, "It is through the invention of a language wherein folly, scandal, and weakness supplant knowing reason, order, and power, and wherein non-being is the only legitimizable affirmation of being, that Christian discourse is articulated. In Paul's eyes, this articulation is incompatible with any prospect (and there has been no shortage of them, almost from the time of his death onward) of a 'Christian philosophy.'"[24]

Paul here seems to be referring to three kinds of knowledge: knowledge given by wisdom, knowledge given by signs, and knowledge given by faith. The first two—if I may simplify Badiou's formulation to terms which I can apprehend more readily—are opposed to faith, precisely because they depend on external verification and not internal conviction.[25] So far I can go along with Badiou and reiterate what seems to me his real contribution to Pauline interpretation, seeing the radicality in his rejection of philosophy and why it is parallel to his rejection of knowledge through signs. Indeed, here is an instance where the non-theological (anti-theological) reader has penetrated more deeply into the text than such theologians as Walter Bauer, who claims that "1 Corinthians is that unit among the major Pauline letters which yields the very least for our understanding of the Pauline faith,"[26] or

Hans Conzelmann, who writes that "the great attraction of I Corinthians, however, lies in the fact that here Paul is practicing applied theology, so to speak."[27] Badiou surely has demonstrated the theological import precisely of Paul's language in 1 Corinthians, import that, it seems, can best be seen by not reading Paul theologically.

In his insistence, however, on only finding philosophical meaning in Paul, meaning that is philosophical (antihistoricist) in its antiphilosophicality, elegantly reproducing in his reading the subtraction which he is taking Paul to be exemplifying, Badiou partly loses sight of some of the political stakes of Paul's writing. Badiou does not ignore the political dimension of Paul's writing (indeed Paul is a veritable poster boy of the political as event in Badiou); rather, Badiou's own notion of the political itself seems to me to evacuate the latter of import as praxis, in its very substitution of militance for praxis. I am *not* arguing for a cynically political Paul—not political in that sense—but a Paul for whom the Christ event has distinct and political stakes in his immediate, historical, and concrete real world, stakes that have to do with the concrete relations, discursive and enacted, of concrete groups of people, named Jews and Greeks, with each other every day. If Badiou, paradoxically, loses the practice from praxis in his reading of 1 Corinthians, the theologians, it seems, lose the theory.

Badiou takes Paul's famous statement in Galatians 3:28, "There is no Jew nor Greek," as being about theories of discourse (not in any Foucauldian sense), modalities of truth, about the subtractability of Truth from any communitarian grasp. For him, when Paul says there is no Jew or Greek, he "institutes 'Christian discourse' only by distinguishing its operations from those of Jewish discourse and Greek discourse." Badiou argues that Jewish and Greek discourses are two sides of the same symbolon: Greek discourse allegedly bases itself "on the cosmic order so as to adjust itself to it, while Jewish discourse bases itself on the exception to this order so as to turn divine transcendence into a sign," and, therefore, "Paul's profound idea is that Jewish discourse and Greek discourse are the two aspects of the same figure of mastery," and, moreover, "neither of the two discourses can be universal because . . . the two discourses share the presupposition that the key to salvation is given to us within the universe."[28]

Although in the passage from Corinthians, the Greek and the Jew indeed abandon former discourses for a new Christian discourse of faith, I submit that discourse is not what Paul is about when he says in Galatians, "There is neither Greek nor Jew because you are one in Christ Jesus" (Gal 3:28). Something else is going on there. When Paul speaks about Jew and

Greek there, it is not "subjective dispositions"[29] but religious identifications and religio-ethnic practices, as I shall try immediately to show. Greek is simply a synecdoche (from a Jewish point of view) for pagan.[30]

Closer reading, in context, is necessary to see what Paul may be saying in that verse. The verse under investigation makes its appearance in the following context: "Now before faith came, we were confined under the law, kept under restraint until faith should be revealed. So that the law was our child-minder[31] until Christ came; that we might be justified by faith. But now that faith has come, we are no longer under a child-minder; For as many of you as were baptized into Christ have put on Christ. There is neither Jew nor Greek, there is neither slave nor free, there is neither male nor female; for you are all one in Christ Jesus. And if you are Christ's, then you are Abraham's offspring, heirs according to promise" (Gal 3:23–29). Paul, I submit, is decidedly not speaking here of epistemology, of how we know or what we know, of discourses, neither Greek nor Jewish, but of peoplehood, precisely the possibility denied by Badiou. The event in question here is as social as it is ontological. Divisions among human beings have been replaced by oneness in the maturation into Christ, from children born of woman and under the law or the equivalent pagan gods to adults adopted by the Father and free of such childish constraints.

The beginning of Galatians 4 is entirely a continuation of the end of chapter 3 and the explanation of the figure of the child-minder, not the beginning of an entirely new section of the letter.[32] The RSV translators get this just right by translating 4:1–2 as "I mean [Λέγω δέ] that the heir, as long as he is a child, is no better than a slave, though he is the owner of all the estate; but he is under guardians and trustees until the date set by the father."[33] This verse clearly hearkens back to (and interprets) verses 23–24 of chapter 3: "Now before faith came, we were confined under the law, kept under restraint until faith should be revealed. So that the law was our child-minder [παιδαγωγός] until Christ came, that we might be justified by faith." In verses 3 and following of chapter 4, Paul begins to give us the application of the parable: "So with us; when we were children, we were slaves to the elemental spirits of the universe, slaves to our child-minder(s), just as the child is. But when the time had fully come, God sent forth his Son, born of woman, born under the law to redeem those who were under the law, so that we might receive adoption as sons." There seems to be a difficulty in this last verse. The question that exercises many commentators is what is "born of woman" doing here? Born under the law to redeem those who were under the law, but why was he born of woman? The verse, according to these commentators and scholars, doesn't tell us. They note that the phrase does not appear anywhere else in Paul and believe that it has no semantic function here and therefore conclude as does, for instance, Betz that "this suggests that it was part of the pre-Pauline material, taken up here by Paul in full and without regard to its usability in the argument."[34] This is, in my humble opinion, entirely to miss the point. The verse is a perfect chiastic structure: Jesus was born of a woman so that we might receive adoption as sons, born under the law to redeem those born under the law. In other words, Jesus' own self-redemptions from those two situations are what make possible the redemption (achieved) by Paul and the redemption of all of us (potential). Born of a woman and therefore of a human genealogy, under the law and therefore as a Jew, Jesus like Paul himself now redeemed (and thus redeeming) from both of those conditions and adopted, on the same basis as the Galatians (and thus all of "us"), as a son of God. Readings which insist that Paul has misadopted a formulation from elsewhere that doesn't fit here are badly missing the mark.[35] It may be, as Longenecker remarks, that "born of woman" is a hapax in Paul, but it cannot be that it is not "really germane to the argument of Galatians," since it is precisely the antithesis to born, by adoption, of the Father.[36] Another way of saying this would be to remark that it is being born of woman and redeemed from that condition that corrects gender difference and instantiates "no man nor woman" in Christ Jesus, just as it is being placed under the law and being redeemed from it that in the resurrection corrects ethnic difference.[37] All now, Jews and Greeks, are only sons by adoption. "Born of woman" could not then be more germane to the argument of Galatians, as it suggests a profoundly soteriological import for an adoptionist Christology. No wonder that readers, more orthodox than I in their Christologies, would wish to exile it from the text.[38] The climax of this adoptionist soteriological Christology is Paul's cry: "And because you are sons, God has sent the Spirit of his Son into our hearts, crying, 'Abba! Father!' So through God you are no longer a slave but a son, and if a son then an heir."

Returning now to the first part of the verse: "So with us; when we were children, we were slaves to the elemental spirits of the universe, slaves to our child-minder(s)," we see much that is puzzling, including the question of who precisely is included in the referent of the utterance. On the one hand, speaking of those under the law strongly suggests that it is Jews to whom Paul addresses these words, but we know that this is not the case; they are written to Galatian gentiles. Secondly, who were slaves to the elemental spirits of the universe, the τά στοιχεῖα τοῦ κόσμου, Jews or Gentiles, and what are these anyway? Third, how to explain Paul's shifts in pronominal reference in the passage from first-person to second-person plural and back again. The answers that we give to these questions will determine the sense that we attribute to the passage as a whole. The interpretation that I will now offer is considerably simpler than the dominant ones within the literature.

It may be that "a large number of scholarly investigations have arrived at the conclusion that these 'elements of the world' represent demonic forces which constitute and control 'this evil aeon,'" but I simply don't believe that that is what Paul is talking about.[39] Pace Betz (and his minions and hosts), it seems to me simply a misreading to wish to see here a whole theory of subjection to demonic forces in nature and negative appreciation of the world that Paul is allegedly finding and condemning in Jews and Greeks; the slavery being the allegedly constant attention to propriation of these "demonic forces." Paul's point is, I think—almost necessarily—much less arcane than that. Nor, however, do I accept that Paul is speaking here of philosophy, of thrall to a science of the cosmos, as Badiou would have it. In order to make sense of the passage as a whole, I think it is necessary to assume that the "elements" here refer to the heavenly bodies, deified in most versions of so-called paganism. Paul is simply referring to the Galatians' former worship of, understood as thralldom to, gods of sun, moon, and stars.[40] The point is, remember, that there is no Greek or Jew, that a distinction understood as terribly significant by Jews, including Jacobean Christians (and now by the Galatians backsliding into Judaism), makes no difference at all. "We" were under thrall to the elements of the universe, all of us, both (former) Jews and (former) Greeks—we through our enslavement to set times and observances controlled by these bodies and you through your sacrifice and worship to them—and now we have all been liberated by the spirit of the son. Being slaves to the elements has to be read as identical in import and significance, but not in denotation, to being under the law in order to make sense of the passage.[41] Paul's shifts between second person and first person are, therefore, precisely the point of his argument, the equivalence of the enslavement of the Jew to the elements of the universe via her observance of days and months and seasons and years to the pagan's enslavement to his celestial no-gods.[42] Hence the "we" of the narrative, the "you" of the address. In the "we" of the narrative, former Jews and former Greeks—Paul's former life in the law as well as the Galatians' former lives as worshipers of divinized elements—are rendered equivalent in order to persuade the Galatians that if they become Torah observers they might just as well have slid back into their former worship.

Continuing to read the passage, we find: "Formerly, when you did not know God, you were in bondage to beings that by nature are no gods; but now that you have come to know God, or rather to be known by God, how can you turn back again to the weak and beggarly elemental spirits, whose slaves you want to be once more? You observe days, and months, and seasons, and years! I am afraid I have labored over you in vain." Despite the machinations of some commentators, to me it seems crystal clear that the last observances to which Paul refers here are the very ordinary Jewish ones of Sabbaths, new moons, Passovers, Tabernacles, and Rosh Hashanah, all of them determined by reference to heavenly bodies. Indeed, these heavenly bodies *rule over* these observances: "And God said, Let there be lights in the heaven to divide between the day and the night and let them be signs for seasons, and days, and years. . . . And God placed them in the heaven to light up the earth and to *rule over* the day and the night" (Gen 1:14–18). In a typically brilliant rhetorical move, Paul declares that such observances of the Torah are functionally equivalent to worshiping these heavenly bodies, these elements of the universe who are no-gods. Therefore the Galatians' acceptance of the Torah (and we see from here that they are already engaging in such observance) constitutes almost literally, argues Paul, a return to paganism, a return to thralldom under the elements of the universe. Here Paul is taking on one of the three major religio-cultural markers that most distinguished the Jews from the Greeks (especially in the eyes of those Greeks)—the observance of the special days and holidays on which Jews did not work (the other two being circumcision and the eating of kosher food thematized in the Jerusalem and Antioch incidents respectively).[43] In this sense Paul can claim parity with the Galatians and they with him. We have all been slave children under the elements of the universe, each in our own way, you with your worship of nature gods that are no gods and I with my observance of Sabbaths, new moons, and solar years, and it is this which explains his use of the first-person plural in verse 3.[44] It is from this thralldom that the son has redeemed all of us; we are no longer children (hence slaves) but free, adopted sons and heirs. Be as I am, as I have become as you are; not a Greek or a Jew and hence a slave but this new thing in Christ which is neither Greek nor Jew.

Badiou, in sum, has more than adequately answered Dawson's challenge to demonstrate that Paul can best be understood in his own terms sometimes by ignoring the particular theological claims that he seems to be making. Badiou's philosophy of the event and fidelity makes better sense of Paul's discourse of faith opposed to the law than any interpretative structure I have seen. At the same time, mindful of the injunction to always historicize, I insist that something vital is lost when Paul is read in a way so disrespecting of time, place, and circumstance, simply repeating Paul's own gesture as if indicative of the non-being of ethnicity, gender, and class. The radically thematized dehistoricizing that constitutes for Badiou the very structure of the event renders all revolution the same revolution and all militance the same militance. It seems to me not unfair to see in this an instantiation of a modernist Platonism of a radical sort in which the event is, unbearably, a newness in the nouemenal world that changes nothing, can change nothing whatsoever, in the phenomenal world. Lenin and Paul are both embodied avatars of the Form of Militance in precisely the same sense that Agathon and Antinous are embodied avatars of the Form of Beauty.

Badiou is entirely on the side of the philosophers when he insists that whatever truth is—Paul's truth, Badiou's true reading of Paul, Badiou's truth—it cannot be a matter of a particular time, place, historical circum- stances, conflicts, and possibilities. It has to be radically subtracted from anything "communitarian." Having been made out to be antiphilosopher, Badiou's Paul ends up strangely philosophical precisely in the insistence that the Truth Procedure involves the radical subtraction of history.[45] As Badiou quite openly states of his own thinking, "The statement 'truths are, for thought, compossible' determines philosophy to the thinking of a unique time of thought, namely, what Plato calls 'the always of time', or eternity, a strictly philosophical concept, which inevitably accompanies the setting-up of the category of Truth."[46] For Badiou, Paul even as antiphilosoper operates precisely in that always of time, in which communal identity is impossible as well, as it is necessarily diachronic. The so-called communitarian is, for Badiou, mere rhetoric: "No real distinguishes the first two discourses [Jew and Greek], and their distinction collapses into rhetoric."[47] Badiou reveals his own philosophical (Platonic) understanding of rhetoric here, one that is uncannily like that of Levinas, who wrote: "Our pedagogical or psychago- gical discourse is rhetoric, taking the position of him who approaches his neighbor with ruse. And this is why the art of the sophist is a theme with reference to which the true conversation concerning truth, or philosophi- cal discourse, is defined. Rhetoric, absent from no discourse, and which philosophical discourse seeks to overcome, resists discourse. . . . But the specific nature of rhetoric (of propaganda, flattery, diplomacy, etc.) consists in corrupting this freedom. It is for this that it is preeminently violence, that is, injustice. . . . And in this sense justice coincides with the overcoming of rhetoric."[48] Badiou, like Levinas, like so many others, has bought Plato's characterization of rhetoric and sophistic wholesale, one in which the mere characterization of speech as "collapsing into rhetoric" is sufficient to dis- credit it. Given such a view, the charge of rhetoricity consists of a charge of cynical manipulation of opinion that has no purchase in "the real."

In a crucial moment for his text (and mine), Badiou mistakes Pascal, the anti-philosopher, for Paul. Pascal (cited by Badiou to disagree with him) writes, "And thus Saint Paul, who came in wisdom and signs, says he came neither in wisdom nor signs, because he came to convert. But those who come only to convince can say that they come in wisdom and signs."[49] Badiou, still in thrall I think to the philosophical condemnation of rhetoric, can only see Pascal's "reticence in the face of Pauline radicalism" as the attribution of insincerity or manipulation on the part of Paul: "For Pascal, Paul hides his true identity." For Badiou this hiding of identity could only be a lack of fidelity to the event. But what if the very concept of a "true identity" is being denied? There is, after all, no Jew or Greek, no slave or free, no man or woman, and Pascal has understood Paul perfectly in this. Pascal's own radicalism would appear in the denial of true identity itself, a denial that is the contribution of rhetoric to the germane discourse of antiphilosophy. This reading of Pascal, at any rate, can be supported by attention to another text of his, a parable:

> A man was cast by a tempest upon an unknown island the inhabitants of which were [anxious] to find their king who was lost; and [bearing] a strong resemblance [both corporally and facially] to this king, he was taken for him and acknowledged in this capacity by all the people. At first he knew not what course to take; but he finally resolved to give himself up to his good fortune. He received all the homage that they chose to render, and suffered himself to be treated as a king.[50]

In Louis Marin's brilliant interpretation of this text, the conclusion (or better, one consequence) of the parable is, "One must act as a king and think as a man, but not because the sociopolitical order, even an upright one, is the truth of man, the place of judgment. . . ."[51] But also, I hasten to add, not because it is false; it is no more false than true. One must act as a Greek (or as a Jew), says Pascalian Paul, but not because the ethnic order is the truth of humanity: "It is because the notion of representation articulates the whole of the astute man's discourse that this discourse can turn the notion of representation back against itself in its contents."[52] For Pascal, I think, we all hide our "true" identity, and the astute man, such as Paul, knows this.

If all identity is performative, as Paul/Pascal would seem to suggest, then being in Greek drag is as good as being in under-the-law drag; both are equally drag performances. The point has been made, of course, by Judith Butler:

> To understand identity as a practice, and as a signifying practice, is to understand culturally intelligible subjects as the resulting effects of a rule-bound discourse that inserts itself in the pervasive and mundane signifying

acts of linguistic acts. Abstractly considered, language refers to an open
system of signs by which intelligibility is incessantly created and contested.
As historically specific organizations of language, discourses present themselves in the plural, coexisting within temporal frames.[53]

This is precisely how Paul enacts being neither Greek nor Jew. Pascal captures
something very important about Paul that Badiou's own Platonic Gedenken
seems unable to grasp. The thought of some Greek thinkers, Gorgias and Protagoras for instance, was shaped by denial of "a metaphysically underpinned
epistemology."[54] This denial is the explicit argument of Gorgias's founding text
against Parmenides (and parodying his title): "On That Which Is Not; or, On
Nature." For thinkers such as these, rhetors indeed, the statement that "no real
distinguishes the first two discourses [Jew and Greek], and their distinction
collapses into rhetoric" is either nonsense or a tautology.[55]

In the final part of this chapter, I hope to adumbrate a shift in our reading of Paul that can result from a re-appreciation of sophistical rhetoric as
an important body of thought, promulgated itself in good faith.[56]

"I decided to know nothing among you except Jesus Christ and him crucified": Paul and the Sophists

For Badiou there is only one kind of Greek and one kind of Jewish discourse,
namely, philosophers on the one hand, prophets on the other. What is common to both is, in my view, commitment to an absolute and knowable truth.
In this sense they are "two aspects of the same figure of mastery." However,
the discourse of philosophy, precisely that to which Badiou would have us
return, does not constitute the whole of Greek discourse; nor does the discourse of the prophet constitute the whole of Jewish discourse—even less
so.[57] Some Jews claim that a sage is superior to a prophet, and some Greeks
that a sophist is to be preferred over a philosopher. Both are articulated explicitly within their own cultural frameworks as antiphilosophers.[58] Badiou
cannot even afford the sophists the name of antiphilosopher—even against
the explicit evidence of one of his heroes, Pascal—and thus his ascription
of the status of antiphilosopher to Paul has to involve an explicit denial
of the sophists: "Every definition of philosophy must distinguish it from
sophistry."[59] Distinguishing itself from sophism—renamed sophistry—is the
founding gesture of philosophy, otherwise known as Plato.[60] If we do not buy
into that gesture, however, or at least not fully so, then perhaps we can read
Paul more richly as antiphilosopher—a sophist. The continuation reads, "For

what the ancient or modern sophist claims to impose is precisely that there is no truth, that the concept of truth is useless and uncertain, since there are only conventions, rules, types of discourse or language games." A fair gloss, I would suggest, on Paul's thought. The prime site for such a reading would be 1 Corinthians, as Badiou has discovered it:

> Has not God made foolish the wisdom of the world? For since, in the wisdom of God, the world did not know God through wisdom, it pleased God through the folly of what we preach to save those who believe. For Jews demand signs and Greeks seek wisdom, but we preach Christ crucified, a stumbling block to Jews and folly to Gentiles, but to those who are called, both Jews and Greeks, Christ the power of God and the wisdom of God. For the foolishness of God is wiser than men, and the weakness of God is stronger than men. (1 Cor 1–20b–25)

Once again, Badiou's summing comment on this passage is, "It is through the invention of a language wherein folly, scandal, and weakness supplant knowing reason, order, and power."[61] Revising his reading in a historicist direction, I hope to preserve what I take to be its signal insight as I have stated above, as well as capture something of its import that is lost in the resolutely antihistoricist mode of Badiou's own reading.

I propose a different context for reading this passage in Paul than the metaphysical one offered by Badiou. There is already a language for Paul, indeed a very ancient one, wherein folly, scandal, and weakness supplant knowing reason, order, and power—the language of sophism. The crucial point is to move beyond the notion of sophists and rhetors as mere teachers of a technique—or worse, charlatans—and to see them as thinkers in their own right. We need to move beyond the negative and pejorative senses that sophistry has had for so many centuries.[62] A recent writer has put this well:

> "sophist" is a dirty word in the history of philosophy (since it is virtually synonymous with "practitioner of rhetoric"); in some mouths it is also virtually synonymous with "liar," "opportunist," or "con man." Nevertheless, if one is willing to treat the term sophist as a descriptive one rather than a pure pejorative—as a description of a group of thinkers expressing a secularism, relativism and pluralism in thought not unlike that with which we are familiar today (rather than those who are inevitably wrong because Socrates and Plato must inevitably be right) the term loses its menace.[63]

Taking a look at Protagoras, the earliest and one of the greatest sophists, we can find an explicit antiphilosopher. A classic (scandalous) example of a term of sophistic art is "making the weaker cause the stronger." Invented by Protagoras, if not by the legendary Corax and Tisias, "making the weaker cause the stronger" has generally been interpreted as making the worse decision or course of action seem the better for reasons of gain or other cynical motive. So fraught with the fraudulent had this term become that it is Aristophanes' charge against Socrates in *The Clouds* (in that play Socrates is himself a sophist par excellence). There is also more than a hint of a suggestion that this charge, derived from Aristophanes, was a major cause of the execution of Socrates only a year or so after the production of the play (*Apology* 18b).

According to Aristotle this topos is almost a metonym of the entire rhetorical/sophistic [eristic] enterprise:

> The *Art* of Corax is made up of this topic; for example, if a weak man were charged with assault, he should be acquitted as not being a likely suspect for the charge; for it is not probably [that a weak man would attack another]. And if he is a likely suspect, for example, if he is strong, [he should also be acquitted]; for it is not likely [that he would start the fight] for the very reason that it was going to seem probable. And similarly in other cases; for necessarily, a person is either a likely suspect or not a likely suspect for a charge. Both alternatives seem probably, but one really is probably, the other so not generally, only in the circumstances mentioned. And this is to "make the weaker seem the better cause." Thus, people were rightly angry at the declaration of Protagoras; for it is a lie and not true but a fallacious probability and a part of no art except rhetoric and eristic. (1402a)[64]

It is worthwhile to spend a little time glossing this passage, for through it we can arrive, against Aristotle's grain, at a more sympathetic reading of the topos and thence to its value for a reading of Paul. For Aristotle, of course, as for philosophical (and authoritarian) thinkers before him, rendering the weaker the stronger is only a matter of a lie. For Aristotle we can know in advance which is the "better" cause; the sophist/rhetor knows that too, and therefore the activity of rhetoric consists merely of slyly overturning the truth with a lie, making the weaker cause *seem* the better.[65] It is this understanding of sophistical rhetoric that motivates philosophical disdain for sophism from Plato to Badiou.

There is, however, a bit of an interpretative puzzle in Aristotle's statement. In the beginning of it, he discusses a certain topos or enthymeme, allegedly invented by Corax, and names it making the weaker cause the better. Then, however, he speaks of the people as being rightly angry at the declaration of Protagoras, an apparent reference to an incident that later (in Diogenes Laertius?) is narrated as a deportation of Protagoras that resulted in his death. However, it seems highly unlikely that it is the making of the weaker cause the better that allegedly caused the Athenian ire, for that is no declaration [τό Πρωταγόρου ἐπάγγελμα] but a practice and, moreover, seemingly attributed by Aristotle to Corax and not Protagoras. It seems that Aristotle refers then to some other declaration of Protagoras that is associated with or productive of or derived from the practice of making the weaker cause the stronger.

As Kennedy points out, there are two candidates for the *declaration* of Protagoras that might have aroused the ire of the Athenian demos.[66] Not choosing between them, but reading both of them together as pieces of a certain *theoretical* whole will further my investigation here. The first is the (in)famous utterance at the opening sentence of Protagoras's lost treatise, *On the Gods,* as reported by Diogenes Laertius and a host of ancient witnesses (Plato being the earliest but only affording a partial quotation or even allusion; *Thaetetus* 162d). The fullest version of the statement as extant in Diogenes reads, "Concerning the gods I cannot know either that they exist or that they do not exist, or what form they might have, for there is much to prevent one's knowing: the obscurity of the subject[67] and the shortness of man's life."[68] According to Diogenes (and Philostratus),[69] it was owing precisely to this statement that Protagoras was exiled from Athens.[70] Edward Schiappa shows, however, that there is little reason to credit this story and, following Werner Jaeger, demonstrates that this fragment is not a statement of agnosticism (or worse, atheism) as it is frequently taken to be but rather a statement of a human-centered (or anthropological) origin for religion, denying only that theology provides knowledge useful for deciding philosophical matters.[71] What is finally to the point (and to my point) is Jaap Mansfield's insight that "as soon as an important thinker says that the notion of 'gods' is epistemologically irrelevant as far as he is concerned, this cannot but have far-reaching consequences for his notion of 'man.'"[72] Given, moreover, that the content of the statement is epistemological, then the shift in the notion of "man" also has to do with man's knowing or not knowing, or, in Badiou's terms, a "truth procedure."

And this brings us neatly to the next prospect for a Protagorean statement that might have made the Athenians angry according to Aristotle, namely, Protagoras's notorious "the human is the measure" fragment: "Of all things, the human is the measure; of that which is, that it is, and of that which is not, that it is not" [καὶ ὁ Π. δὲ βούλεται πάντων χρημάτων εἶναι μέτρων τὸν ἄνθρωπον τῶν μὲν ὄντων ὡς ἔστιν, τῶν δὲ οὐκ ὄντων ὡς οὐκ ἔστιν].[73] Although this is not the place to go into the myriad philological and philosophical issues involved in the interpretation of this passage,[74] what is crucial for my argument here is to note the close relation between the denial of human knowledge of gods and the insistence that (subjective or relative)[75] human perception is the only criterion that there is. If we take the two statements together (which they seem rarely to be), we can see an epistemological theory begin to emerge at least inchoately. Since the gods are epistemologically irrelevant (i.e., gods may exist but we don't know anything about them), therefore there is no criterion by which judgments can be made other than human perception (although this latter term may be anachronistic).[76]

In other words, the major focus of each of Protagoras's two most famous declarations is entirely epistemological and moves in the direction of an indeterminacy principle. It follows that in any given forensic contest or in any given metaphysical inquiry, since we know nothing of the gods *and* human experience is the measure of truth, there can be no determination of absolute truth through logic alone. Combining the analysis of these two famous Protagorean utterances, we can easily understand why "[Protagoras] was the first to say that on every issue there are two arguments opposed to each other.[77] [Καὶ πρῶτος ἔφη δύο λόγους εἶναι περὶ παντὸς πράγματος ἀντικειμένους αλλήλοις [DL 9.51]." As a recent critical legal scholar, Michael Dzialo, has defined it, this comes startling close to the modern doctrine of legal indeterminacy: "legal doctrine can never determine a legal outcome because every argument in favor of a particular outcome can be met with an equally valid counterargument."[78] Now, however, we must return to Aristotle, for according to the passage, there is a direct entailment between these snippets of Protagoras's epistemology and the practice of the sophists of making the weaker cause the stronger. What is that entailment?

Reading directly against the grain of Aristotle's text, I would answer this question in a way that credits the sophists and does not discredit them. In any given situation, one side or the other may appear stronger at the outset. Rather than glossing the weaker and stronger argument phrase as Aristotle does, then, as making the weaker cause appear the stronger, one could easily gloss it as making the apparently weaker cause the stronger. This, then, ascribes great ethical and political force to the Protagorean practice and training, for it involves the systematic critical overturning of what appears to people to be the truth, not, however, as in Platonic terms, where the real truth, the "really real," *episteme,* will be revealed but rather in the interest of an educated *doxa*, of an educated decision regarding probability within a given particular situation. As Johan Vos has shown, the practice "says nothing about the true or intrinsic values of the arguments. An argument can be weaker simply because the majority do not accept it or because the opponent has better argumentative skills."[79] Following this reasoning, even Socrates (i.e., "the real" Socrates) may have professed this practice as well and the charges against him at his trial would then be well founded, at least as well founded as those allegedly brought against Protagoras of impiety and the fulmination of social change. Clearly a case can be made for reading Protagoras's theory and his practice as an invitation to change the weaker cause and render it the stronger.[80] On this reading, the interpretation from Aristophanes forward, that it consists of making the worse argument (i.e., the ethically worse or less just argument) defeat the better one through fancy rhetoric and fallacies, is nothing but a parodic slander on the genuine practice of the sophists.

How might we read Paul in such a context? Through analysis of a vitally important documentary papyrus, Bruce Winter establishes the importance and prestige of sophists in first-century Alexandria: "The sophists emerge from *P.Oxy.* 2190 as an important group in the Alexandrian educational system. In an age in which declamation was deemed the best method for advanced education, the sophists were in great demand. . . . The sophists had always charged fees, which distinguished them from the philosophers. It mattered little that philosophers denigrated their professional ability: parents who paid substantial amounts to sophists were acknowledging their primacy in *paideia*."[81] In the first century sophists were among the leaders of the Alexandrian *politeia,* prefiguring their explicit role in the second sophistic of a century later.[82] Dio also provides important evidence for the central role of rhetors/sophists at Tarsus in the first century, as well.[83] Nor, as Winter amply demonstrates, is *sophist* a negative term for Dio. He attacks weak and deceptive sophists but not sophists per se. Indeed, for him the seven vaunted sages are sophists.[84] Winter also makes a highly persuasive case for the prevalence and prestige of sophists/rhetors in Corinth as well.[85] Later thinkers (such as Plutarch) who were not sophists also did not use the phrase pejoratively, discussing, rather, particular groups of sophists and rhetors who were charlatans and not the sophistic movement as a whole.[86]

All of this attests the likelihood that Saul/Paul had imbibed the thought of the sophists with his mother's milk, as it were. If this meant only that he knew techniques of formal rhetoric as might appear from some recent scholarship, it would remain rather inert knowledge in my opinion. The significance of the observation that Paul inhabited a sophistic world will only come to the fore when we take into account the deep theoretical import of sophism and its own challenge to any form of epistemological certainty, whether prophetic or philosophical. Although for Winter, Paul is the anti-sophist, I believe this judgment needs nuancing.

Given this back story, we can return to the crucial passage in 1 Corinthians, not losing, I hope, Badiou's genuine insight into it but seeing the value of the discarded nameless impurities of historicism. Winter quite brilliantly argues that in verses 3–5 of chapter 2, when Paul writes, "And I was with you in weakness and in much fear and trembling; and my speech and my message were not in plausible words of wisdom [οὐκ ἐν πειθοῖς σοφηίας λόγοις], but in demonstration of the Spirit and of power [ἀποδείξει πνεύματος καὶ δυνάμεως], that your faith might not rest in the wisdom of men but in the power of God," what Paul is actually doing is eschewing the ethos, logos, and pathos of traditional rhetorical training. He will not establish his own worthiness to persuade, nor depend on the power of his logos, nor seek to create an emotional effect in his listeners. And yet he does seek to achieve conviction [πίστις], meaning "proof" in general Greek usage but "faith" in Pauline usage,[87] which is, after all, the goal of the ethos, pathos, and logos of rhetoric.[88] (In a convincing demonstration, Mark Given has shown the Paul of Acts 17:31 playing ironically on this double meaning.)[89] But this claim does not indicate a total rejection of the epistemological position and especially the anti-foundationalism that characterized the sophists as thinkers. As Given has written, "Paul's epistemology, especially as illustrated by his Christology and theology, did not discourage but rather encouraged the use of an ambiguous, cunning, and deceptive rhetoric of both body and voice,"[90] without—and this is precisely the point—allowing these terms any pejorative force whatsoever, difficult as that may be for us, accidental Platonists all.[91]

Paul may claim, for rhetorical purposes, not to use rhetoric in his discourse, but the claim is, of course, impossible to sustain.[92] Paul is rhetor nonpareil.[93] Indeed, one is tempted to compare his declarations of rhetorical inability in his own and his opponents' voices as so much rhetoric, much like Isocrates' repeated similar declarations five hundred years earlier.[94] To see these verses of 1 Corinthians as only a polemic against sophists or an encouragement to the untutored to express themselves is to miss their major theological force, which Badiou has captured so well. In overstressing Paul's oppositional position to sophistical rhetoric, as if that were the goal of his speech rather than an instrument toward something else, Winter misses the mark, I think.[95]

Given has written, "Suffice it so say for now that I believe that deception (ἀπάτη) is of great importance for understanding Paul's apocalyptic epistemology and rhetorical strategies, and it leads us into deep and sometimes disturbing aspects of his theology, Christology, soteriology, anthropology, missiology, and ecclesiology."[96] Given goes on to analyze the first chapters of 1 Corinthians as an instance of Paul's adoption of sophistical rhetoric,

"True rhetoric," as his discursive mode, showing how Paul carefully adopts language of double meaning to do his persuasive work. Moreover, in this context we can best understand Paul's famous (or infamous) utterance in 1 Corinthians 9:19–23 that he becomes all things to all people, like a Jew to the Jews and lawless to the lawless, in order to win and save souls. After disputing various major lines of interpretation with respect to this passage, Given himself writes that "just as Plato's Socrates feels free to break the rules of dialectic if necessary in order to win an argument, and Aristotle can counsel the use of sophistic *elenchus* to defeat sophists on their own terms, so Paul feels free to leave the world of being for that of seeming, 'to become all things to everyone,' in order to propagate the Truth, his gospel Truth. However different the reasons for their conviction that Truth is real and knowable, however differently they define the Truth, the rhetorical effect is rather analogous: a willingness to employ intentional ambiguity, cunning, and deception to disseminate the Truth, a willingness to employ True rhetoric."[97] The difference between Plato's (and Paul's) "true" rhetoric and the false rhetoric of sophists comes down, then, to a matter of intention alone; Socrates and Paul do it for the Truth, the sophists for the money, but for this latter judgment we have only the word of their enemies. I would rather suggest that the difference lies here: the sophists in their travels from place to place, from culture to culture, have learned that everywhere folks have different customs. They relativize truth and teach an art of living well and honestly in a world in which there are two sides to every question, while Plato finally cannot stand such a world and thus escapes to another one in which finally there is an ex-tramundane, extralogical source of Truth, the Forms. Paul is all things for all people, among sophists a sophist, but like Plato in that he too finally seeks that extramundane absolute truth—for Paul, Christ and him crucified. As Susan Jarratt has put it, "Their effectiveness in teaching this *techne* derived in part from their experiences of different cultures; they behaved and taught that no-tions of 'truth' had to be adjusted to fit the ways of a particular audience in a certain time and with a certain set of beliefs and laws."[98] The ancient sophists too were all things to all people.[99]

Paul is aware of the weakness of his position from the point of view of logic [wisdom] and scripture/Jesus' tradition [signs], and yet seeks mightily to make the weaker cause the stronger. Moreover, as Vos points out, Paul is explicitly aware—Protagoras-like—that at many points equally good arguments could be produced for the other side, or alternatively that his own arguments could lead to results that he hardly wants.[100] μὴ γένοιτο! Paul explicitly describes his own logos as well as his own ethos and even that of his Corinthian congregation as the weaker, "nevertheless, Paul presented his position so strongly that he convinced the majority of Christian believers from his time until the present day" and hence made the weaker cause the stronger.[101]

Having come this far, however, Vos's argument now breaks down into an attack on Paul's integrity. Vos completely accepts the philosophically pejorative characterization of the praxis of making the weaker cause the stronger, simply describing Paul in as negative a guise as any ancient philosophical anti-rhetor could wish, concluding that "all [the] characteristics of the 'malartful arts' of rhetoric mentioned by Sextus Empiricus can be found in Paul's interpretation."[102] Invoking rather the defense of Protagoras that I have briefly adumbrated above, I would concur in seeing Paul as a sophist (at least at times), rejecting entirely (as I do for Protagoras) any of the pejorative connotations of that term. Or better and more modestly put, it seems to me that Paul is to be found at least as much among those ancient antiphilosophers, the sophists, as among the philosophers, and in my usage, the sophists are explicitly antiphilosophers. At least as much as Paul calls for fidelity to an event, he envisions also social change in which the weak are made strong: "If rhetoric is to mean anything as a practice, a theory of discourse, or a philosophy by which to understand the world, it must be given the potential to transform the world. If there is to be a substantive difference between 'rhetoric' and 'propaganda,' then it must start from the following distinction: propaganda is the invitation to envision the world according to the people who own and rule it. Rhetoric is the invitation to change the world."[103]

In this context, Paul's weakness made strong can be read anew, as we can read anew his Hellenicity among Greeks and his Jewishness among Jews. Paul's challenge to Greek wisdom is an attack on the epistemological certainty that is the hallmark of the bulk of philosophy (to be sure, there are *sophisticated* versions of philosophy which interrogate that as well). Both his capacity for making the weaker cause the stronger and his being all things to all people can be read in this sophistical context as having positive political import, providing surprisingly a way beyond, a poros through the aporiae of ethnic particularism and liberal universalism. Paul's seeming equivocation on this issue, both asserting the value of Jewish difference and totally disdaining it almost at one and the same moment, would be seen on this account as a negotiation of difference, precisely in a sophistical and rhetorical manner—both in form and in substance, insofar as it is one of the very substantive characteristics of sophists to understand that they can be Athenians in Athens and Corinthians in Corinth—and not the adoption of a position.[104] This is then a somewhat different Paul from the Paul of my own Paul book too, in which I read him rather too definitely as a Platonist. I would argue now that as both theorist of the event and a practicing sophist, Paul is not laying claim to a "Hellenizing" universal truth as knowledge-to-be-possessed but performing an act of faith or fidelity in or to the radical transformations that may be effected within the rhetorical negotiation of difference. This Paul would be then a postcolonial sophist and also a Paul who could conceivably provide more of a resource for negotiations of democratic differences as well. At the same time, I cannot abandon my sense that even such a more complexly theorized Paul still evacuates of significance histories, memories, practices, discourses that I hold most dear as my own. There *is* something troubling about itinerant sophists who relativize everything in both their cosmopolitanism and insistence that for everything there are two *logoi*.

In his own zeal against the sophists—which could indeed be another title for his *Manifesto*—Badiou cannot see the sophist in Paul, and, this proud adherent of the third sophistic would argue, therefore misses much that is valuable for thought in the epistles. The task is (and I agree with Badiou that it is) somehow to make sense of a Paul for those of us who do not know Christ and him crucified. But it is precisely here that I don't somehow "get" Badiou. To my mind in the subtraction of everything but militance itself and fidelity, Badiou leaves us with almost nothing of value. Having subtracted everything of the contingent, the historical, even the individual in his account of Paul, he is left knowing nothing but Paul asserting Jesus Christ and him crucified (or resurrected). It is finally unclear from Badiou's Paul book, especially when read in the context of the Badiouish corpus as a whole, whether Paul is to be seen as a positively marked figure, antiphilosophical but in his militance on the side of those compossibilities that constitute the conditions of philosophy for Badiou, or as on the negative side of those enemies of truth whom Badiou denounces as adherents of the great sophistry. Once again, we are thrown back on Badiou's professed Platonism[105] in realizing that it doesn't matter to him what Paul says at all.[106] The manner of his militance, the dehistoricization of all truth, is critical. It is not fortuitous. For Badiou in some profound sense, all historicism is the antithesis of truth: "Philosophy must break, from within itself, with historicism. . . . It must be bold enough to present its concepts without first bringing them in from the tribunal of their historical moment."[107] In denying the name philosophy to Wittgenstein and Derrida (whom he referred to as neo-sophists), Badiou reproduces the Platonic denial of the name *philosophy* to Gorgias, Protagoras, and Isocrates, claiming it only for his brand of "transversal" thinking. For this sophist, at any rate, such philosophy will always be a dead letter or at least an unreadable one.

Notes

1. Alain Badiou, *Manifesto for Philosophy Followed by Two Essays: "The (Re)Turn of Philosophy Itself" and "Definition of Philosophy,"* ed. and trans. Norman Madarasz (Albany: State University of New York Press, 1999), 33.

2. Blaise Pascal, *Thoughts,* trans. O. W. Wight, Mary L. Booth, and W. F. Trotter (New York: Collier, 1910), 513, cited in Louis Marin, "On the Interpretation of Ordinary Language: A Parable of Pascal," in *Textual Strategies: Perspectives in Post-Structuralist Criticism,* ed. Josue Harari (Ithaca, N.Y.: Cornell University Press, 1979), 255.

3. I understand Dawson's dilemma as well as his frustration. It is not unsimilar to the frustration of those who criticized Mel Gibson's film, since their critique simply reinforced the very message of the film over and over again.

4. John David Dawson, *Christian Figural Reading and the Fashioning of Identity* (Berkeley: University of California Press, 2002), 20.

5. Daniel Boyarin, *A Radical Jew: Paul and the Politics of Identity,* Contraversions: Critical Studies in Jewish Literature, Culture, and Society (Berkeley: University of California Press, 1994).

6. See too Alain Badiou, *Saint Paul: The Foundation of Universalism,* trans. Ray Brassier, Cultural Memory in the Present (Stanford, Calif.: Stanford University Press, 2003), 4–5. I agree wholeheartedly with Badiou that any version of a subjectivism that says: "You must be an X to understand X-ness" is worse than pernicious. For an elegant counter to that version of identitarianism, see David M. Halperin, *Saint Foucault: Towards a Gay Hagiography* (Oxford: Oxford University Press, 1995), 62.

7. Boyarin, *Radical Jew,* 228.

8. Badiou, *Saint,* 1.

9. Badiou, *Saint,* 2.

10. Alain Badiou, *Infinite Thought: Truth and the Return to Philosophy,* ed. and trans. Justin Clemens and Oliver Feltham, intro. Justin Clemens and Oliver Feltham (New York: Continuum, 2003), 6.

11. Badiou, *Saint,* 2 (emphasis added).

12. Badiou, *Infinite,* 23.

13. See the subtitle of Badiou's *Infinite Thought: Truth and the Return to Philosophy.*

14. Badiou, *Manifesto,* 96.

15. Badiou, *Saint,* 5.

16. Alain Badiou, *L'être et l'événement,* Ordre philosophique (Paris: Seuil, 1988), 68.

17. Badiou, *Infinite,* 15–16.

18. On the other hand, when Badiou goes off, he does so spectacularly as well: "It is John who, by turning the logos into a principle, will synthetically inscribe Christianity within the space of the Greek logos, thereby subordinating it to anti-Judaism," Badiou, *Saint,* 43. I simply cannot imagine a Johannine passage that could possibly be glossed as "turning the logos into a principle"!

19. See discussion in Mark Douglas Given, *Paul's True Rhetoric: Ambiguity, Cunning, and Deception in Greece and Rome,* Emory Studies in Early Christianity (Harrisburg, Pa.: Trinity Press International, 2001), 97 n. 54.

20. For this opposition, see Badiou, *Manifesto,* 29: "It is thus entirely conceivable that the determination of Nazism—for example, of Nazism as political—be removed

de jure from the specific form of thinking which, since Plato, has deserved the name of philosophy."

21. Margaret Mitchell has pointed out, partly following Tertullian, that Peter was behaving in a manner not entirely un-Pauline here; indeed, he was being all things to all people, "Pauline Accommodation and 'Condescension' (συγκατάβασις): 1 Cor 9:19–23 and the History of Influence," in *Paul Beyond the Judaism/Hellenism Divide*, ed. Troels Engberg-Pedersen (Louisville: Westminster/John Knox Press, 2001), 202–203.

22. Compare Badiou's own reading of the Antioch episode (Badiou, *Saint*, 26).

23. Badiou, *Saint*, 27.

24. Badiou, *Saint*, 47.

25. Hans Conzelmann, *1 Corinthians: A Commentary on the First Epistle to the Corinthians*, ed. George W. S. J. MacRae, trans. James W. Leitch, Hermeneia (Philadelphia: Fortress, 1976), 47.

26. Walter Bauer, Gerhard Krodel, and Robert A. Kraft, *Orthodoxy and Heresy in Earliest Christianity*, ed. Gerhard Krodel (Philadelphia: Fortress, 1971), 69, cited in Conzelmann, *1 Corinthians*, 9.

27. Conzelmann, *1 Corinthians*, 9.

28. Badiou, *Saint*, 41–42.

29. Badiou, *Saint*, 41.

30. Conzelmann gets this just right, "The classifying of mankind from the standpoint of salvation history as Jews and Greeks is a Jewish equivalent for the Greek classification 'Greeks and barbarians,'" Conzelmann, *1 Corinthians*, 46.

31. I depart here from the RSV's "custodian." The *paidagogos* was a slave who took the child back and forth from school.

32. As Betz would have it, Hans Dieter Betz, *Galatians: A Commentary on Paul's Letter to the Church in Galatia*, Hermeneia (Philadelphia: Fortress, 1979), 202. Burton too claims that the thought of chapter 3 is complete with verse 29 and that Paul now "takes up again the thought of the inferiority of the condition under law" (Ernest De Witt Burton, *A Critical and Exegetical Commentary on The Epistle to the Galatians*, International Critical Commentary [1920; Edinburgh: T & T Clark, 1988], 211), quite missing the point, thus, in my opinion, that this is precisely an interpretation of the somewhat cryptic "there is no Greek nor Jew" at the end of chapter 3. Even Longenecker, who seems to me so often right and sure in his exegetical judgment, does not regard the end of the passage (vv. 8–11) as anything more than a virtual appendix to it (Richard N. Longenecker, *Galatians*, vol. 41 of Word Biblical Commentary [Dallas: Word, 1990], 178–79), whereas I am arguing that it is only with these verses that the point of the whole illustration becomes at all clear or do we see, in any way, what the elements of the universe, to which we have been enthralled, are.

33. Longenecker, *Galatians*, 162 also captures this connection perfectly, as do Frank J. Matera and Daniel J. Harrington, *Galatians* (Collegeville, Minn.: Liturgical, 1992), 148.

34. Betz, *Galatians*, 207.

35. See Betz, *Galatians*, 207 n. 55 documenting many.

36. Longenecker, *Galatians*, 166.

37. Compare Richard Hays, who writes, "I began this study under the assumption that Gal 4:4–5 was in fact a fragment of pre-Pauline tradition; this investigation has substantially undermined my confidence in this assumption, as most of the features which have been thought to mark it off from the 'grain' of Paul's thought have been shown to be capable of explanation in other ways." Richard B. Hays, *The Faith of*

Jesus Christ: An Investigation of the Narrative Substructure of Galatians 3:1–4:11, SBL Dissertation Series (Chico, Calif.: Scholars, 1983), 135 n. 80

38. See the many examples in Bart D. Ehrman, *The Orthodox Corruption of Scripture: The Effect of Early Christological Controversies on the Text of the New Testament* (Oxford: Oxford University Press, 1993).

39. Betz, *Galatians,* 204.

40. That this is one of the possible acceptations of the term, as shown clearly by usages in Diogenes Laertius and Justin Martyr, Burton, *Critical and Exegetical Commentary on The Epistle to the Galatians,* 512–13. I believe it is the only sense that enables Paul's comparison of the observance of the law to pagan worship of gods who are not gods, the στοιχεῖα. This is the interpretation of Theodoret, generally adopted by most of the fathers (Burton, *Critical and Exegetical Commentary on the Epistle to the Galatians,* 515), and should never have been strayed from, in my perhaps less than humble opinion. Burton himself rejects this view, but I find nothing of his objections telling, certainly not in the face of the eminent sense that this reading makes of Paul's rhetoric. Burton interprets (following Tertullian): "the rudimentary religious teachings possessed by the race," thus completely undermining Paul's argument and rhetoric, making nonsense of his allegation that keeping the law is equivalent, literally, to returning to pagan worship! I have similar concerns with Longenecker's interpretation of the elements of the world themselves as being "the Mosaic Law" (Longenecker, *Galatians,* 165–66), taking the στοιχεῖα, once again, as Burton does, as "basic principles of religion," which also seems to me to fatally weaken Paul's argument against the Galatians that by keeping the law they are reverting to their former state of paganism. It is *not* that the Torah is the στοικεῖα, but that by adopting the Torah, with its observances based on the movements of heavenly bodies, the Galatians have returned, in effect, to their former worship of these heavenly bodies themselves. To miss this is to miss the whole force of Paul's bitterly ironic argument (cf. Longenecker, *Galatians,* 181). I would argue similarly against F. F. Bruce, *Commentary on Galatians,* New International Greek Testament Commentary (Exeter: Paternoster, 1990), 193. If the elements are the Torah, then the whole rhetorical force of the bitter comparison is lost. It is not finally the point that "if former pagans accepted the Jewish calendar, old astral associations could easily reassert themselves" (Bruce, *Commentary on Galatians,* 206–207), but that in Paul's rhetoric, they are already asserting themselves by the very fact of such observances.

41. Betz, *Galatians,* 205. Burton gets this right: "Jews and Gentiles are therefore classed together as being before the coming of Christ in the childhood of the race, and in bondage, and the knowledge of religion which the Jews possessed in the law is classed with that which the Gentiles possessed without it under the common title, 'the elements of the world.'" Burton, *Critical and Exegetical Commentary on the Epistle to the Galatians,* 212. For a veritable inventory of complicated and distracting interpretations, see Bruce, *Commentary on Galatians,* 202–204.

42. Longenecker, *Galatians,* 164.

43. Burton misses this point when he writes that the letter to the Galatians is silent "about any statute of the law except circumcision, which they had not yet adopted, and the fasts and feasts, which they had, there being, for example, no mention in connection with the situation in Galatia of the law of foods" (Burton, *Critical and Exegetical Commentary on the Epistle to the Galatians,* 233). As already noted, I believe that the law of foods is precisely what is thematized in the report of the Antioch incident. I agree, however, that it seems most likely from Paul's language that the

Galatians were already observing the holy days but not circumcision or kashrut laws. This makes sense from what we know, in general, of the attractiveness of the Jewish holy days to gentiles. The "opponents" now seem to be pressing about circumcision, with kashrut perhaps less urgently on the agenda.

44. Of course, as Betz points out, the Jacobean tutors of the Galatians would not agree here that observance of the Torah constitutes paganizing worship in effect, but that hardly justifies Betz's conclusion that "the opponents understand their religion as a cultic-ritualistic system of protection against the forces of evil," Betz, *Galatians*, 217. I would have said that this is as distorting a reading of Judaism (not justified even in Paul) as any produced to date, except that Betz writes "the cultic activities described in v. 10 are *not* typical of Judaism (including Jewish Christianity), although they are known to both Judaism and Christianity" (emphasis added). What can he mean? What cultic activities are described in verse 10 if not the ordinary Jewish (and Jewish-Christian) ones of observance of the Sabbaths, new moons, and festivals determined by the sun and the moon? Betz could not be more mistaken, in my view, in seeing Paul's critique of the Galatians as being for "religious scrupulosity" or "superstition." Betz, *Galatians*, 218. Paul must be referring here to his own former observances that put him, in his own view, in the same situation as that of the Galatians in their own former life. Thus he was equal to them in need of redemption, and they equal to him in the finding of redemption through Christ if they do not slip into his (Paul's) own former lifestyle. Hence, I have become like you; do you remain as I am (in this, v. 12).

45. Compare Badiou's own demurral (*Saint*, 108).

46. Alain Badiou, "The (Re)Turn of Philosophy *Itself*," in *Manifesto for Philosophy Followed by Two Essays: "The (Re)Turn of Philosophy Itself" and "Definition of Philosophy*," ed. and trans. Norman Madarasz (Albany: State University of New York Press, 1999), 123.

47. Badiou, *Saint*, 57.

48. Emmanuel Levinas, *Totality and Infinity: An Essay on Exteriority,* trans. Alphonso Lingis (Pittsburgh: Duquesne University Press, 1969), 72–74. For this citation and a brilliant discussion of Levinas on rhetoric, see Susan E. Shapiro, "Rhetoric, Ideology, and Idolatry in the Writings of Emmanuel Levinas," in *Rhetorical Invention and Religious Inquiry: New Perspectives,* ed. Walter Jost and Wendy Olmsted (New Haven, Conn.: Yale University Press, 2000), 254–78.

49. Badiou, *Saint*, 50.

50. Pascal, *Thoughts,* 382. I willingly confess that I, almost innocent of any claim to knowledge of Pascal, came across this passage decades ago in an essay of Louis Marin, "Interpretation," and barely know any other. I took that essay and its analysis of the parable to be parabolic of parables; now I use it for another purpose.

51. Marin, "Interpretation," 244 (ellipses original).

52. Marin, "Interpretation," 246–47.

53. Judith Butler, *Gender Trouble: Feminism and the Subversion of Identity,* Thinking Gender (London: Routledge, 1990), 145. I am grateful to Dina Stein for reminding me of this passage.

54. Given, *Paul's True Rhetoric,* 20.

55. Badiou, *Saint*, 57.

56. Badiou is well aware of the possibility of such recuperation and dismisses it a priori: "Philosophy today, caught in its historicist malaise, is very weak in the face of modern sophists. Most often, it even considers the great sophists—for there are

great sophists—as great philosophers. Exactly as if we were to consider that the great philosophers of Antiquity were not Plato and Aristotle, but Gorgias and Protagoras," Badiou, "(Re)Turn," 116. Well, yes. Yes, precisely, that's it.

57. I say this because there are Greeks for whom the discourse of philosophy constituted the whole of discourse but there were no historical Jews for whom prophecy was all and everything.

58. Serguei Dolgopolsky, "The Rhetoric of the Talmud in the Perspective of Post-Structuralism" (Ph.D. diss., University of California, 2004).

59. Badiou, "(Re)Turn," 119.

60. Badiou, *Manifesto*, 34.

61. Badiou, *Saint*, 47.

62. This is an intellectual project that has been going on now for a century, largely inspired, it seems, by Nietzsche. See, inter alia, John Poulakos, *Sophistical Rhetoric in Classical Greece,* Studies in Rhetoric/Communication (Columbia: University of South Carolina Press, 1995). Paul's own affinities to Nietzsche have been adumbrated by Badiou in ways that are different from my own sense of these. On Nietzsche himself as the originator of contemporary anti-Platonism (that which I am pleased to call the third sophistic), see Badiou, *Manifesto*, 99.

63. Michael G. Dzialo, "Legal and Philosophical Fictions: At the Line Where the Two Become One," *Argumentation* 12 (1998): 219.

64. Aristotle, *On Rhetoric: A Theory of Civic Discourse,* trans. George Alexander Kennedy (New York: Oxford University Press, 1991), 210.

65. Compare the discussion of epistemological confidence in Given, *Paul's True Rhetoric,* 34.

66. Aristotle, *On Rhetoric: A Theory of Civic Discourse,* 210 n. 254.

67. On this phrase, Schiappa writes, "What Protagoras had in mind as 'the obscurity of the subject' is difficult to say. *Adêlotês,* translated above as 'obscurity,' can also imply uncertainty, to be in the dark about, or not evident to sense. One can imagine a number of reasons why the gods are a 'subject' too obscure to reason about confidently," Edward Schiappa, *Protagoras and Logos* (Columbia: University of South Carolina Press, 1991), 143.

68. Hermann Diels and Rosamond Kent Sprague, *The Older Sophists,* ed. Rosamond Kent Sprague (Columbia: University of South Carolina Press, 1972), 20. On this last phrase, Schiappa (*Protagoras,* 143) has compared Empedocles' claim that life is too short to acquire knowledge of "the whole."

69. Diels and Sprague, *Older Sophists,* 6.

70. Diels and Sprague, *Older Sophists,* 4.

71. Schiappa, *Protagoras,* 144–48.

72. Jaap Mansfield, "Protagoras on Epistemological Obstacles and Persons," in *The Sophists and Their Legacy,* ed. G. B. Kerferd (Wiesbaden: Franz Steiner Verlag, 1981), 43.

73. Hermann Diels and Walther Kranz, *Die Fragmente der Vorsokratiker, Griechisch und Deutsch,* ed. Walther Kranz (Zürich: Weidmann, 1966), 258 in Sextus's formulation. Once again, we have an earlier Platonic citation of the principle as well.

74. For which, see Schiappa, *Protagoras,* 117–33.

75. For this distinction, see Schiappa, *Protagoras,* 129–30.

76. When this is combined with Protagoras's evident continued practice of worship of the gods and other observances, one might dream up an early version of Pascal's wager, but a highly sophisticated one.

77. Diels and Sprague, *Older Sophists,* 21. Schiappa discusses at length difficul-

ties with this translation (a traditional one) in that it reduces "all sophistic teaching to rhetoric" (Schiappa, *Protagoras,* 90), by which he means rhetoric itself in its least elevated acceptation, essentially how Kennedy takes it as sort of a founding charter for debating societies, i.e., simply it is possible to organize a debate on any topic. I cannot make short work of Schiappa's compelling discussion but suffice it to say that by the end Protagoras's statement makes a profound philosophical point (Schiappa, *Protagoras,* 91–100), in which, again we find Protagoras on the side of Heraclitus against Parmenides (Schiappa, *Protagoras,* 92). This is a discussion for another venue, however, and I hope to come back to it.

78. Dzialo, "Legal," 217.

79. Johan S. Vos, "'To Make the Weaker Argument Defeat the Stronger': Sophistical Argumentation in Paul's Letter to the Romans," in *Rhetorical Argumentation in Biblical Texts,* ed. Anders Eriksson, Thomas H. Olbricht, and Walter Übelacker (Harrisburg, Pa.: Trinity Press International, 2002), 217–31.

80. John Poulakos, "Rhetoric, the Sophists, and the Possible," *Communications Monographs* 51 (1984): 215–25.

81. Bruce W. Winter, *Philo and Paul among the Sophists: Alexandrian and Corinthian Responses to a Julio-Claudian Movement,* 2nd ed. (Grand Rapids, Mich.: Eerdmans, 2002), 39. It seems not inapposite to note that Winter's translation of the pair παιδεία καὶ λόγος as "education and rhetoric" (Winter, *Philo and Paul,* 45) implies that rhetoric (like sophism) for him is merely an art of speaking and not a theoretical enterprise of thinking. Interestingly, in another collocation, πειθὸς καὶ λόγος, Winter translates the latter as "reason" (Winter, *Philo and Paul,* 47). On page 53 of the same work, *logos* is translated "reason" even in the first collocation. This all makes a difference.

82. Winter, *Philo and Paul,* 49.

83. Winter, *Philo and Paul,* 54–55.

84. Winter, *Philo and Paul,* 56. See Winter's strong arguments that the term "sophist" is not pejorative for Dio. While Winter is correct to emphasize that reading it as such, as C. P. Jones does, involves an anachronism, Winter only sees the anachronism as proceeding from the fact that later on, *sophistes* is pejorative, but is this not the case for Plato already? This provides support for the view defended in my current work that the Platonic value system was not as dominant as we might think. On the other hand, Winter seems to suggest on page 58 that Dio's usage is consonant with Plato's, and he may, of course, be correct in this.

Winter makes an important point when he argues that the distinction between philosophers and sophists was not as sharp as some would like it to be. See his discussion on this question, in which he comes down on the side of Stanton's insistence that the distinction is blurred. Winter, *Philo and Paul,* 116 n. 11; Graham R. Stanton, "Sophists and Philosophers: Problems of Classification," *American Journal of Philology* 94, no. 4 (1973): 304–306; and Stanley K. Stowers, "Social Status, Public Speaking, and Private Teaching," *Novum Testamentum* 26 (1984): 59–82.

85. Winter, *Philo and Paul,* 140, for a summary of his case. Winter's argument goes to the heart of the methodological question raised by Mitchell, that any argument for a specific Hellenistic background in Paul be evaluated by the likelihood that he was aware of that background. Mitchell, "Pauline Accommodation," 199.

86. Winter, *Philo and Paul,* 139, is unclear on these points, seeming almost to contradict himself on the same page. Reading the original texts, as I will do presently, bears out the judgments I presented above.

87. Not only in him, of course, and the question of whose faith, ours or Jesus', is not germane here.

88. Winter, *Philo and Paul,* 157–60.

89. Given, *Paul's True Rhetoric,* 74.

90. Given, *Paul's True Rhetoric,* 8.

91. "What," I hear a voice saying, "speak for yourself, Platonist!" For decades I have maintained in a more than intuitive, less than scholarly way that in very important ways Plato and Aristotle are one, or, better put, Aristotle is a Platonist too. It is gratifying indeed to be vindicated by Lloyd P. Gerson, *Aristotle and Other Platonists* (Ithaca: Cornell University Press, 2005). The practice of dividing the world of thought into Platonists and Aristotelians is, from where I sit, as much an ideological exclusion of sophism as it is a real division within philosophy.

92. Apparently pace Winter, *Philo and Paul,* 185.

93. Johannes Weiss, "Beiträge zur Paulinischen Rhetorik," in *Theologische Studien Herrn Wirkl. Oberkonsistorialrath Professor D. Bernhard Weiss zu seinem 70. Geburtstage dargebracht,* ed. Bernhard Weiss and Caspar René Gregory (Göttingen: Vandenhoeck & Ruprecht, 1897), 165–247.

94. This point was originally made by Hans Dieter Betz; see Given, *Paul's True Rhetoric,* 13.

95. Compare too Given, *Paul's True Rhetoric,* 99 n. 58.

96. Given, *Paul's True Rhetoric,* 5.

97. Given, *Paul's True Rhetoric,* 117.

98. Susan C. Jarratt, *Rereading the Sophists: Classical Rhetoric Refigured* (Carbondale, Ill.: Southern Illinois University Press, 1991), xv.

99. Interestingly, notwithstanding the seven options for "Hellenistic" background for this verse cited by Mitchell, "Pauline Accommodation," 198, the one that does not figure at all, is not even mentioned, is sophism. Nor does Mitchell, in her excellent and illuminating discussion, even pick up on Clement of Alexandria's explicit mention of the sophists in this context (*Strom.* 7.9), despite citing the Clementine passage, "Pauline Accommodation," 204. Rehabilitating sophism will be very much to the point, I think.

100. Vos, "To Make."

101. Vos, "To Make."

102. Vos, "To Make." If I have misread Vos here, I withdraw this point.

103. Omar Swartz, *The Rise of Rhetoric and Its Intersections with Contemporary Critical Thought,* Polemics Series (Boulder, Colo.: Westview, 1998), 40. Would that this book, frequently stirring and more than occasionally illuminating, had undergone editing, even copyediting, before being published.

104. I am grateful to Virginia Burrus for conversations that led to this formulation.

105. "Today the Nietzschean diagnosis must be toppled. The century and Europe must imperatively be cured of anti-Platonism. Philosophy shall only exist insofar as it proposes, to match the needs of our times, a new step in the history of the category of truth," Badiou, *Manifesto,* 101.

106. Badiou, "(Re)Turn," 128–31.

107. Badiou, "(Re)Turn," 114.

Bibliography

Aristotle. *On Rhetoric: A Theory of Civic Discourse.* Translated by George Alexander Kennedy. New York: Oxford University Press, 1991.

Badiou, Alain. *Infinite Thought: Truth and the Return to Philosophy.* Edited and translated by Justin Clemens and Oliver Feltham. With an introduction by Justin Clemens and Oliver Feltham. New York: Continuum, 2003.

———. *L'être et l'événement.* Ordre philosophique. Paris: Seuil, 1988.

———. *Manifesto for Philosophy Followed by Two Essays: "The (Re)Turn of Philosophy Itself" and "Definition of Philosophy."* Edited and translated by Norman Madarasz. Albany: State University of New York Press, 1999.

———. "The (Re)Turn of Philosophy *Itself.*" In *Manifesto for Philosophy Followed by Two Essays: "The (Re)Turn of Philosophy Itself" and "Definition of Philosophy,"* edited and translated by Norman Madarasz, 113–38. Albany: State University of New York Press, 1999.

———. *Saint Paul: The Foundation of Universalism.* Translated by Ray Brassier. Cultural Memory in the Present. Stanford, Calif.: Stanford University Press, 2003.

Bauer, Walter, Gerhard Krodel, and Robert A. Kraft. *Orthodoxy and Heresy in Earliest Christianity.* Edited by Gerhard Krodel. Philadelphia: Fortress, 1971.

Betz, Hans Dieter. *Galatians: A Commentary on Paul's Letter to the Church in Galatia.* Hermeneia. Philadelphia: Fortress, 1979.

Boyarin, Daniel. *A Radical Jew: Paul and the Politics of Identity.* Contraversions: Critical Studies in Jewish Literature, Culture, and Society. Berkeley: University of California Press, 1994.

Bruce, F. F. *Commentary on Galatians.* 1982. New International Greek Testament Commentary. Exeter: Paternoster, 1990.

Burton, Ernest De Witt. *A Critical and Exegetical Commentary on the Epistle to the Galatians.* International Critical Commentary. 1920. Edinburgh: T & T Clark, 1988.

Conzelmann, Hans. *1 Corinthians: A Commentary on the First Epistle to the Corinthians.* Edited by George W. MacRae. Translated by James W. Leitch. Bibliography and references prepared by James W. Dunkly. Hermeneia. Philadelphia: Fortress, 1976.

Dawson, John David. *Christian Figural Reading and the Fashioning of Identity.* Berkeley: University of California Press, 2002.

Diels, Hermann, and Walther Kranz. *Die Fragmente der Vorsokratiker, Griechisch und Deutsch.* Edited by Walther Kranz. Zürich: Weidmann, 1966.

Diels, Hermann, and Rosamond Kent Sprague. *The Older Sophists.* Edited by Rosamond Kent Sprague. Columbia: University of South Carolina Press, 1972.

Dolgopolsky, Serguei. "The Rhetoric of the Talmud in the Perspective of Post-Structuralism." Ph.D. diss., University of California, 2004.

Dzialo, Michael G. "Legal and Philosophical Fictions: At the Line Where the Two Become One." *Argumentation* 12 (1998): 217–32.

Gerson, Lloyd P. *Aristotle and Other Platonists.* Ithaca: Cornell University Press, 2005.

Given, Mark Douglas. *Paul's True Rhetoric: Ambiguity, Cunning, and Deception in Greece and Rome.* Emory Studies in Early Christianity. Harrisburg, Pa.: Trinity Press International, 2001.

Halperin, David M. *Saint Foucault: Towards a Gay Hagiography.* Oxford: Oxford University Press, 1995.

Hays, Richard B. *The Faith of Jesus Christ: An Investigation of the Narrative Substructure of Galatians 3:1–4:11.* SBL Dissertation Series. Chico, Calif.: Scholars, 1983.

Jarratt, Susan C. *Rereading the Sophists: Classical Rhetoric Refigured.* Carbondale, Ill.: Southern Illinois University Press, 1991.

Levinas, Emmanuel. *Totality and Infinity: An Essay on Exteriority.* Translated by Alphonso Lingis. Pittsburgh: Duquesne University Press, 1969.

Longenecker, Richard N. *Galatians.* Word Biblical Commentary. Dallas: Word, 1990.

Mansfield, Jaap. "Protagoras on Epistemological Obstacles and Persons." In *The Sophists and Their Legacy,* edited by G. B. Kerferd, 38–53. Wiesbaden: Franz Steiner Verlag, 1981.

Marin, Louis. "On the Interpretation of Ordinary Language: A Parable of Pascal." In *Textual Strategies: Perspectives in Post-Structuralist Criticism,* edited by Josue Harari, 239–59. Ithaca: Cornell University Press, 1979.

Matera, Frank J., and Daniel J. Harrington. *Galatians.* Collegeville, Minn.: Liturgical, 1992.

Mitchell, Margaret M. "Pauline Accommodation and 'Condescension' (συγκατάβασις): 1 Cor 9:19–23 and the History of Influence." In *Paul Beyond the Judaism/Hellenism Divide,* edited by Troels Engberg-Pedersen, 197–214. Louisville: Westminster/John Knox, 2001.

Pascal, Blaise. *Thoughts.* Translated by O. W. Wight, Mary L. Booth, and W. F. Trotter. New York: Collier, 1910.

Poulakos, John. "Rhetoric, the Sophists, and the Possible." *Communications Monographs* 51 (1984): 215–25.

———. *Sophistical Rhetoric in Classical Greece.* Studies in Rhetoric/Communication. Columbia: University of South Carolina Press, 1995.

Schiappa, Edward. *Protagoras and Logos.* Columbia: University of South Carolina Press, 1991.

Shapiro, Susan E. "Rhetoric, Ideology, and Idolatry in the Writings of Emmanuel Levinas." In *Rhetorical Invention and Religious Inquiry: New Perspectives,* edited by Walter Jost and Wendy Olmsted, 254–78. New Haven, Conn.: Yale University Press, 2000.

Stanton, Graham R. "Sophists and Philosophers: Problems of Classification." *American Journal of Philology* 94, no. 4 (1973): 304–306.

Stowers, Stanley K. "Social Status, Public Speaking and Private Teaching." *Novum Testamentum* 26 (1984): 59–82.

Swartz, Omar. *The Rise of Rhetoric and Its Intersections with Contemporary Critical Thought.* Polemics Series. Boulder, Colo.: Westview, 1998.

Vos, Johan S. "'To Make the Weaker Argument Defeat the Stronger': Sophistical Argumentation in Paul's Letter to the Romans." In *Rhetorical Argumentation in Biblical Texts,* edited by Anders Eriksson, Thomas H. Olbricht, and Walter Übelacker, 217–31. Harrisburg, Pa.: Trinity Press International, 2002.

Weiss, Johannes. "Beiträge zur Paulinischen Rhetorik." In *Theologische Studien Herrn Wirkl. Oberkonsistorialrath Professor D. Bernhard Weiss zu seinem 70. Geburtstage dargebracht,* ed. Bernhard Weiss and Caspar René Gregory, 165–247. Göttingen: Vandenhoeck & Ruprecht, 1897.

Winter, Bruce W. *Philo and Paul among the Sophists: Alexandrian and Corinthian Responses to a Julio-Claudian Movement.* 2nd ed. Grand Rapids, Mich.: Eerdmans, 2002.

SEVEN

Paul's Notion of *Dunamis:* Between the Possible and the Impossible

RICHARD KEARNEY

Paul's writings on divine *dunamis* draw from the biblical message that what is impossible for us is possible for God. In various letters to the Corinthians and Romans, Paul invokes the transformative character of the possibilizing power of the Spirit (*dunamis pneumatos*). The radical nature of this message, I submit, lies in reversing the ontological *dunamis* of power in favor of an eschatological *dunamis* of possibility. This reversal is expressed in Paul's startling claim in 2 Corinthians 12:9 that "strength accomplishes itself in weakness." The *dunamis* announced by Christianity inverts, says Paul, the logic of worldly dominion and empire by liberating and redeeming the "least of creatures" (*elachistos*). "I came among you in weakness," as Paul says in 1 Corinthians 2:4, "in fear and great trembling, and what I spoke and proclaimed was not meant to convince by philosophical argument but to demonstrate the convincing power of the Spirit [*pneuma tes dunameos*], so that your faith should depend not on human wisdom but on the power of God [*dunamis theou*]." As Gerhard Kittel suggests in the *Dictionary of the New Testament,* this power of God is to be understood as the "divine possible" which "expresses itself as the support or gift of the Spirit which manifests itself in the *personal* rapport between Christ and man . . . accessible through faith."[1]

Paul construes this *dunamis* accordingly as a divine call to become children of God. He sees it as ushering in a new concept of natality and filiality which understands progeny as eschatological rather than merely biological or tribal, as procreation from the future rather than causal generation from the past. As such, it points beyond divisions between Jew and gentile, Greek and non-Greek, Athens and Jerusalem to a new universal kingdom which includes each human creature as a son or daughter of the returning God. No longer mere offspring of archaic ancestors or demi-gods, the faithful are now invited to become descendants of a future still to come, strangers reborn as neighbors in the Word, adopted children of the *deus adventurus*—the God of the Possible.[2]

The Messianic Possible

The Pauline notion of messianic possibility is prefigured in several scriptural passages. In Mark 10, for example, we are told that while entry to God's kingdom seems impossible for humans, all things are made possible by God: "For humans it is impossible but not for God; because for God everything is possible" (*panta gar dunata para to theo*) (Mk 10:27). In a similar vein, we are told in St. John's prologue that our ability to become sons of God in the kingdom is made possible by Christ: "Light shone in darkness and to all who received it was given the possibility (*dunamis*) to become sons of God." The term *dunamis* is crucial and can be translated either as power or possibility—a semantic ambivalence to which we shall return below. But perhaps the most dramatic instance of the term is found in the Annunciation scene where Mary is told by the angel that the *dunamis* of God will overshadow her and she will bear the son of God, "for nothing is impossible [*a-dunaton*] with God" (Lk 1).

In all these examples, divinity—as Father, Son, or Spirit—is described as a possibilizing of divine love in the order of human history where it would otherwise have been impossible. The divine reveals itself here as the possibility of the kingdom or as the *impossibility of impossibility*. This is a *deus capax* who in turn calls out to the *homo capax* of history in order to be made flesh, again and again—each moment we confront the face of the other, welcome the stranger, open ourselves to the incoming of the infinite in and through the finite here and now. A capacitating God who is capable of all things cannot actually be or become incarnate until we say yes.

Paul is clearly inspired by the early Christian idioms of eschatological promise. These figures almost invariably refer to a God of "small things," to borrow from the wonderful title of Arundhati Roy's novel. Not only do we have the association of the kingdom with the vulnerable openness and trust of little children, as in the Matthew 10 passage cited above, but we also have the images of the yeast in the flour (Lk 13), the tiny pearl of invaluable price (Mt 13), and perhaps most suggestive of all, the mustard seed (Mk 4)—a minuscule grain that blooms and flourishes into a capacious tree. The kingdom of God, this last text tells us, is "like a mustard seed that, when it is sown in the ground, is the smallest of all the seeds on the earth. But once it is sown, it springs up and becomes the largest of plants and puts forth large branches, so that the birds of the sky can dwell in its shade."

I am tempted to read Paul's eschatological reading of *dunamis*—as the last, least, or littlest of things—as a *micro-eschatology* to the extent that it resists the standard macro-eschatology of the kingdom as emblem of sovereignty, omnipotence, and ecclesiastical triumph. Crucial here are the frequent references in the Gospel accounts to the judgment of the kingdom being related to how we respond in history, here and now, to the "least of these" (*elachistos*) (e.g., Mt 25:40). The loving renunciation of absolute power by Christ's emptying of the Godhead (*kenosis*) to assume the most vulnerable form of humanity (a naked infant repudiated by the world) is echoed by the eschatological reminder that it is easier for the defenseless and powerless to enter the kingdom than the rich and mighty. And I think it is telling—as Dostoyevsky reminds us in the Grand Inquisitor episode of the *Brothers Karamazov*—that the greatest temptation Christ must overcome, after his forty days in the desert, is the will to become master and possessor of the universe. This is a temptation he faces again and again right up to his transfiguration on Mount Tabor when his disciples want to apotheosize and crown him by building a cult temple there on the mountain (Lk 9). Instead, Christ proceeds to a second kenotic act of giving, refusing the short route to immediate triumph and embracing the *via crucis* that demonstrates what it means for the seed to die before it is reborn as a flowering tree which hosts all living creatures. As king, he enters Jerusalem not with conquering armies but "seated upon an ass's colt" (John 12). He upturns the inherited hierarchies of force, fulfilling Isaiah's prophecy that he would bring justice to the world, not by "shouting aloud in the street" but as a "bruised reed that shall not break, a smoldering wick that shall not quench" (Isa 42:1–4).

But in addition to these *spatial* metaphors of the kingdom exemplified by little things—yeast, a mustard seed, a pearl, a reed, an infant, the "least of these"—a hermeneutic poetics of the kingdom might also look to the *temporal* figures of eschatology which Paul's notion of messianic time foregrounds. These invariably take the form of a certain *achronicity*. I am thinking here of the numerous references to the fact that even though the kingdom has *already come*—and is incarnate *here and now* in the loving gestures of Christ and all those who give, or receive, a cup of water—it still always remains a possibility *yet to come*. This is what Emmanuel Levinas calls the "paradox of posterior anteriority," and it is cogently illustrated in an aphorism of Walter Benjamin which combines the spatial figure of the portal with the eschatological figure of futurity: "This future does not correspond to homogeneous empty time; because at the heart of every moment of the future is contained the little door through which the Messiah may enter."[3]

As "eternal," the kingdom transcends all chronologies of time. Christ indicates this when he affirms that "before Abraham was, I am" (John 8:58); and again when he promises a second coming when he will return again. In short, the kingdom is both (1) *already* there as historical *possibility* and (2) *not yet* there as historically realized kingdom "come on earth." This is why we choose to translate the canonical theophany of God to Moses on Mount Sinai (*esher ayeh esher*) not only as "I am who am" (*ego sum qui sum*) but also as "I am who may be." God is saying something like this: I will show up as promised but I cannot *be* in time and history, I cannot become fully *embodied* in the flesh of the world, unless you show up—unless you answer my call "where are you?" with the response "here I am." I am the possibility of making the impossible possible in history, but you are the ones to realize it!

Aristotle and Aquinas

What kind of possibility is Paul speaking of exactly when he talks about the *dunamis theou*? It clearly takes its primary inspiration from Jerusalem. But is there a sense in which it might, contrary to received wisdom, also be inspired by Athens?

Aristotle outlines two different kinds of *dunamis* in the *De Anima*—generic and effective. An example of generic *dunamis* is the potentiality of a child to grow up and acquire the skill of a musician or mathematician. By contrast, effective *dunamis* refers to the potentiality of an adult who has acquired such skills to exercise them or not. In the first instance, the act of realizing the potency means abolishing and passing beyond *dunamis,* whereas in the second it means conserving (*soteria*) the potency in and through its actualization, as something of a gift of potentiality to itself (*epidosis eis heauto*). (We shall return to this distinction in the discussion of Agamben's reading of Paul below.) Whereas the standard metaphysical reading of *dunamis* talks of a potency which realizes and abolishes itself as act, the idea of effective *dunamis* is one which survives the passage into act and therefore sustains the moment of actualization within the larger horizon of possibilities—the possibility to play or not to play music, to continue playing or cease playing, and so on. (I suspect that Nicholas of Cusa has something quite similar, if more explicitly theological, in mind when he suggests that the highest name for God is *Possest,* that is, the coexisting and combining of both *posse* and *esse.* In this manner divinity may be rethought as being *all that it is able to be.* We will return to this intriguing idea in the conclusion.)

Paul's reading of divine *dunamis* is more in line with this second sense, whereas most Christian readings of Aristotle focus on the former understanding of potency as a lesser and ultimately inferior state than act. Nowhere is this more obvious than in Aquinas, who defines God as pure act without possibility of any kind. In the first chapter of the *Summa Theologia,* entitled "What God Is Not," Thomas offers some of the most influential and persuasive arguments against the idea of divine *potentiality* or *posse.* He argues that "the starting point for all existence must be wholly real and not potential in any way" (*esse est id quod est primum ens esse in actu et nullo modo in potentia;* I.3.1). Aquinas rejects the idea that God could be material, or "matter under a certain form," for matter is defined by its potentiality to take on forms, while God is wholly realized (I.3.2). God, he claims, is the absolute, underived, immaterial form of pure activity. "Deus est actus purus non habens aliquid de potentialitate." Or again, "Impossible est igitur quod in Deo sit aliquid in potentia" (I.3.2).

In the second chapter of the *Summa,* Aquinas elaborates on this line of thinking in a section entitled "God Acts." Here he distinguishes between "active power," namely, the ability to act upon another, and "passive potentiality" or the "ability to be acted upon by another" (II.25.1). In this strict division of active and passive, God emerges as an omnipotency of pure act—impassive and invulnerable to all that is other than himself, human or otherwise. God is the *ipsum esse subsistens.* Pure agency without any potency whatsoever (*ergo agens primum, quod est Deus, est absque potentia*). Divinity is the thought that thinks itself. The cause that causes itself. The love that loves itself. The power that powers itself. Thomas's reasoning goes like this: "Active power is not contrasted with actuality but depends on it; things act only if actualized. But passive potentiality contrasts with actuality; things are acted upon only in the respects in which they are not yet actualized but potential. God then cannot have potentialities but must have active power. In God power and action are the same and both are his substance and existence" (II.25.1). To say that God is at once both act and potency (as Cusanus would do) is contradictory for Aquinas. And God cannot be in contradiction with himself. Thomas concludes by saying that "God is said to be all-powerful in the sense that he can do whatever can be done" (II.25.3). So what we have is a God that is pure *esse* with no need of *posse.* Pure power without the slightest trace of potentiality.

The unequivocal exclusion of possibility from God is based accordingly on four main grounds: (1) God is immaterial; (2) God is impassive; (3) God is non-contradictory; and (4) God is omnipotent.[4] To attribute possibility to the divine absolute would violate these four principles.

In short, the Pauline reading of *dunamis* presented above is clearly different from Aquinas's understanding of *potentia* in the *Summa* and in *De Potentia Dei.*

Badiou: Paul as Militant Subject

My reading of Pauline *dunamis* in terms of micro-eschatology is informed by an ongoing conversation with a number of recent thinkers who have stressed the vulnerability and powerlessness of the divine, for example, Stanislas Breton's reflections on the meontological mystery of the crucified Christ as *germen nihili,* Derrida's notion of a divine *désir au-dela du désir,* Caputo's weak God, and of course Levinas's God as trace and nudity of the stranger. These all derive, in their different ways, from certain debates within the phenomenology of religion (including its deconstructive guises). And in this respect I have also been influenced, as I acknowledge in *The God Who May Be* and elsewhere, by earlier phenomenologies of the possible found in Husserl and Heidegger. In this section, I wish to extend this conversation to two philosophers who have published what might be termed postmodern readings of Paul in a curiously a-theological and a-phenomenological style. I believe that both these thinkers—Badiou and Agamben—lend support to our own eschatological reading of Pauline *dunamis* while stopping short at some crucial points.

In *Saint Paul: The Foundation of Universalism,* Badiou highlights the revolutionary implications of Paul's power of weakness as it is pitted against the power of this world, namely, the power of empire and dominion. His reading is essentially political—with a certain psychoanalytic dash. Badiou argues that Christian resurrection is above all a subjective possibility that subverts the standard norms of history:

> The Resurrection is not, in Paul's own eyes, of the order of fact, falsifiable or demonstrable. It is pure event, opening of an epoch, transformation of the relations between the possible and the impossible. For the interest of Christ's resurrection does not lie in itself, as it would in the case of a particular, or miraculous, fact. Its genuine meaning is that it testifies to the possible victory over death, a death that Paul envisages . . . not in terms of facticity, but in terms of subjective disposition. Whence the necessity of constantly

linking resurrection to *our* resurrection, of proceeding from singularity to
universality and vice versa: "If the dead do not resurrect, Christ is not resurrected either. And if Christ is not resurrected, your faith is in vain" (1 Cor.
I, 15–16). In contrast to the *fact,* the *event* is measurable only in accordance
with the universal multiplicity whose possibility it prescribes. It is in this
sense that it is grace, and not history.[5]

For Paul the basic wager of Christian *dunamis* is the good news that it is
now *possible* to overcome the *impossible*—to defy what Heidegger would
call the impossibility of possibility, namely *death.* Paul's discourse is one of
fidelity to the "possibility opened by the event," that is, to the possibility of
the impossible: victory over death.[6] This faith transgresses and transcends
knowledge as such, for we are dealing here with an unheard-of possibility,
what Badiou following Kierkegaard calls a "subjective possibility," without
logical proof, conceptual consistency, or empirical verification. Unlike the
philosopher, the advocate of the Resurrection announces a radically novel
discourse breaking with all inherited customs and categories. And this is
why Paul declares that with the advent of the possibility of the resurrection,
"knowledge disappears" (1 Cor 13:8).

Based on this line of thinking, Paul concludes that the ultimate *dunamis*
of God is the power of the powerless, or, as he puts it, the strength of weakness: "For the foolishness of God is wiser than men and the weakness of God
is stronger than men" (1 Cor 1:17–28). Thus the message of Christ crucified
(and resurrected) represents both a stumbling block (*skandalon*) to the legal-
ism of Jerusalem and a folly (*moria*) to the reason of Athens. But "to those
who are called, both Jews and Greeks, [it represents] Christ the power of God
(*theou dunamin?*)" (1 Cor 1:17–28). Why? According to what logic? According
to the logic of the eschatological *posse:* For "God chose the foolish things of
the world to confound the wise, and God chose the weak things of the world
to confound the strong: God chose what is base and despised in the world,
and even things that are not (*ta me onta*), to bring to naught things that are
(*ta onta*), so that one might glorify himself in his presence."[7]

So what is this power (*dunamis*) of the cross that Paul speaks of? It is the
surplus of Spirit which defies the laws of rational understanding, represented
by the Greek philosophical *logos.* Invoking the language of Lacanian psychoanalysis, Badiou interprets this Christ-event in terms of the real which
cuts across the law of language. And in the spirit of Heidegger he claims
that this event exceeds the old metaphysics of being. In fact, Badiou holds that
the Pauline profession of Christian *dunamis* amounts to an antiphilosophy

of radical subjectivity and decision which will be taken up later by certain existentialists. "That the Christ-event causes non-beings rather than beings to arise as attesting to God; that it consists in the abolition of what all previous discourses held as existing, or being, gives a measure of the ontological subversion to which Paul's antiphilosophy invites the declarant or militant. It is through the invention of a language wherein folly, scandal and weakness supplant knowing reason, order and power, and wherein non-being is the only legitimizable affirmation of being, that Christian discourse is articulated."[8]

Christ is read by Badiou, accordingly, as a radically new beginning which suspends the Law of the Father and invites us to a universal becoming-son. Through this event we are freed from slavery into filial equality. And it is this same logic which surfaces even more forcefully in 2 Corinthians 12:9–11: "The Lord said to me: 'My grace is sufficient for you, for my strength is made perfect in weakness.' I will all the more gladly glory in my weakness, that the power of Christ (*dunamis tou christou*) may rest upon me . . . for when I am weak, then I am strong."

There is, of course, a profound paradox here: strength in weakness, power in powerlessness, glory in folly, meekness, and non-being. But that is precisely Paul's point. And rather than retreat into mystical silence before the unfathomable, unutterable, unimaginable enigma, Paul resolves to speak out, to invent a new discourse of the naked event, of radical beginning. He determines to declare the irreducible aporia that "power is fulfilled in weakness itself."[9] Again, his is no ordinary *dunamis*—caught in the ontology of potency and act—but an unprecedented *dunamis* that goes beyond all metaphysical and historical categories of possible-impossible to declare another kind of power altogether: "For the weapons of our warfare are not carnal," Paul hastens to remind us, "but they have divine power to pull down strongholds" (2 Cor 10:4–5). Interestingly, Badiou considers these aporias and paradoxes to be completely irreducible to hermeneutic mediation of any kind.

For all the evangelical rhetoric, however, Badiou is more interested in making a militant structural subject out of Paul than an apostle of divine *caritas*. If Badiou were a believer—which he does not profess to be—it would be more in the spirit of Cromwell than St. Francis. The truth of Christ is converted into what he calls the fable of Christianity. Revelation becomes the blind rupture of the event and the subjective decision that it provokes. And law is equally so sacrificed. So Badiou's Paul, we might say, supersedes both the *logos* of the Greeks and the law of the Jews. He steers an uncharted path beyond Athens and Jerusalem. Badiou is, it seems, an atheist of event rather than a theist of advent. More militant than mystic. More a follower of Lacan and Lenin than of Eckhart or Eriugena.

Agamben: On Potentiality

In his commentary on Paul's letter to the Romans, entitled *The Time That Remains,* Giorgio Agamben offers a more arcane, if equally postmodern reading of Pauline *dunamis.* Taking his cue from Paul's claim that strength accomplishes itself in weakness (*dunamis en astheneia teleitai;* 2 Cor 12:9), Agamben interprets the exigency of messianic potentiality in terms of what he calls impotentiality.[10] Where Leibniz, as well as the metaphysical tradition generally, construed possibility as something that demanded to be realized, Agamben reverses the formula and sees existing realities as exigencies to become possible! Relating this to the Christian notion of salvation, he sees Paul's preference for what is not (*ta me onta*) over what is (*ta onta*) as a way of overcoming traditional notions of human power and potency in favor of a redemption of our sinful being—an impotentiality which becomes miraculously possible in and through the *dunamis* of God, that is, through the powerless power of Christ's resurrection. This co-existence of impotentiality with potentiality is, he argues, precisely what characterizes the paradox of messianic time.[11] Just as the forgotten demands to be unforgettable, so too the fallen, sinful, finite time of this world demands to be redeemable. Impotentiality demands the potentiality (*dunamis*) of Spirit and is indispensably precontained within it.[12]

Agamben stresses that what mattered for Paul was less the historical Jesus of flesh and blood than the Messiah, "who in terms of the spirit and of holiness was designated Son of God in *dunamis* by resurrection from the dead" (Rom 1:3–4). This is a *dunamis* which unrealizes the realized and realizes the unrealized. This is a "potentiality" which is accomplished and actualized not as force (*ergon*) but as weakness (*astheneia*). This messianic inversion of the traditional metaphysical relationship between potency and act—*dunamis en astheneia teleitai*/when I am weak then I am strong (2 Cor 12:19–20)—is, for Agamben, the kernel of Paul's revolutionary reading of *dunamis.*[13]

But what is the *telos* of this potency which accomplishes itself as weakness? Agamben asks this question in relation to the passage about the word of faith in Romans 10:9–10 as a "potentiality which exists as potentiality" (*puissance qui existe comme puissance*). Guided by Origen, Agamben returns here to a much-neglected Aristotelian insight that impotentiality (*adunamis*) or privation (*steresis*) is, in spite of all, a species of potentiality. As we already had occasion to mention, there are two passages in the *Metaphysics*—1019b, 9–10 and 1046a, 32—where Aristotle claims that potentiality and impotentiality can *co-exist* in one and the same person or thing. He spells this out in the *De Anima* (417a, 21), as also noted, when he distinguishes between generic and effective *dunamis*. In this latter case of effective *dunamis,* according to Agamben, the potentiality of the Word is preserved in the act of realization alongside its impotentiality.

Origen had used this differentiation between generic and effective *dunamis* to distinguish between the virtual proximity of the divine Word to each creature, and the effective existence and expression of this word through the mouth of the believer who has received this Word and professed the resurrection of the dead.[14] The word of messianic faith thus presents itself as the effective experience of the pure potentiality of saying, which goes beyond all functions of denotation or proof. And it is in this sense that the goal of messianic potentiality (*dunamis*) finds its strength (*dunamis*) in weakness. Such a profession of faith, in other words, is not about formulating true propositions about God and the world nor about prescribing juridical principles.

> Believing in Christ the Messiah is not about believing something about him (*legein ti kata tinos*) . . . The potentiality of saying (*puissance de dire*) is messianic and weak in that it remains close to the word, exceeding not only every spoken thing, but equally the very act of saying, the performative power of language. It is the remainder of potency which does not exhaust itself in actualization, but is each time conserved and preserved in its acts. If this remaindered or remaindering potency is in this sense weak, if it cannot be accumulated into a knowledge or dogma, nor impose itself as a law (*droit*), it is neither passive nor inert: on the contrary, it operates precisely by virtue of its very weakness, in *rendering the world of the law inoperative,* in de-creating and deposing the conditions of fact and law, which means becoming capable of their liberal usage. *Katargein* and *Chresthai* comprise the act of a potency which accomplishes itself in weakness. But the fact that this potency finds its very *telos* in its weakness does not mean that it remains simply suspended in infinite deferral; on the contrary, returning onto itself, it accomplishes and deactivates the very excess of signification in every signified, the "falling silent of languages" (I Cor 13, 8); and it bears witness accordingly to what, non-expressed and non-signified, remains forever within the close usage of the word.[15]

The potential not to be is, for Agamben, the secret of the Aristotelian doctrine of potentiality, as later radicalized by Paul in the light of revelation. Agamben makes much of Aristotle's claim in the *Metaphysics* (1050b, 10) that what is "potential can both be and not be." This potential not to be transforms every potentiality in itself into an impotentiality, says Agamben. Something cannot be capable of something else if it is not also and at the same time capable of its own incapacity. In *On Potentiality*, Agamben interprets this to mean that in its originary structure, potentiality (*dunamis*) is the potential to be in relation to its own incapacity.[16] Agamben offers this reading: "If a potential to not-be originally belongs to all potentiality, then there is truly potentiality only where the potential to not-be does not lag behind actuality but passes fully into it *as such*."[17] Actuality may thus be seen as nothing other than the full realization of the potential not to be.[18]

Actuality is thus indistinguishable from potentiality—in a manner similar to Cusanus's *possest*—to the extent that it preserves and redeems potentiality. For if "all potentiality is originally impotentiality, and if actuality is a conservation of potentiality itself, then it follows that actuality is nothing else than a potentiality to a second degree, a potentiality that, in Aristotle's phrase, 'is the gift of the self to itself.'"[19] In the final analysis, therefore, actuality turns out to be simply a potential-not-to-be turned back on itself in an act of double negation, namely, capable of *not* not being—and thereby granting the existence of what is actual. Pure potentiality and pure actuality thus become two faces of the same thing—and what is possible and what is real can no longer be clearly distinguished. It is only because language is capable of not saying that it is truly sayable; so that to speak is, in fact, the capacity to suspend one's own incapacity or impotentiality to speak. Just as it is only because our memory can forget that we can truly remember. Likewise the realization of the kingdom, as the promise of divine *dunamis,* is nothing other than the self-suspension of its own potentiality to not-be. This, one could argue, is a sure guarantee against the omnipotent theodicy of metaphysicians such as Hegel and Leibniz.

The coming community of the kingdom, announced by Paul in specifically eschatological and messianic terms, reveals itself accordingly as pure potentiality. For Paul messianic potentiality does not exhaust itself in its *ergon,* but remains capacitating (*puissante*) under the guise of weakness. Commenting on Paul's statement that "God chose the weak things of the world to confound the strong" (1 Cor 1:27), Agamben concludes that "Messianic *dunamis* is in this sense constitutionally 'weak'—and it is precisely through its weakness that it exercises its effects."[20]

But before signing off on this subject, Agamben identifies additional and quite intriguing instances of messianic inversion, namely, the fact that the messianic *dunamis* renders the law (*nomos*) and its works inoperative without annulling them. The messianic restores acts to their potency or non-operativeness not to destroy them but to elevate them to their higher purpose. This is why Paul can say at one and the same time that the Messiah (1) deactivates (*katargese*) every power and authority (1 Cor 15:24), and (2) constitutes the *telos* of the law (Rom 10:4). It is only by transmuting the law from actuality to a renewed sense of potentiality that it can represent the *telos* of the law as both end and accomplishment. For the Messiah is, Paul tells us, the fulfillment of the deactivated (*telos tou katargoumenou*), the promise to accomplish what is liberated from act back into potency. That is what Paul means, according to Agamben, when he declares in Romans 3:31: "Are we saying that the law has been made pointless (*katargoumen*) by faith? Not at all: we are saying that the law has been placed on its true footing." To re-potentialize the *energeia* of law is not to deny it but to reestablish it in view of its true fulfillment. Or as John Chrysostom put it, the Pauline sense of deactivation (*katargesis*) should not be understood as a destruction but as a "growth and gift towards what is better," as an "accomplishment (*plerosis*) and an addition towards the best (*pros to meizon epidosis*)."[21] In short, Paul's notion of messianic *katargesis* should be construed less as abolition *tout court* than as a catalyst of fulfillment in a process of active capacitating.

This marks a clear departure from Badiou's reading of Pauline universalism as a repudiation of the politics of difference which, according to Badiou, infects the universal with laws, signs, and particularities (i.e., the legacy of Jerusalem). For Agamben, by contrast, Paul's notion of *katargesis* is less about an "indifference to differences" (Badiou's position) than an "indistinction of differences" that serves to respect the notions of law and wisdom which Christ supersedes by re-capacitating them in their Messianic *dunamis*. In sum, the Pauline Christ does not dispense with law and wisdom but restores them to their pure potentiality. It reveals the *logos* as say*able* before it is said, express*ible* before it is expressed, communic*able* before it is communicated. It exposes the hidden "to be able" at the heart of reality. Paul's Messiah thus becomes the "to be capable" par excellence.

Agamben's analysis opens many intriguing perspectives on Paul's notion of *dunamis*. He revivifies these oft-quoted passages from Romans and Corinthians and restores, in accord with my own modest efforts, the power-possibility paradox of Pauline eschatology at the center of contemporary thinking about religion. But I have three main reservations.

First, I feel that his emphasis on deficit terms like "impotentiality," "deactivation," and "non-signifiability" lends a certain negativity and pessimism to his conclusions, not altogether different from the apocalyptic tone found in certain postmodern thinkers who privilege the impossible over the possible. Moreover, his seeming preference for idioms of apocalypse, negation, and privation serves to deflect Pauline *dunamis* from the existing paths of history and reconciliation in favor of alternative options of sublime rupture. This theory of the impotential leads in Agamben's other writings to an ethics and politics of what he calls "bare life," which while admirably engaged with the "least of these," seems to embrace a scenario of impossible citizenship and disinheritance—bordering at times on a morbid obsession with the dehumanized and disenfranchised. I have some problems with this ethics of the abject, though I admit I may be missing something here. One almost longs for more of Badiou's militant universalism!

Second, it is not clear (at least to me) from Agamben's analysis that the question of atheism or theism actually matters. For someone who dwells at such length on the importance for Paul of *commitment* to the news of the resurrection, the author himself seems remarkably non-committed. If I put the hermeneutic question to Agamben's text—*d'ou parlez-vous?*—I am not certain I hear a response. But again, maybe I need to be attuned to a finer acoustic.

Third, and perhaps not unrelated, it is not clear to me what kind of human subject we are talking about in Agamben's messianic atheology. In marked contrast to Badiou's militant revolutionary of the kingdom, and my own notion of an ethically committed person/persona, Agamben's messianic witness often seems so destitute and passive as to be utterly inactive and impotent. But in spite of these reservations, what I share with both Badiou and Agamben is a commitment to a new understanding of the eschatological relationship between power and possibility latent within Paul's notion of *dunamis*.

Conclusion: Toward a Micro-Eschatology of the Possible

I conclude by looking at a number of religious thinkers down through the centuries who have developed notion of "possibility" in line with the Pauline legacy. Unlike metaphysical thinkers who presuppose an ontological priority of actuality over possibility, these more poetic or mystical minds reverse the traditional priority and point to a new category of possibility—divine possibility—*beyond* the traditional opposition between the possible and the impossible.

Let me begin with the intriguing maxim of Angelus Silesius: "God is possible as the more than impossible." Here Silesius—a German mystical thinker often cited by Heidegger and Derrida—points toward an eschatological notion of possibility which might be said to transcend the three conventional concepts of the possible: (1) as an epistemological category of modal

logic, along with necessity and actuality (Kant); (2) as a substantialist category of *potentia* lacking its fulfillment as *actus* (mainstream Aristotle and
the scholastics); and (3) as a rationalist category of *possibilitas* conceived as a
representation of the mind (Leibniz and the idealists). All such categories fall
within the old metaphysical dualism of possibility versus impossibility. But
Silesius intimates a new role for the possible as a ludic and liberal outpouring
of divine play: "God is possible as the more than impossible. . . . God plays
with Creation/All that is play that the deity gives itself It has imagined the
creature for its pleasure." Creation here is depicted as an endless giving of
possibility which calls us toward the kingdom.

I think the early medieval Jewish commentator, Rashi, also had something
like this in mind when he interpreted Isaiah's God calling to his creatures, "I
cannot be God unless you are my witnesses." He takes this to mean, "I am the
God who will be whenever you bear witness to love and justice in the world."[22]
Holocaust victim Etty Hillesum was gesturing toward a similar notion when,
just weeks before her death in a concentration camp, she wrote, "You God
cannot help us but we must help you and defend your dwelling place inside
us to the last."[23] Both Rashi and Hillesum were witnessing to the *dunamis* of
God as *the power of the powerless*. This clearly is not the imperial power of a
sovereign; it is a dynamic call to love that possibilizes and enables humans
to transform their world by giving itself to the least of these, by empathizing
with the disinherited and the dispossessed, by refusing the path of might and
violence, by transfiguring the mustard seed into the kingdom, each moment
at a time, one act after an other, each step of the way. This is the path heralded
by the Pauline God of "nothings and nobodies" (*ta me onta*) excluded from
the triumphal pre-eminence of totality (*ta onta*)—a kenotic, self-emptying,
crucified God whose weakness is stronger than human strength (1 Cor 1:25). It
signals the option for the poor, for non-violent resistance and revolution taken
by peacemakers and dissenting "holy fools" from ancient to modern times. It
is the message of suffering rather than doing evil, of loving one's adversaries,
of no enemies, of soul force (*satyagraha*). One thinks of a long heritage rang-
ing from Isaiah, Jesus, Siddartha, and Socrates to such contemporary figures
as Gandhi, Vaclav Havel, Dorothy Day, Jean Vanier, Ernesto Cardinal, Thich
Nhat Hahn, and Martin Luther King, among others. The God witnessed here
goes beyond the will to power.

Nicholas of Cusa offers some radical insights into this eschatological
God when he declares that "God alone is all he is able to be" (*Trialogus de
Possest*).[24] Unlike the God of metaphysical omnipotence, underlying the per-
verse logic of theodicy which seeks to justify evil as part of the divine will,

this notion of God as an "abling to be" (*posse* or *possest*) points in a radically different direction. Let us pause for a moment to unpack the phrase, "God is all he is able to be." Since God is all good, God is not able to be non-good, that is, non-God—defect or evil. In other words, God is *not* omnipotent in the traditional metaphysical sense understood by Leibniz and Hegel. The Divine is not some being able to be all good *and* evil things. That is why God could not help Etty Hillesum and other victims of evil. God is not responsible for evil. And Hillesum understood this all too well when she turned the old hierarchies on their head and declared that it is *we* who must help God to be God.

Was Hillesum not in fact subscribing here to a long—if often neglected— biblical heritage? After all, if Elijah had not heard the still small voice of God in his cave, we would never have received the wisdom of his prophecy. If a young woman from Nazareth had said no to the angel of the Annunciation, the Word would not have become flesh. If certain fishermen, tax collectors, and prostitutes had not heard the call to follow the Son of Man, there would have been no Son of God—and no gospel witness. So too, if Hillesum and others like her had not let God be God by defending the divine dwelling place of *caritas* within them, even in those most hellish moments of Holocaust horror, there would have been no measure of love—albeit as tiny as the mustard seed—to defy the hate of the Gestapo. For if God's loving is indeed unconditional, the realization of that loving *posse* in this world is conditional upon our response. If we are waiting for God, God is waiting for us. Waiting for us to say yes, to hear the call and to act, to bear witness, to answer the *posse* with *esse,* to make the word flesh—even in the darkest moments.

I think Dionysius the Areopagite could be said to add to our understanding of this great enigma when he speaks, in book 7 of the *Divine Names,* of a "possibility beyond being" (*hyperousias dunameos*) which engenders our desire to live more abundantly and seek the good. "Being itself," he writes, "only has the possibility to be from the possibility beyond being." And he adds that it is "from the infinitely good posse (*dunamis*) of what it sends to them (that) they have received their power (*dunamis*)."[25] I am tempted to relate this notion of an infinitely good possibilizing of God to another extraordinary passage in the *Divine Names*—this time book 9, section 3—where Dionysius writes of the God of little things, "God is said to be small as leaving every mass and distance behind and proceeding unhindered through all. Indeed the small is the cause of all the elements, for you will find none of these that have not participated in the form of smallness. Thus, smallness is to be interpreted with respect to God as its wandering and operating in all and through all without hindrance 'penetrating down to the division of the soul, spirit, joint and marrow', and discerning thoughts and 'intentions of the heart', and indeed of all beings. 'For there is no creation which is invisible to its face' (Heb 4, 12). This smallness is without quantity, without quality, without restraint, unlimited, undefined, and all embracing although it is unembraced."[26] Is this extraordinary passage by Dionysius not a passionate invitation to embrace a micro-theology of the kingdom? Is it not a solicitation to embrace an eschatology of little things—mustard seeds, grains of yeast, tiny pearls, cups of water, infinitesimal everyday acts of love and witness? It appears so.

Moreover, I think it is just this kind of micro-theology that Gerard Manley Hopkins had in mind when he recorded God's grace in small and scattered epiphanies of the quotidian, for example, God's "pied beauty" being manifest in various "dappled things," from "finches wings" and "rose-moles all in stipple upon trout that swim" to "all things counter, original, spare, strange;/Whatever is fickle, freckled—who knows how?" ("Pied Beauty"). For Hopkins, it is not the mighty and triumphant Monarch that epitomizes the pearl of the kingdom ("immortal diamond") but, contrariwise, the court fool, the joker in the pack, the least and last of these. Here is Hopkins's take on the eschatological kingdom:

> In a flash, at a trumpet crash,
> I am all at once what Christ is, since he was what I am,
> And
> This Jack, Joke, poor potsherd, patch, matchwood,
> Immortal diamond,
> Is immortal diamond.

Hopkins's Deity is one of transfiguration rather than coercion, of *posse* rather than power, of little rather than large things.[27] I suspect Paul might have cited this poem in one of his letters to the Corinthians or Romans had he had the opportunity to read it.

Notes

1. Cited and commented in Richard Kearney, *Poétique du Possible* (Paris: Beauchesne, 1984).
2. See the chapter entitled "Possibilizing God" in Kearney, *God Who May Be* (Bloomington: Indiana University Press, 2001), 80f.
3. Walter Benjamin, "Theologico-Political Fragment" (1921), in *One Way Street*

(London: NLB, 1979), 155f.

4. These points are elaborated by Aquinas in greater detail in *Questiones Disputatae De Potentia Dei/On the Power of God* (Westminster, Md.: Newman, 1952). See especially Question 1, VII, "Is God Almighty?"

5. Alain Badiou, *Saint Paul: The Foundation of Universalism* (Stanford, Calif.: Stanford University Press, 2003), 45.

6. Badiou, *Saint Paul*, 45.

7. Badiou, *Saint Paul*, 45.

8. Badiou, *Saint Paul*, 47.

9. Badiou, *Saint Paul*, 52.

10. Giorgio Agamben, *The Time That Remains* (Stanford, Calif.: Stanford University Press, 2005). My own translations and paginations below are from the earlier French edition, *Le Temps qui Reste*, ed. Judith Revel (Paris: Bibliothèque Rivages, 2000), 65f.

11. "Celui qui se tient dans la vocation messianique . . . sait que, dans le temps messianique, le monde sauvé coincide exactement avec le monde perdu . . . il sait qu'il doit vivre réellement dans un monde sans Dieu et qu'il ne lui est en aucun cas permis de camoufler cet etre-sans-Dieu du monde, car le Dieu qui le sauve est le Dieu qui l'abandone . . . Le sujet messanique ne contemple pas le monde comme s'il était sauvé. Pour reprendre les mots de Benjamin, il ne contemple le salut que dans la mesure où il se perd dans ce qui ne peut etre sauvé. L'expérience de la *klesis* est aussi compliquée que cela; et demeurer dans l'appel est aussi difficile que cela" (*Le Temps qui Reste*, 72).

12. Agamben returns to this difficult but decisive paradox of *dunamis* in a later section of the book entitled *euaggelion* or "the announcement." The epistle to the Romans, he argues, is the impossibility of separating the Good News and its content. The declaration of the promise of salvation is identical with salvation itself. The announcement is thus inextricably linked with the response of faith (*pistis*). "The Gospel is the possibility (*dunamis*) of salvation for all those who believe (*Rm I, 16*). This definition seems to imply that the *euvaggelion*—as *dunamis*—potentiality . . . needs faith in order to be effective. Paul is well aware of the opposition—perfectly Greek and which plays at once on both the categories of language and of thought—between potency (*dunamis*) and act (*energeia*), and makes reference to it in several passages (*eph 3, 7; ph 3, 21*). What is more, Paul often places faith and *energeia, being-in-act*, beside each other: vis-à-vis potency, faith is '*energumene*' par excellence, the principle of actuality and enactment (Gal 5, 6 refers to faith that is actualized by love; Col. 1, 29: 'according to its *energeia*—of the Messiah—that which operates (*energoumene*) in my potency'). But this principle is not for Paul something external to the announcement; it is rather that which actualizes the potency (Gal 3,4: 'That which actualizes your potencies—*energon dunameis*—comes from the harkening of faith') and can therefore be presented as the content of the announcement (Gal 1, 23 . . .). That which is announced, it is faith which realizes the potency of the announcement itself. Faith is being in act, the *energeia* of the Gospel" (p. 145). Citing Paul's example of Abraham, Agamben goes on to observe the necessary connection between the promise and its realization. Abraham was someone fully convinced that the one who promised was equally capable of doing. Agamben concludes that "the announcement is the form that the promise takes in the contraction of messianic time" (p. 146).

13. On this Pauline notion of the "weakness of God," see John D. Caputo, *The Weakness of God* (Bloomington: Indiana University Press, 2006); and Joseph S. O'Leary, "The Empty Christ," in *Religious Pluralism and Christian Truth* (Edinburgh:

Edinburgh University Press, 1996).

14. Origen, *Commentarii in Epistulam ad Romanos;* cited in Agamben, *Le Temps,* 213.

15. Agamben, *Le Temps,* 213–14.

16. Agamben, *Potentialities* (Stanford, Calif.: Stanford University Press, 1999), 16.

17. Agamben, *Potentialities,* 17.

18. For potentiality to pass over into actuality it must set aside its own impotential to be. That is, it must suspend its potential not to be potential any longer. Therefore to set im-potentiality aside in this way is not to destroy it but to fulfill it, to "turn potentiality back upon itself in order to give itself to itself." Agamben, *Homo Sacer* (Stanford, Calif.: Stanford University Press, 1998), 46.

19. Agamben, *Potentialities,* 18.

20. Agamben, *Potentialities,* 155.

21. John Chrysostom, *On the Incomprehensibility of God;* cited in Agamben, *Potentialities,* 157–58.

22. Rashi, *The Torah: With Rashi's Commentary* (New York: Mesorah, 1997). It would be interesting to relate Rashi's rabbinical interpretation with Isaac Luria's Kabbalist reading of God in terms of a generous withholding or "withdrawal" (*zimzum*) which invites human creatures to subsequently retrieve and reanimate the fragments of the broken vessels of divine love which lie scattered like tiny seeds throughout the created universe. This reading, which exerted a deep influence on Hassidic thinkers as well as on philosophers like Simone Weil, seems to confirm our own account of God's refusal to impose himself on creation—as some kind of omnipotent fulfilled being (*Ipsum Esse subsistens*), Sufficient Reason or Supreme Cause (*ens causa sui*)—preferring instead to relate to humans in the realm of the possible rather than of the purely actual or necessary. I am grateful to my Boston College colleague, Marty Cohen, for bringing the insights of the Lurianic Kabbala to my attention. See Cohen, "Sarach's Harp," *Parabola,* Fall 1997.

23. Etty Hillesum, *An Interrupted Life* (New York: Owl, 1996), 176.

24. Nicholas of Cusa, *Trialogus de Possest* in *A Concise Introduction to the Philosophy of Nicholas of Cusa* (Minneapolis: University of Minnesota Press, 1980), 69. The original Latin reads: "Deus est omne id quod esse potest."

25. Pseudo-Dionysius the Areopagite, *The Divine Names and Mystical Theology,* trans. J. D. Jones (Milwaukee: Marquette University Press, 1980), 182. For a further exploration of the link between neo-Platonic negative theology and our micro-eschatology, see Stanislas Breton, *The Word and the Cross* (New York: Fordham University Press, 2002), 8–11, 49–50, 60–70, 80–91, 112–14. See in particular Breton's radical claim that we must give to God the being he has not, qua thirsting, kenotic, crucified stranger (121–22). The *dunamis* of God is here identified with the *germen nihili* or "power of nothing" that reveals itself as a double nothingness and powerlessness which liberates those oppressed by the power of *ta onta,* sowing the seed of non-being epitomized by the Beatitudes so that the eschatological tree of love and justice may flower and flourish (pp. 80–84; xxiv–xxvi) . For it is in and as a seed of non-being that, in Eckhart's resonant phrase, "God becomes verdant in all the honor of his being" (p. 80).

26. Pseudo-Dionysius, *Divine Names,* 188.

27. See the illuminating reading of Hopkins in Mark Patrick Hederman, *Anchoring the Altar: Christianity and the Work of Art* (Dublin: Veritas, 2002), 131f.

EIGHT

Concluding Roundtable: St. Paul among the Historians and the Systematizers

Linda Martín Alcoff: We have had an interesting but implicit conversation among our participants for the last two and a half days. Now we want to make that conversation more explicit and dialogical. I will start out with a couple of general topics and then Jack Caputo will begin with a direct question.

The overarching topic of this conference is the revival of Paul as an authority in contemporary political, moral, and philosophical debates. And into this debate have entered the historians, who have raised questions about the interpretations, and the theory of interpretation, which have grounded these various philosophers' uses of Paul. A lot of people here have apologized for not being philosophers and for just being historians and scholars of religion. I have to apologize for just being a philosopher and not a religion scholar. The historians, I think, have been very important in counseling us that the invocation of Paul by the philosophers as both a resource and an authority needs to be tempered by some interpretive humility. We need to acknowledge the incoherences of the text and we need to be more historically reflective in our interpretations. A traditional philosophical response to that would be to point out the different logics that operate in these different discourses of history and philosophy. The traditional philosophical position is to say, "What motivates a philosopher's use of any authoritative figure or textual tradition is not, ultimately, to understand that figure or textual tradition accurately or correctly but simply to use that figure or text to prompt a series of questions of normativity—questions like, What is the truth? What is the right? and What is the good?' But I think that what we've seen here is that this response of traditional philosophers can't work. The philosopher's invocation of Paul has to be held accountable to an interpretive plausibility, but even more than that it has to be held accountable rhetorically and politically. By invoking Paul as an authority we have to be responsible for everything that is being invoked there, all of the meanings that are being put into play. One of the principal issues in Paul that is being put into play by Žižek and Badiou is the issue of universalism—a revival of universalism—but the question has been what version of universalism. On one reading of the debate we could say that we have advocates of a substantive, concrete, and situated universalism pitted against the advocates of a more abstract, contentless—the subtracted—universalism. That's one way to see the debate. I think some people see it another way, as a debate between two alternative substantive universalisms: one that seeks to make everyone essentially the same through subtraction, the other one that tries to include everyone essentially the same through an addition. One that privileges the Christian tradition as the unique site, or the unique discursive tradition that can produce universal justice—that's the sort of supersessionist idea—and another that leaves open the possibility that there's more than one discursive tradition that can produce universal justice. I invoke here the concern with Eurocentrism. I think if our task is, as Professor Badiou says, to invent a new present, surely we need more than anything else to avoid reinvoking Eurocentric constructions of justice once again.

John D. Caputo: Following up on Linda's point, I would like to address a question to Professor Badiou, which goes back to the question that Dale Martin raised in his paper. If I understood Dale Martin, Paul is not arguing for a universality from which ethnicity has been subtracted. Paul is preaching a particular people of God, Israel, through whom God has found a way to save all people, so that Israel—not Babylonia and not Egypt—will become all in all. At the end of time, all people—that is the universalism—will be grafted onto the olive tree of Israel, of a particular people. So, Paul was not trying to find a new and homogeneous universality, but he sees himself poised at the beginning of the end time, in which Israel will be brought to completion. Dale Martin said one might even recast the old formula *extra ecclesiam nulla salus est* to say *extra Israel nulla salus est.* That seems to me a central point and I am interested in how you would respond to that?

Alain Badiou: The question for me is the relation between universalism and something like the burst, the appearing of universality. Because there is always something like newness, something like creation, in universality, only what is created, always in certain circumstances, can become universal. So the difficulty, the philosophical-conceptual difficulty, is to completely understand, first, that every new form of universality is born in one place, in some circumstances, in some determination; after that, the becoming of that particular creation is addressed to everybody. That is why the question of universality is not a grammatical one, is not a question of a logical framework, not a question of abstract universality, but is always a question of a process, a question of creation, of becoming in a spatial context. So, finally, in the case of Paul, I never have said that the circumstances are nothing in the development of universality, of Pauline universality. Certainly we have a sort of necessity of the place, Palestine, the Roman Empire, concrete conflicts, the religious situation, and so on. And the material of the choice made by Paul is completely embedded in a concrete place. The language is the language of Judaism, the metaphors are completely the metaphors of that sort of text, reflecting the disposition of the communities inside the Roman Empire, which is for Paul the totality of the world. So, we have the creation of Paul which is in complete relation with the historical, geographical, and political situation. After that, we have something like a transfiguration of all that in the creation of a new form of universality. It's not really something like a separation of all the circumstances, on one side, and the birth of universality on the other side. It's a process of transformation and, as always, transformation is also creation. But in that sort of creation we have to understand simultaneously the situation and the transformation of the situation. And so, my conception of universality is not at all an abstract one. On the contrary, universality is something which appears like the real, which is hidden in the concrete circumstances, which is also *in* the concrete circumstances. There is also in the Pauline gospel something which is like an address, an address to everybody. The question of subtraction is, finally, a question of address. Something universal is always something which finishes some difference. There is always a difference or some differences which, after the creation of something new—which is a universal—are not really differences like before. There are differences which become indifferent, and the becoming indifferent of some differences is exactly the process of the universalization of the situation. Finally, when Paul says that in the new truth there is neither Jew nor Greek, male nor female, it is not naturally and empirically constituted. Paul knows perfectly that there are Jews and Greeks and that the concrete world is made up of those sort of differences. He is only saying to us, to everybody, that in the element of the new creation, of the new truth, those sorts of differences, which exist, which are perfectly real, are indifferent, or become indifferent. So, it's a transformation of differences into something indifferent which is like a signal of a new universality.

Dale Martin: I find that helpful. I should clarify that what I am trying to do in my own paper is not to say that I felt that the picture drawn by Professor Badiou was not accurate because it was not historically sensitive enough, not historically accurate. I was responding to something that recurs, not in all philosophy but in a certain kind of philosophical tradition, in which a dualism of Judaism and Hellenism, or the Jew and the Greek, comes to stand for much larger ways of thinking. At certain points, the Jew and the Greek represent different ways of thinking. The point I was trying to raise in my paper was this. In my view, Paul's vision is not one of completely overcoming ethnicity for the sake of a nonethnic universal but the grafting of the gentiles into the stock of Israel. In a sense, Paul is making the ethnicity of Israel *the* universal ethnicity, which of course would be a contradiction in terms in the ancient world, because the very category of ethnicity in the ancient world is something in which humanity is split up. I urge us to think about what it would mean to think about the universal on this grafting model, grafting onto ethnicity, rather than the subsuming of ethnicity. I urge us to think about that not because, as a historian, I am saying this is a more accurate understanding of Paul, but because I thought that might spark our creative imaginations and help us get away from a certain nineteenth- and twentieth-century biblical scholarship way of putting Paul in between Hellenism and Judaism, or saying that Paul overcomes Hellenism and Judaism. That is one thing. The other thing I am trying to do is to reflect the fact that a lot of us biblical scholars do not want to deny the newness that is in Paul. I was trying to go back and look at the many times Paul uses the word "new" in his letters. I don't have a concordance with me but I was just flipping through the Greek text. He does talk about "the new creation" quite a bit, and in Galatians he says that there is "neither circumcision nor uncircumcision but a new creation (*kaine ktisis*) is everything" (Gal 6:15). He never talks about a new people or a new religion—nothing like that—it is always the person who is new, or the creation that is new, but never a new people. Pauline scholars over the last twenty years, especially in North America, have been emphasizing a narrative of continuity, of Paul with Israel, rather than of discontinuity. And again, I don't want to push that just because I think it is historically accurate but because it has forced me to exercise my historical imagination differently, as far as how I might appropriate Paul, not as the founder of Christianity, not as the founder of a new religion, but as expressing a continuity with the God of Israel. What do I do with that?

Slavoj Žižek: I accept and deeply appreciate everything you said, but I think that, given the way you put it, you have made Paul even more radical, because you had to use these contradictory terms—like it's ethnicity but it's no longer ethnicity. Something much more radical than simple expansion to universality is going on there.

Martin: Yes.

Žižek: So I would propose a kind of dialectical compromise formula: in order to see the radical break of Paul, one has to read him precisely as a Jew, from within, not already adopting the Christian terms, to put it in Kierkegaardian terms, not in being Christian but Christianity in becoming, what Christianity was before it became Christianity. I would like to read your work. I found this very interesting. I thought the debate was going to be, Do you really believe in God? Instead of that type of naive question, we have totally different ones.

Caputo: That was going to be my next question!

Žižek: I accept it and I will reply with a personal anecdote from you. You [Caputo] told me that when your teenage son once told you, "I don't believe in God" you told him, "That's okay, just as long as you're not a Republican." So, I think this answers the question. Okay, sorry, let me go on. I am interested in the focus on two interconnected questions: the one more methodological, the other more abstract-philosophical, the status of universalism. To put it bluntly, by asserting universalism, are not some of us coming close to imposing some uniform, potentially even terroristic encompassing entity? Connected to this is the problem of historicism: are we anachronistically imposing some notions? So, very briefly since I talk too much, I think that, although we have had our internal struggles, both of us nonetheless share—maybe we did not explain it well enough—a very precise sense of universality. For us universality is not simply this abstract link: we have many phenomena, let's abstract from them and look at what they share. I would like to translate this into my Hegelian/Marxist terminology of universality and use a crucial distinction between universality as such and 'appearing' universality. Now, the question is, What does this mean? Let me, as an old-fashioned Marxist, give you two strange but perfect examples from Marx, just to make the point clear. We find in Marx two contradictory things. First, at the very beginning of *The Communist Manifesto*, "All societies hitherto are class societies." But wait a minute, a little bit later he says, "The bourgeoisie is the first class in the history of humanity." What does he mean? He means that, of course there was always a class distinction, but it was obfuscated; the differences were not differentiated. So, it's one thing to say that all societies were class societies but in order for this universality to appear, it appears at that precise, particular moment. Which is why we have these wonderful anti-evolutionary formulas of Marx, "the anatomy of men is the key to the anatomy of the ape," which is to say that it's only from the veil of bourgeois society that you get the key to analyze properly the previous societies. Or, for example, apropos of work, Marx says, of course, universal work was always here, different people work at different things, but they were all working. But Marx says that only in the proletariat condition, the condition where workers are selling their labor force, does this universality appear as such. Why? Because the worker, who is selling his work for an abstract entity, is not just being his work, but experiences himself as an abstract worker who is selling his work. That's the first very precise catch to add. I see this Hegelian moment, that universality appears. The problem is where universality appears, which leads to the second point, that universality is always a struggling universality. Universality does not mean, "We are different, let's find a common language." Universality means that within a certain social totality there is a specific element. Let's focus on the logic. Why is it that for Marx the proletariat is the universal class? Because it is a class without its proper place, thwarted in its identity, and the point for Marx is, precisely as such, it does not fit into it—it *stands* for universality. It's a kind of struggling, fighting universality. I find this in Paul. Maybe I'm anachronistic; I accept that. But this is what I am looking for in Paul, a universality that is not "let's all be together," but a fighting universality. I found this distinctly two-sided logic in the gospel. On the one hand Christ brings peace, but then also, of course, as an old Stalinist, my favorite Christ, the one who says, "I bring the sword, not peace," "If you don't hate your father and mother," and so on. These are strictly two sides of the same coin—to become universal means, hate your mother and father. So, you see that the point is to have universality not as this blank notion of 'we are all together in it, we all share it.' Then we get caught in this totally boring pseudo-Habermasian problematic, "If each of us is in our own universe, how can we be sure that we share some same horizon?" If you ask this type of question, of course, you never arrive at it, but if you fight together, you get it.

Alcoff: But that move, to hate your mother and father, sounds like a statement that's overtly counter to everything feminism has tried to develop theoretically over the last century. In the move from "born of woman" to "adopted by the father" there's a rejection of the genealogical tie, there's a rejection of materiality and semantic tie, and that rejection of the materiality and the genealogical is always a rejection of the female and the mother. To paraphrase Irigaray, it's an old dream of transcendence. Is this the price of universalism: a revival of old-fashioned patriarchy?

Žižek: I will answer very briefly and then I'll shut up. What I intended to say is the exact opposite. In pre-Cartesian societies women had their allotted place, but it was a fixed place. I think that only with the radical Cartesian *cogito* is the place for modern feminism opened up. In order to experience your sexual orientation, gender, and so on, as something ultimately arbitrary and contingent, you have to go through this point of hatred, which means untying this concrete type. Women were ecstatic with Cartesianism, not only the queen of Sweden but others. They said, "My God, for the first time—at least officially— the *cogito* has no sex." Now you can engage in historicist hermeneutics and say that, well, we all know that secretly, in a codified way, *cogito,* the Cartesian *cogito* really privileges male heterosexual normativity. I agree. But I claim that the very space from which you criticize it was opened by Descartes himself. Without Descartes, no modern feminism. All you get is this old New Age feminism, this Jungian obscurantism, where I think the death penalty is justified. "We are to march under the sway of masculine principle of domination; we need more of the feminine principle"—here you have this big problematic of sexualized cosmology which I think is the worst thing that can happen to feminism. If I were to be a woman, what I would fear today is not a man telling me, "Listen, you women are inferior." That you can manage; you can retrain him. I would fear a man who tells me, "I am a man, a Cartesian imperialist, embodying the logic of domination; you really have a greater sensitivity for dialogue." That's a far more dangerous position, I think. It's the same as with racism. Today's neoracism always has been the celebration, the false celebration, of alterity. I became converted to this when I read some old apartheid South African propaganda. It was not "blacks are less," it was "why should we impose on them our universal, Western civilization—it's so precious their specific culture, they are much better than us in their goodness, and so on." The greatness of Mandela (I have other problems with him) is that he never fell for it. He insisted on universality. I know that what I'm saying is provocative, but it's my nature. I will shut up now.

Caputo: Daniel Boyarin, in your paper at the conference and in your writing in the past, you have been especially eloquent on this question of the right of a community to be different and to maintain the identity of its local practices, as well as on a certain fear that the universal inspires of erasing difference. I was wondering if you would like to add something at this point?

Daniel Boyarin: A friend of mine, who thirty years ago moved to Israel and got an administrative position, could not understand why when she said to the secretary who was working for her, "Would you like to write a letter for me?" the woman thought it was perfectly okay to say, "No, I'm not in the mood." She thought she was being asked the question of would you *like* to write a letter and answered the question. No, but I *would* like to, so thank you. I will probably speak overly long like Slavoj, or like Slavoj says he does. I'll come obliquely to the question you asked, Jack, but I must share that when my son came to me, at the age of seventeen, and said that he was no longer a Sabbath observer, and I was shocked, he said, "But Abba, I'm not a Zionist." And then, "What were you expecting, a clone?"

I want to start by reflecting on one of the themes that has come up. I think Paula Fredriksen's paper focused something for me very clearly. We sometimes think, and we were tempted to slip back into thinking, that the difference between the reading of a philosopher (I will complicate that in a second) and the reading of a historian is this. The historian claims to be making a systematizable reading of the text by saying that the historian's systematized reading of the text is more accurate, is more correctly that systematization of the text that, either, the author originally meant or the hearers originally heard. That's one way in which we are sometimes tempted to pit these two different styles of reading against each other. But Paula actually reached inside her discourse for something more original and more helpful than that—the place to see the difference is on the question of systematization per se. What marks the historians' reading—and I'm merely mirroring back what she said—is the refusal to systematize, on the assumption that discourses and texts are being produced that are *eo ipso,* not systematic, except perhaps for those rare instances of discourse which set out to be philosophical or systematic. The difference is not between one systematization and another, between one statement of "this is what Paul says" against other statements of "this is what Paul says." The role of the historian is to focus on the messiness, the contradictoriness, the ways in which there are multiple things going on, which Ed Sanders beautifully laid out for us as a shift in development. So the opposition is between the historian's reading, which is not systematic, and all systematic readings, whether those of theologians, philosophers, cultural critics, and so on.

If the distinction is acceptable in that way, then there is simply no room to place in contradiction the readings of philosophers, theologians, cultural critics, and the readings of historians. They don't contradict each other; rather, they are two entirely different enterprises. This is not to say that the two cannot learn from each other, or that they can't coexist in the same person. The same person can be doing both readings, historical readings, defined in this way, and systematizable readings. Given that, I would characterize the reading I usually do as systematic; my reading is not that of a historian but a systematic one. I learned this actually from someone who is in this room, Professor Antoinette Wire, my colleague at Berkeley, at the Graduate Theological Union, who characterized my Paul book, in a quotation on the cover, as a work of systematic theology. That totally blew me away, because it's the last way that I would have described myself ten years ago. But Paula's characterization of what it is that makes a historical reading historical helped me see that.

Now, if that's the case then the issue on the table for me with Alain Badiou is not that I claim to do something more accurate, more Greek, more historical, more archaeological. I might want to play that game under other circumstances, for other purposes, but that's not the game I'm playing here. When I talk about historicism—and I think Alain Badiou understands very well what I am doing—I am arguing against his antihistoricist position but within a universe of systematics. I don't want to call it philosophy, because "philosophy" is the contested term here. Is philosophy the only practice of systematic thinking or are there other practices of systematic thinking that are not philosophy, like rhetoric or sophism? And the question for me finally is—and this is where I come, in a sense, at least obliquely, to what you asked me directly—what kind of thinking at this particular moment, at this particular juncture, is going to feed more people, have fewer people dead, end the domination and torture of the Palestinians? I just take that example because that's the one that's nearest, dearest to my particular political heart and in that sense I think that we're on the same side in terms of the enterprise. There is no opposition in terms of the enterprise. But this is thinking as praxis—and I don't mean practice, I mean praxis in the fully technical Marxist sense—and a struggle to see what kind of thinking makes the best politics. My response is that Protagoras and Gorgias have more to offer us for a politics of the present than Plato does and that is where I'm taking my stance. At least now.

Badiou: I completely disagree with your conclusion because I think that sophistry, which is without a conception of truth, which is something like anachronic pragmatism, is the dominant ideology of the democratic Western world. We are all sophists in fact. And so, the real question for me, the real political, concrete question, is on the side of Plato, although the side of Plato is really a metaphor. It's on the side of something like a fixed point in a world which is a world of circulation, of communication, of market. We have an absolute resolution to find something like a fixed point, and you cannot find a fixed point in the field of sophistry, and that is why in my vision of

Paul, the fundamental point is that of faith. Not faith like a subjective determination of psychological want, but like the possibility to have relation to a fixed point in the concrete experience of the world. In my concrete life I am a political activist. I confess that sort of thing to you. I spend much more time with workers, with the poor, and so on than in the philosophy colloquia, but I also like these colloquia. The difference between us, and you know that, is not about the urgency of political activism. I am of the conviction that the question of the birth of a new truth, the question of the transformation of the political field today, the question of the fixed point is of great necessity for us in all concrete political situations. And so there is something strange for me in our disagreement. I agree with you on the political situation and I disagree with you on something very essential, which is something like the abstract conditions of political engagement. And now there is a difference— a very hard difference—between Platonism and sophistry.

Caputo: Is that how you understand your differences, Daniel?

Boyarin: I was trying to bring to a level of clarity what's at stake for me here in this particular conversation and to focus the point that for me it is a matter of a more robust sense of *doxa,* a more robust sense of the possibility of speech, communication—and I do not mean that in the Habermasian sense—not a fixed point that will provide purchase for political newness. And so simply having that lifted up—or "thematized," as my friends up on Holy Hill say—is enough, I think, for me.

Caputo: Richard, you look like you want to get into this.

Richard Kearney: I want to pick a fight with Slavoj, if I may—a friendly one. I struggle with the concept of the fighting universal, which is a very robust one, but belligerent too if I understand it. If there is a debate emerging, I find myself more on the side of Daniel and Linda than you and Alain. But let me focus on something you said about the fighting universal, because I detect in it a certain celebration of toughness, violence, belligerence, and you invoke the Stalinist thing as a joke, but at another level this is not a joke. If the fighting universal is really what you say it is—a *fighting* universal—it's a violent universal. It's a universal that wants to affirm its view of what the universal is over other views of what the universal is or isn't. My question is this, coming back to a point raised by Daniel: What philosophy or what concept of the universal is going to contribute most to peace in our world, and to addressing poverty and injustice? From that point of view, I wonder if the fighting universal you are invoking, with Marx and Hegel and their dialectic of the labor of the negative, while a brilliant dialectic, is going to be conducive to interreligious dialogue, since we are talking about religion. As was pointed out by several speakers, like Karen Armstrong and Paula Fredriksen, we live in a time when most wars are caused by religions and a certain perverse religious imaginary. How are we to address the possibility of an interreligious dialogue that can actually operate on the basis of an interconfessional hospitality?

I would add this: you made the remark, again humorously but in fact seriously, "I hope that nobody's going to ask me what I believe." But I think this is an incredibly important question to ask at a certain point. Particularly if we're discussing St. Paul; not that we should be less philosophically rigorous or less scientifically exact, but because that, as I understand it, is part of our hermeneutic situation. I think a theist is probably going to read St. Paul's letters in a way that an atheist isn't. Sometimes, when I read this spate of atheistic philosophers writing about St. Paul, I, as a theist, see it as a breath of fresh air because I see a certain liberty in an atheistic method, like a phenomenological bracketing of presuppositions which allows for readings that I think are difficult sometimes for those who are too confessionally committed. But I think that atheism is also a form of confession. I think that you come with a Marxist-Hegelian reading, and Alain with a Platonic-Lacanian reading, and Linda comes with a feminist reading and Daniel comes with a Jewish reading. We all come with a hermeneutic. I think it is extremely salutary in the debate to own up at some point to those hermeneutic presuppositions. If we're talking about mathematics, these presuppositions are irrelevant, but not if we're talking about St. Paul. This is a time when the stakes of peace and violence with regard to religion, with regard to confessions, and with regard to the possibility of a hermeneutics of interconfessional hospitality are crucial.

Žižek: This is a wonderful question. Again, I will try to be short. But if I speak too long you are responsible, because you ask an essential question. I will very honestly try in a very naive way to go at the level of the disagreement. You know that when people fight, the greatest difficulty often is simply to really locate the place of disagreement. I may disagree with you that the fundamental conflicts today are at this, let's call it, horizontal level. There are different groups, ethnic groups, religious groups—the point is how to find communication and so on. Of course! I'm not an idiot. Of course, at this level, I'm for understanding communication. Why? Here I will defer to the politics of subtraction, because my fighting universal is not: "I have the truth. Other religions don't. Kill them." What does Paul do? Here again my model for Paul is Paul. It is not "We have Jews; we have Greeks and so on, let us see what unites them." No. He cuts a kind of a diagonal which cuts across each and all of them. So my answer to you would be that the only possibility, for me, to bring together all these different confessions, lifestyles, whatever, it's not this Habermasian game—I'm not accusing you of being Habermasian, but Habermasians are an appropriate target—to see what unites us, to find some universality. It's let's see what struggle cuts across all of us. That would be fighting universality for me. It's not to claim that we Christians are more than Jews, are more than others, but there is a same fight going diagonally across the both of us.

That also is my problem with this mantra against class essentialism. To put it in extremely simplified terms, I always am suspicious about it and people accuse me of class essentialism but I am not guilty, because my point is not that class struggle is somehow more important. I agree with all the economic debates—Does it exist at all?—but don't you notice that the difference is formal? When we speak about ethnic struggle for ethnic recognition, sexual recognition, and so on, these must be put—the way you describe them—as horizontal struggles. The aim of ethnic struggle is not that one race should kill another. The aim of antiracist struggle is how each different partner should recognize the other. The aim, for example, of antisexist struggle, feminist struggle, is not that women should castrate men. It is to find the space where women can be fully women and realize their potential, and men can be fully men and so on and so on. Sorry, but class struggle is not the same. The goal in class struggle is not that capitalists should be fully capitalists and proletarians should be fully proletarians. It's "I want to cut their throat." And this is for me the fighting universal. I think that paradoxically I totally agree with Daniel when he says, yes, Jewish identity crucial for him, Palestinian identity, and so on. But the only way in the precise sense of praxis that you evoke, of practical identity, is a common struggle that runs across all of us.

One brief remark to make it very clear that I have here a very refined notion of "fighting universality." A simple example taken from Fredric Jameson which I think works perfectly. Fred Jameson elaborated recently a wonderful criticism of the fashionable notion of alternate modernities, which appears very progressive. "Let's not appear Eurocentric, let's not impose on others our form of modernity, which is the liberal-capitalist. There are other modernities, Latino-American, Asian, whatever." And Jameson explodes, exclaiming, "No, this is a worse ideology!" I think he is right. Why? His idea is that in this apparently honest, historicist reaction something happens. What are the true stakes of these theories of alternate modernities? It is to relativize something. Modernity is a code word for capitalism; we all know this. The theory of alternate modernities says, "no, it's the subliberal capitalism that is objectionable; we can have another capitalism which wouldn't be so bad." So, my big argument is I've had enough of alternate modernities because we in Europe knew very well in the twentieth century, in the middle, one form of alternate modernity which was called fascism. Fascism was precisely an alternate modernity in the sense that, "We can have modernization but an alternate one avoiding all that."

So, okay, what's the point here? It's not simply that we have some simple universal essence of capitalism with merely different modernities. It is to introduce an appropriate dialectical tension between universality and particularity in the sense that different modernities—our liberal modernity, fascist modernity, Indian modernity, Latin American—are not simply neutral examples of a universal notion of modernity but are attempts to resolve, pacify, articulate, come to terms with, a certain tension which is inscribed into the very concept of modernity. So we have multiple modernities, not in the sense that all life is complicated or complex, but because there is an antagonism, a tension, inscribed into modernity itself. Fascism is one way of trying to resolve this antagonism. Liberal capitalism is another way, and so on. So you see what the appropriate dialectical notion is here. It's not that universality is a neutral cover, as it were, and then particular struggle. Struggle is at the level of universality, and particulars are in kind of a dialectic (tension with their own universality). Particular examples of universality are attempts to cope with, to pacify, a tension which is inscribed at the level of universality itself. This would be for me an example of what I mean by struggling universality. But again I think that you should use your own example. I hope we agree here. I appeal to your Irish, Catholic, militant attitude. I think that the worst thing, something totally empty, the death of any religion is this cheap ecumenical spirit: "Aren't they all secretly referring to the same God?" That's the end. That's more dangerous to any meaningful religious experience than the most vulgar materialism.

Kearney: A quick reply if I may, since you have provoked the militant Catholic Irishman in me. I am totally for ecumenism, and that includes the relationship between Ireland and Northern Ireland, but what I'm against is ecumenism as "you-come-in-ism." I think that the ability of Protestants and Catholics in Northern Ireland to reach across borders and boundaries—not toward some wishy-washy, Habermasian ideal-speech situation—but out of their very differences, the ability to exchange memories and narratives and traditions and to get into each other's skins was hugely important. I think there are two ways of conversing and of being a host in a conversation. One is where the other is an adversary. That's the host as hostility, to borrow from Derrida's play on this root word *hostis*. The other is the host as a giver of hospitality. And in Northern Ireland it was very important to be the host that accepted the difference of the other and be prepared to try to exchange places with the other, so that John Hume went and shook hands with Gerry Adams. Right? That is like Begin and Sadat.

Boyarin: No, it isn't. Don't invoke that.

Kearney: Okay, I'll leave Palestine out of it. You know Palestine better than I do. I'll talk about what I know in Northern Ireland. That was the movement of a leader of a republican nationalist democratic movement, John Hume, who shook the hand of a terrorist. That was huge. He was decried by the churches, by the British government, but it brought about the Good Friday agreement and that is why we now have politically and constitutionally a document that says you can be British or Irish or both. That's the move of hospitality, rather than hostility, that brought about peace in Northern Ireland. I don't know what would bring about peace in Palestine. I'm sure you're as committed to it as I am. But I think it is hospitality toward the other, an enemy, an adversary, rather than hostility.

Boyarin: I just want to say two things here, first of all. I am not committed to peace in Palestine; I'm committed to justice in Palestine. Peace will always only follow from justice.

Kearney: Well, I don't intend peace without justice.

Boyarin: I know that and I am not accusing you of that. But I think that we have to be clear in our language, and in that sense I am certainly not associating myself with any pacifist doctrine. I see now emerging a fairly sharp difference between Badiou and Žižek precisely on the question of historicism. You cannot, in one moment, be invoking Jameson, and in another moment citing page after page in the *Manifesto* against historicism and claim that you are saying the same thing. That, you know. If we are having a conversation here among militants and activists about theoretical positions, the discussion has to do with historicism or antihistoricism. Not pacifism or militancy.

Žižek: I totally disagree with Jameson's big motto "historicize." But here specifically his point is precisely nonhistoricist. It's that in order to account for a certain historical dynamic, you have to refer to some antagonism which is precisely, in a sense, a nonhistorical universal. I think that Jameson, here, comes to the limits of his own historicism, which is why I like this example.

Caputo: Ed Sanders, why don't you pick up the gauntlet here and bring us back to Paul?

E. P. Sanders: How about a nice exegetical question? Dale, I have an exegetical bone to pick with you. You decided to include the gentiles in Paul's universalism at a late moment in your lecture, but the image you have built on does not actually do for you what you want it to do. To be grafted into the stock of Israel—this is the figure of the vine, or of the olive tree (Romans 11). The olive tree is there; this is originally the people of Israel. Some limbs are cut out and they fall, and some limbs are grafted on. The limbs grafted on are gentiles. The issue is faith, by which I assume Paul means faith in Christ. The limbs are cut out and they fall if they don't have faith; they're grafted on if they do have faith. But this does not add up to the universal inclusion of all gentiles in the people of Israel. To the contrary, it's a tripartite figure, where you have the tree and you have two batches of dead limbs. That is, as I see it, Paul's general view when he is thinking of the period of his own apostolic labors. There are three groups: the new people of God, and then there are the Jews who don't accept Christ, and the gentiles who don't accept Christ. I don't see him making a truly universal move until he switches time zones. He switches out of the period of the apostolic labors when some people turn him down and when he says, "You will be destroyed," to the time when the Redeemer comes from Mount Zion. Is this a fair correction, would you say?

Martin: Yes. I would say that I was making some hermeneutical moves at the same time as I was making exegetical moves.

Sanders: But in this case it is not that Israel is all in all. When you come to the concluding verses of Romans 11 where you have the universalistic statement "All Israel will be saved" (Rom 11:26), and God "will be merciful to all" (11:32), you do not have an in-grafting passage in between. The in-grafting is back up earlier in the chapter, referring to the period of the apostolic labors. So I don't know that Israel is all in all. God saves his entire creation.

Martin: God does save his entire creation. But the idea seems to be that there ends up being almost nothing but Israel. I am fudging with exactly how to say it because I don't think that Paul ever comes out and says what he really conceives is going to happen. So I don't want to oversystematize him.

Sanders: Right.

Martin: I think the big problem is—and this is found in other parts of Paul—that he uses the term "gentiles" almost always in a completely derogatory sense for people outside the church. He doesn't have the term "Christians." When he talks about the latter, they're "brothers," "saints," all kinds of things. I'm just pointing out that while he never really tells us that everybody will be Israel, his logic and his rhetoric don't seem to leave any other choice.

Sanders: His principal name for his group is *hoi pisteuentes:* "those who believe." It's an active participle used as a substantive. We would translate it as "the faith-ers" or "the believers" or something of the sort. That's the most common name for them, but it clearly differentiates that in-group from the other two left-out groups.

Martin: That's right. This is why I was fudging. I'm not saying that Paul's a universalist when it comes to all of humanity. I said that I am perfectly willing to go with you on that, if we're going to talk about that. I don't have anything against it. But I really don't know. I don't think he's clear enough about *that*. But if there's going to be any kind of universal salvation, I do believe it's in that time, not in this time.

Sanders: Yes, right. We've got it.

Žižek: Can I make one just very quick remark? The two of you just spoke as historians. But this was a purely systematic analysis and a hermeneutical help to us in understanding. So it's not so simple. I think the image should be complicated. On the one hand, it's too simple to say that historians discover inconsistent views. To say that something is inconsistent is already systematizing. But the point which interests me, and this is where I think we historians and systematizers can creatively interact, is when you find an inconsistency, and you prove that this inconsistency is systematic, necessary. It's not just that the guy grew old, was drunk, developed, and so on, but it's a structural inconsistency which is productive, which is pushing it. There we can collaborate, I think. Again, the problem is the status of inconsistency. Is this just that the guy was confused or is it inscribed into the very system?

Martin: This is one of the things I liked very much and said so about both your treatments: it's that you come to Paul recognizing that you can't treat him like a philosopher and you can't treat him like a systematic theologian. And I think that's great. I think to read Paul that way and still to read him as a resource is really what I applaud completely.

Sanders: I might say, just from the point of view of your last remark, that I think there is a deep inconsistency built into Paul's basic structure, and it is a systematic inconsistency. He believes two opposite things at the same time. One of them is that God called Israel and gave the law to Moses and the law is good and the people of Israel are chosen. The other is, God decided to send Jesus to save the entire world without reference to whether or not anyone was Jewish or obeyed the law. And it's when he tried to hold these two things together that you get these really complicated passages like Romans 7 and Romans 9–11, I think. There is a basic inconsistency and it is systematic, I think.

Alcoff: Before we open this up to the audience, does Paula Fredriksen or Karen Armstrong want to get her two cents in?

Karen Armstrong: I am neither a philosopher nor a Paulinist nor a New Testament historicist, and I'm not an academic either. I'm an amateur, and I use the word amateur advisedly: the word means one that loves. I love what I'm doing and stumbled into it *unsystematically*. I'm with Richard Kearney on the question of ecumenism, though I don't like all this boiling down to finding common denominators. The handshake means an encounter, that the other is other, that there is as it were a collision of hands there in the moment of meeting. It's not a oneness, it is an encounter. The fact that there is a handshake implies a history of antagonism. And I think too that we've got to remember that all this is a process. Ed was just talking about Paul holding two contradictory ideas in his head at the same time. We're in a moment of historical transition where there are going to be these kinds of contradictions that are not going to be resolved immediately. Culture is always contested. There are always people who are going to revolt against the prevailing cultural norm, and now we've got this on the global sphere, too. There's going to be antagonism and we must work through it, but I think we must work through it with a model of peace at the end, and respect. I liked Kearney's idea that hospitality is respect and justice. This is something that always has to be introduced into any discussion of any religious system. At their best the religions speak of this kind of respect for the sacred inviolability of the other. So on that, I think, we can work together. Not endlessly gazing at one another saying, "How do we understand each other?" but working alongside one another to promote some kind of respectful understanding. When we gaze into each other's eyes and talk about our differences, it all becomes self-conscious and can reinforce us, ingrain us, in positions. But if we are working alongside to meet common problems we discover commonalities without embracing some kind of false unity. I'm sorry to be the picture of a silent woman—it's not my normal mode. But as I say, this is not a normal gathering for me, although I've very much enjoyed the conversation.

Paula Fredriksen: You're an impossible act to follow. Nonetheless, I will try to say something. One of the ways I try to get my students—most of whom are personally Christian—to look at their own sacred scriptures historically and not simply religiously or fideistically is to invite them to think of what Paul is doing and talking about as an extreme form of Judaism. If you bracket out the idea of Christianity, if you force yourself to translate *ekklesia* as "assembly" or "the group" instead of "the church," if you imagine yourself back into Paul's time frame, when he was expecting the return of the Son within his own lifetime, then the letters begin to sound very different.

For example, Paul the "radical" has gotten a lot of mileage out of the sound bite in Galatians 3:28: "There is neither Jew nor Greek, there is neither slave nor free, there is neither male nor female; for you are all one in Christ Jesus." This sentence about radical equality reverberates so much with what we want to think of as the best in all of us. But when we get down to it, what was he saying about the people who were traditionally religious in terms of majority Mediterranean culture (a.k.a. the idol worshipers)? He didn't respect them. He didn't embrace their alterity. He said that, come the end of the age, they were going to fry. And what was Paul demanding that his gentiles, his saints, his "believing ones" do? They had to cut themselves off from their own roots. Why? Because Paul based his argument about Jesus on an unsystematic reading of his own sacred scriptures. *Paul is not obligated to history* because he is so convinced that he's right about the eschatological timetable on the strength of the fact that he thinks he has seen the risen Christ. Paul's indictment of majority Mediterranean culture in the first chapter of Romans is horrific. These people—most of the humanity he is acquainted with—are given to unnatural sexual practices, he says; they are morons, because they look at the sky but they do not infer anything about the God of Israel who made the sky, and so on. And Paul has seen a second miracle that confirms to him that he is absolutely right about what time it is on God's clock. He is getting people from this wicked pagan group to quit their low-down heathen ways and do something that only one other people in the empire do, namely, the Jews. I'm going to mess up the old Protestant "ritual versus ethics" distinction, where ethics are nice and ritual is grotty (or, worse, ritual is "Catholic."). Paul makes a *ritual* demand of his gentiles: no more idol worship. Finished. And the fact that these gentiles are able to do this, despite the debilitating environment of their own native culture, confirms for Paul yet again that the kingdom of God is going to arrive in Paul's own lifetime.

Now let me segue from this point to the one that Danny raised a short while earlier, namely, the difference between the type of interpretation of ancient texts that occurs when you are systematizing versus the type that goes on when you are doing history. Anybody who is traditionally religious—anybody who places herself or himself within a religious tradition, wherein you read these really ancient texts and you attempt to make sense of them now, in the present day— anyone who does this is performing a hermeneutical and in a sense a theological act. This is what you have to do. The other choice would be to abandon these texts, to stop being traditionally religious, if you say, "The Bible was a good book but I'd rather read something else that makes more sense to me." Anachronism in the interpretation of ancient texts is not an indictment of all interpretative acts. But anachronistic interpretation is fatal to doing history. It is a cheat.

But if, as a systematician—as a philosopher, say, or as a critic of culture— you say, "This is what Paul means" and then go on to say something that Paul could not possibly have meant, then that is also a cheat, though a different form of cheating. That move is about proposing your own, modern statement of what matters to you, and borrowing authority from some ancient texts by claiming that "Paul" said and thought the same. *That* was the point I was try- ing to make.

Žižek: I agree with you. We often bluff, we philosophers. I will admit it; many philosophers often bluff. Nonetheless—how should I put it?—I will not make the usual arrogant, philosophical reply which is, that nonetheless in every historical analysis you already apply certain notions. That's the first point. I'm not saying anything specifically about you but how I see, in a very naive, philosophical way, the limits of historicism, the limits of historical contex- tualization. The first problem is that most of the historicists I know are not historicist enough, in the sense that they don't really historicize the very con- ceptual apparatus that they use when they analyze. For example, religion: my God, what is religion? What is art? Are we aware that, for example—we all know this, it's ridiculous—to repeat Marx's analysis, when we speak today about art and analyze ancient Greek art and so on as art, we are effectively us- ing the term "art," which probably didn't emerge until the eighteenth century or something like this. So I think that if one plays the historicist game one should really be a historicist. And there is, for me, something that is precisely a historicist anachronism, in the sense that it is precisely when you guess what was really meant there, that the very apparatus, categories, that you use do not belong to that time period. The second problem is that I would like to think about inconsistency, especially about systematic inconsistencies. What, nonetheless, for me, gives a certain amount of legitimacy to anachronism is this. The problem for me is not that we should understand what Paul really meant. It's that—and here is the conclusion I accept from you—Paul probably didn't understand what he meant himself, that he was inconsistent. And I am tempted to read this in the Walter Benjaminian way, in the sense that this gives a kind of opening toward the future. At a certain level—I know these are dangerous waters and if you go too far you can justify anything—but at a certain level you can say that past texts are certain kinds of open traces where we can understand them better than the authors understood themselves. For me, it's crystal clear that Paul is doing this to Christ. What if Christ were to be informed, "There is this guy Paul who writes this and this about you"? I don't think he would like it. What I'm trying to say, how should I put it, is that what always fascinated me in the history of thought is how something which comes later and looks at first like an obvious misreading can nonetheless bring out something which was a repressed dimension in the original text itself. Let me formulate this as a way of celebrating you Americans who are so often despised by arrogant Frenchmen. It is absolutely obvious that the first genera- tion of reception in the United States of Derrida, and of Foucault even more, was a total misreading. But it's interesting how, at a certain point, Derrida and Foucault themselves started to imitate this American misunderstanding in a very productive way. Consider the whole progress of the politicization of Derrida and of Foucault. Before Derrida became Americanized he was a rather boring, academic philosopher. What I'm saying is that we cannot simply say that Derrida got misread. He was fascinated by the political potentials, which changed his position. There was a kind of ambiguity potential already in there. As Derrida would have put it (I'm not a Derridean, although here I agree with him), contexts are never really fully contextualized. For example, let's return to my previous example. Yes, I know, human rights ideology was, from the beginning, an ideological product. But what always fascinates me is not the standard process of decadence—how an authentic position gets degenerated— but how precisely something which historically started as a fake, as a brutally imposed ideology, becomes authentic, for example, the Virgin of Guadalupe in Mexico. It's clear that at the beginning Christianity was brutally imposed on Mexicans, but at that point it was reappropriated; there was a potential in it. So, again, I totally agree that we philosophers are prone to many sins. Nonetheless I do believe in this kind of historical opening, in the sense that contextualization is not the ultimate answer. There is a kind of opening. Texts always have an open spot, as it were—they say more than they think they say. And this provides for me the opening of later misreadings, different readings, productive readings, and so on.

Caputo: Let's take some questions from the floor.

Question: I appreciate your comments, Dr. Žižek. I particularly like this idea that Paul didn't understand himself fully and this allowed for openness toward the future. There was a question that arose among you, and I'm not sure exactly who posed it, but it concerned what kind of thinking makes for the best politics. I got this sense that we have this antecedent thing we understand as political, certain political ends we want to achieve, and then we use these as a kind of litmus test to figure out which of us is being the best philosopher. That was the sense that I got. I felt Professor Žižek resisting this, specifically with his reading of Paul. But I wonder if we couldn't apply this to our conversation here. To what extent are we open to not understanding ourselves and our conversation? It's an open-ended question, but let me direct this to Professor Kearney and Professor Boyarin. What kind of thinking do you think makes the best politics? And, is this the right question?

Kearney: I was citing Daniel approvingly, that there should be some connection between Paul's writings and the effects of those writings on the world. It was true of his day, for better and for worse, and it's true today, for better and for worse. So the stakes of a discussion of St. Paul are not completely neutral, politically and ethically, but have in addition to their theoretical interest, a certain pragmatic value—of protest and of commitment to violence or nonviolence. That's what I was trying to say.

Boyarin: Yes, I'll stay with my position. It's a variant, a gloss, on Marx's famous statement that "Up till now philosophers have understood their task to explain the world and now it is the task of philosophy to change the world." I think this is the only worthy task that remains for human endeavor, whether in science, love, politics, and art. So yes, I remain with that. One more sentence, though, that I think needs to be clear here—and I'm sure it's clear to you, Slavoj—and it's that, of course, historicism is not the same thing as the work of historians, and this might have gotten a little confused. There are ways in which historicism is in opposition to what historians do.

Question: I'm interested in this talk of the relationship between politics and philosophy. One of the things I think hasn't been addressed explicitly enough is the place that universality goes to after you've developed class solidarity. To be extremely brief, I think that the Tiananmen Square incident is a great way to codify the situation. There you have this extremely well organized group of students and workers from around China, and peasants were coming in toward the end, and you have this well organized group which is outside Tiananmen and all they wanted was to have a meeting. Well, they got their meeting, things fell apart, and afterward they were standing outside the gates not knowing what to do. So, you have to establish this sort of universal solidarity, a kind of fighting solidarity. But at that moment, when what you are asking for fails to be delivered, what do you do after that? Then the tanks started coming in and all of a sudden a highly organized group—you had artists who had the time to come up with a Styrofoam "Our Goddess of Democracy," you had old people cooking in their houses and bringing food out to the students—and their organization was scattered. They had to consider the question of what they wanted, and what they wanted could not deliver on its promise. So I think that the Pauline gesture that Dr. Martin addressed most explicitly is this creative dimension where new concepts, new ways of organizing the community, were developed out of this unique situation. Beyond a fighting universality, I think we should also have a creative universality as well. So maybe Dr. Martin can comment on that?

Martin: I don't have any comment. I think you were very eloquent.

Question: I'd like to ask Professor Boyarin about Paul's conception of Jew and gentile. There are two views I've heard thus far, one the Platonic/Hegelian mode, where ethnic difference is resolved at a higher level even while it's preserved. And then the sophistic/negative mode, where difference is preserved and not resolved. What I want to ask is, Could there be sort of a resolution between these two views if you take into account Paul's apocalypticism, that at the end of history you have an eschatological vision of unity, while for now, in the world, Paul sees separation?

Boyarin: What do you gain by taking such a position?

Question: I'm just wondering if it fits the text.

Boyarin: I'm not enough of a scholar to answer that.

Question: This question is addressed to anyone who wants to answer, but especially to Karen Armstrong. The title of this conference was slightly misleading. Fully half of the participants apologized for not being philosophers. Nevertheless, there was perhaps one perspective that was not included, that of the passionate adherent to the message of Christianity. So my question is,

What is it that you give up or gain by looking at St. Paul as a scholar and not, say, as a Christian? Does this approach risk sacrificing the praxis of Christianity, and instead looking on it as in a sort of knowing condescension.

Martin: I would like to object to the question because I am a passionate adherent, and I never said I wasn't. That doesn't mean I'm uncritical of the tradition, but I never pretended not to be invested. Nor you, Richard.

Žižek: Well, this is rather paradoxical, probably unacceptable for most of you, but my position is that I am also a passionate adherent of what I see represented in Badiou's book, and much more accidentally in some of my books, as the centrality of Paul's achievement. I think, to put it very brutally, that this achievement, what is truly great in Paul, is not alive today in the Church as an institution. That's my point. In a good revolutionary moment, you find much more of what is progressive in a messianic idea of Paul than in today's churches and institutions. I don't see any contradiction in this.

Fredriksen: I also want to object to the imperialism of referring to "the" Christian mentality. It is just as silly as talking about "the" Jews. I have a friend, Amy Levine, who studied early Christianity at Duke. When she was in a seminar led by W. D. Davies, he would turn to her and say, "And what do the Jews think of this, Miss Levine?" All she could answer for was what one Jew thought. We are being reductive. It's not all right to say what "the Jews" think or what "the Greeks" think, and there are also many, many different types of Christians as well, and that's not going to change, no matter how ideologically pure we want to be.

Armstrong: I was asked to say something and I will say simply that I started at the very beginning of my career reading Paul when I was utterly antagonistic to every kind of religion and just weary and sickened by it. My study of Paul was like a minnow compared to other people at this table. But, nevertheless, it was the passion of the man, the commitment of the man, that I found so engaging that it started me on a journey back to a faith that is not confined to Christianity, or to Judaism, or to Islam or Buddhism. I'm still convalescent, I think. My study, my scholarship, can be a spiritual discipline, can be a form of prayer, that's not necessarily oriented in a sectarian way. I couldn't agree more that St. Paul puts a lot of religious people to shame, as does any creative or passionate or deep thinking philosopher.

Question: I pose this question to Professor Martin. At the beginning of this roundtable discussion Professor Badiou said that the question of universalism is not a grammatical one but a question of process and becoming. Does this contradict your understanding of universalism?

Martin: No. In fact, that's part of what I very much value. The only part of the universalism of Paul that I have questions about is whether it really has very much epistemological leverage when you have a debate among people about what is the politically right thing to do. But as far as seeing Paul as an event that provokes us to action, that is militant and is an opening, I think, that is exactly right.

Alcoff: Let's conclude by thanking all of our speakers and thanking all of you for coming.

CONTRIBUTORS

Linda Martín Alcoff is professor of philosophy at Hunter College and the City University of New York. She has authored and edited many books, including *Singing in the Fire: Tales of Women in Philosophy*; *Visible Identities: Race, Gender, and the Self*; *Identity Politics Reconsidered*; and *The Blackwell Guide to Feminist Philosophy* (with Eva Feder Kittay).

Karen Armstrong is an internationally recognized author of widely read books on Christianity, Judaism, Islam, and Buddhism. She participated in this conference, but her presentation is not included in the published volume.

Alain Badiou, professor of philosophy at the École Normale Superieure and the Collège de Philosophie, is author of *St. Paul: The Foundation of Universalism*, which ignited the current philosophical interest in St. Paul; his magnum opus recently appeared in English translation: *Being and Event*.

Daniel Boyarin is Taubman Professor of Talmudic Culture at the University of California–Berkeley. His work on Judaism and Christianity as a single religious polysystem has appeared so far in three monographs, including *A Radical Jew: Paul and the Politics of Identity*; *Dying for God: Martyrdom and the Making of Judaism and Christianity*; and *Border Lines: The Partition of Judaeo-Christianity*, winner of the 2006 American Academy of Religion award for books in the history of religion.

John D. Caputo is Thomas J. Watson Professor of Religion and Humanities at Syracuse University. His most recent books include *The Weakness of*

God: A Theology of the Event (Indiana University Press, 2006), winner of a 2007 American Academy of Religion book ("constructive studies"); *After the Death of God,* with Gianni Vattimo; *What Would Jesus Deconstruct?*; *How to Read Kierkegaard;* and *Philosophy and Theology.*

Paula Fredriksen is Aurelio Professor of Scripture at Boston University. Her books include *Augustine on Romans; From Jesus to Christ; Jesus of Nazareth, King of the Jews;* and, mostly recently, *Augustine and the Jews.*

Richard Kearney is Charles B. Seelig Chair of Philosophy at Boston College. He has authored more than twenty books on European philosophy, two novels, and a volume of poetry, and has edited or co-edited fifteen more. His most recent work in philosophy comprises a trilogy entitled *Philosophy at the Limit.* The three volumes are *On Stories; The God Who May Be* (Indiana University Press, 2001); and *Strangers, Gods, and Monsters.*

Dale B. Martin is Woolsey Professor of Religious Studies at Yale University. His books include *The Corinthian Body; The Invention of Superstition: From the Hippocratics to the Christians; Sex and the Single Savior: Sexuality and Gender in Biblical Interpretation; and Pedagogy and the Bible: An Analysis and Proposal.*

E. P. Sanders is Arts and Sciences Professor Emeritus of Religion at Duke University. The author, coauthor, or editor of twelve books as well as numerous articles, he has received several awards and prizes, including the Grawemeyer Award for the best book on religion published in the 1980s (*Jesus and Judaism*). His work has been translated into eleven languages.

Slavoj Žižek is senior researcher in the Department of Philosophy, University of Ljubljana (Slovenia) and co director of the Center for Humanities, Birbeck College, University of London. He has recently produced a major work of theory, *The Parallax View.*

INDEX

Winter, Bruce W., 128, 129
Wittgenstein, Ludwig, 132
woman, 117, 118, 165–166, 167
world, 15, 16, 19, 21, 27–29, 32, 36, 42, 44,
    48, 63, 66, 67, 68, 76, 77, 86, 92, 101,
    102, 131, 147, 151, 155, 156, 162, 168,
    169, 176, 180

Yoder, John Howard, 10

Zeno of Elea, 82
Zion, Mount, 85, 86, 174
Žižek, Slavoj, 9–18, 20, 21, 91, 92, 94, 95,
    98, 102, 161, 163, 164, 166, 170, 173,
    175, 178, 180

CPSIA information can be obtained at www.ICGtesting.com
Printed in the USA
LVOW101431210912

299738LV00003B/1/P

9 780253 220837